MW00780064

HELL
IN
BOOTS

HELL
IN
BOOTS

CLAWING
MY WAY
THROUGH
NINE
LIVES

SARAYA-JADE BEVIS

with **BERNADETTE MURPHY**

GALLERY BOOKS

New York   Amsterdam/Antwerp   London   Toronto   Sydney   New Delhi

Gallery Books
An Imprint of Simon & Schuster, LLC
1230 Avenue of the Americas
New York, NY 10020

First Gallery Books hardcover edition March 2025

GALLERY BOOKS and colophon are registered trademarks
of Simon & Schuster, LLC

For information about special discounts for bulk purchases,
please contact Simon & Schuster Special Sales at 1-866-506-1949
or business@simonandschuster.com.

The Simon & Schuster Speakers Bureau can bring authors
to your live event. For more information or to book an event,
contact the Simon & Schuster Speakers Bureau at 1-866-248-3049
or visit our website at www.simonspeakers.com.

Interior design by Karla Schweer

Manufactured in the United States of America

10   9   8   7   6   5   4   3   2   1

Library of Congress Cataloging-in-Publication Data is available.

ISBN 978-1-6680-2784-4
ISBN 978-1-6680-2786-8 (ebook)

For Mum and Daddio

CONTENTS

FOREWORD BY RENEE PAQUETTE IX

PROLOGUE 1

PART *One*

1 PRIDE AND JOY 7

2 RAISED BY WOLVES 15

3 GYPSY 25

4 FADE TO BLACK 39

5 FIGHT FOR YOUR RIGHT TO PARTY 47

6 RUNAWAY 65

7 GIRLS, GIRLS, GIRLS 81

PART *Two*

8 LOSE YOURSELF 99

9 THIS IS ME 115

10 GET THE PARTY STARTED 125

11 ALL I WANTED 141

12 YOUTH GONE WILD 151

13 POPULAR MONSTER 161

14 WHERE IS MY MIND? 169

PART *Three*

15 IF YOU COULD READ MY MIND, LOVE 177

16 UNDER PRESSURE 189

17 WATCH THE WORLD BURN 197

18 STAYIN' ALIVE 203

19 MY WAY 219

20 GIVE 'EM HELL, KID 225

21 ONE WAY OR ANOTHER 235

22 WE ARE THE CHAMPIONS 245

EPILOGUE 253

ACKNOWLEDGMENTS 257

FOREWORD

Hello! I'm so honored I have been asked to write the foreword for this book. I'm someone who has known Saraya most of her adult life—bearing in mind that she's still only in her early thirties—but, damn, has she made the most of those years. I met her when she was nineteen years old, and I was immediately drawn to her. I wanted to know who she was; I wanted to know how this magnetic, electric person made her way through the world. We became fast friends. I don't know if it was some commonwealth connection or what. But it was instant. I've seen the good, the bad, the ugly. I've celebrated successes with her and done my best to pick her up when she needed it. I've known her as Paige; I know her as Saraya. So for you, reader, who has also been fascinated by this "raven-haired lady" I can't wait for you to hear her story. From her mouth. Her story has been told by so many other people. From big fancy movie studios to leaked footage to articles written about her, hell, even just word of mouth. But this is her story, from her perspective, finally.

Now, I'd like to turn this over on a more personal note, with a letter to my friend.

Raya,

Hey, buddy! Firstly, let me just say how proud I am of you. Not only for putting pen to paper and getting your story out there but just for you merely existing. I can remember the first day I met you. It was the summer of 2013, in Orlando, Florida, at Full Sail University for a taping of *NXT*. I was just dipping my toe into the world of professional wrestling and meeting a shit ton of people. So. Many. People! But then I saw you. Man, did you stand out. Not only because of your jet-black hair and snow-white skin—it was you. Your energy. Your vibration. The way people were drawn to you, listening to you. You are the center of attention in any room you're in. Not in an annoying way, ha ha, but in a way that we all want to be a part of it—hoping a little bit of your magic might rub off on us. In fact, I've seen some real motherfuckers try to suck that magic right out of you.

I've always felt this older-sister protectiveness over you. I've seen you go down some treacherous paths, knowing full well it was probably a bad idea. But also knowing you'd figure it out. You're a badass. You're your mother's daughter. I've never seen anyone with the strength you have. You had worldwide fame so early in your life. Literally changing the landscape of professional wrestling. Thrown into the pressure cooker and thriving. You had private videos leaked to the world. You licked your wounds and came back to stare everyone in the face. You were in horrible relationships that you escaped by the grace of some greater power. You put your pieces back together. You broke your neck in front of a sold-out crowd. And, girl, you healed and fucking came back. The fight in you is so incredible. And through all of this, you still remain one of the most loving, warm people I know. Unless of course someone happens to fall on your bad side, and in that case, I send them my thoughts and prayers.

You wear your scars, but you are not your scars. You have so much more of your story to tell. This is all still your first act. I can't wait to see what books two, three, and four look like. I'll always be here for you. I love you. Blondie and Joan Jett forever. Thanks for letting me live in your magic.

Love,

Renee Paquette

PROLOGUE

I'm hiding in a fucking hedge outside a grocery store, praying no one sees me, my arms scratched from the branches and the sun baking the shit out of my skull. The day is hot, and the adrenaline running through my body has me sweating everywhere. When I sweat in the ring it's different—cleaner, more wholesome, the product of hard work. But it's been months since I've wrestled, thanks to a neck injury, and this odor I'm emitting reeks to high heaven. It's anxiety and fucking panic, making my stomach knot. The hedge is thick enough to shield me from the glances of shoppers entering the store with their trollies, all of them going about their daily chores as if the sky hasn't begun to break into a million pieces and fall on my head.

Just an hour ago, sex tapes of me as a nineteen-year-old with two male World Wrestling Entertainment (WWE) wrestlers were leaked to the internet. There I am, completely naked for all the world to see. The wrestler I'd been seeing at the time, Maddox, was older, nearly thirty. Before him, I had almost no experience with boyfriends—I was too busy wrestling and training to get caught up with guys. I didn't know I might need to protect myself from this kind of shit: emotional manipulation and mind-fucking. He wanted to film or photograph just about everything sexual we did, and I was too young, too naive, maybe too much of a twat to object.

At one point about six years ago, he wanted to have a threesome with me, him, and Woods, one of the other WWE wrestlers. Woods was sweet and in no way took advantage of me, but in truth, I went along with the plan solely to shut up Maddox.

And now, what the fuck, that threesome is being shared on social media, going viral so fast my head is spinning. Who leaked the fucking thing and why? More important, how in the hell am I going to live this down? After my injury and two suspensions for drug use, my career is hanging by a thread. WWE is gonna get fed up with my shit soon, and it'll all be over.

People might think that because I'm a badass wrestler who's proven myself in the ring that I'm in control of my life, that I know what the fuck I'm doing. That used to be true. But lately, this life has broken me. I don't have any fight left.

When the tapes were released, I freaked out and fucking took off out the front door, not sure where I was going or why. I just needed to get away. But now I feel even more exposed. I hadn't taken my driver's license or credit cards. I started walking the long road that led to the local shops, a busy mile-long, four-lane street. I just needed to keep putting one foot in front of the other, dragging them toward I didn't know where, my Converse turning gray from the dirt.

Once I made it to H-E-B, I worried I might be recognized. Maybe everyone I passed had already seen that fucking leaked video. I might be a tad bit paranoid, but it was possible. I didn't know what else to do, so I ducked into this hedge in the grocery store's parking lot to hide and get myself sorted, to try to make a plan. How will I ever escape this fucking mess, even if it was the result of my own bad choices?

My phone keeps pinging, though, blowing up now that the word has gotten out, now that everyone has seen me butt-naked, in the most compromising positions possible. I want to disappear, maybe even die. To fall asleep and never wake up again sounds like a fucking relief.

I'm sitting in the dirt, with my stupid white jeans getting filthy. I'm practically emaciated, far too underweight for my height and bone structure—down to 115 pounds from my usual 135 to 140. A wrestler needs some bulk and muscle for strength, and mass to absorb the bumps in the ring. Anytime I make a public appearance these days, people ask if I've seen a doctor. It's not good.

The coke certainly isn't helping. I've been snorting so much lately, every time I sneeze I'm spraying blood. Even my voice seems to be disappearing, literally and figuratively. I've forgotten how to speak up for myself. And when I try, my voice doesn't sound like my own anymore.

But what else can I do? Being awake to my life as it unfolds is simply too painful. . . . The drugs and drinking numb me out for a few moments at a time, allowing me some moments of relief, making it possible for me to keep going. God, I've lost the plot here, haven't I?

I'm not sure I can keep it together anymore. I'm twenty-five years old and have everything I ever wanted. I am a two-time WWE Divas Champion—the youngest ever!—and the inaugural NXT Women's Champion. I was the only woman to hold both titles at the same time. WWE was *my* house, and I was a household name.

But I was a household name as Paige, a character created for me. And who am I now? I don't even know who Paige is at this point.

As I sit in the dirt behind this hedge, I wonder, *How the fuck did I get here?* I used to be *Paige*, the WWE wrestler who's an action figure, beloved by young wrestling fans across the nation for being a badass. I don't feel so badass right now; I'm a nervous fucking wreck.

Maybe I'm still Britani Knight, the name I chose in 2005 when I started wrestling at thirteen, living with my family back in Norwich, England. She was tough, too, not afraid to stick up for herself. But she got left behind somewhere along the way when I came to the States.

Sometimes, I wonder what happened to the real me, Saraya-Jade, the person who's buried somewhere inside. Where is she in all this mess?

My hands shake so badly that I can hardly scroll through the messages on my phone. Renee and my other female wrestling friends are all checking in on me. They love me and are worried. Mark Carrano, the talent-relations guy at WWE, reassures me by text.

Everything's going to be ok. We'll figure this out.

All I want is to hear the voice of my father, to listen to his love and support in my ear, to feel the comforting squeeze of his massive bear hug, making everything okay again. He's always over the moon about my successes.

But since I've been spiraling, I've kept a distance from my family, so afraid of seeing their disappointment in me. I've ignored the WhatsApp notifications on my phone, and now I'm afraid to look, afraid to see what they have to say. God, they'll be so fucking mortified. All these years, my parents and my brothers, Zak and Roy, have been my most loyal supporters. They're the reason I've come so far. They'll be fucking gutted with these leaked videos. They've forgiven me for so much over the years, made allowances for me, loved me through so much fucking shit. Surely, this is too much.

I stare at my phone, paralyzed, convinced that this will be the time they'll finally reject me. I'm positive I'm worthless and a failure. That nobody loves me. My whole life, I've only wanted to make Dad proud. And now I've gone too far; I've made an absolute fucking mess of my life.

I type in "Daddio." I can hear the phone ringing five thousand miles away in their little house in Norwich, the one place that feels like home. I'm terrified of what they'll have to say. If he can't forgive me for this, I don't want to live anymore. I hold my breath and wait for someone to answer.

PART One

PRIDE AND JOY

Picture yourself standing in the middle of an arena, a huge crowd stretching high above you from every angle. Some of them hate you with every fiber of their being, some of them love you to the point of obsession, and all of them are screaming at the top of their lungs. Music is blaring against your eardrums. The smoky scent of a firework that's just exploded into a million tiny embers hovers in the air. Every nerve in your body feels electric. You breathe deep into your lungs. And just then, the bottom of someone's boot connects square with your jaw.

Believe it or not: This is the Best. Feeling. *Ever.*

There's nothing in the world that comes close to the buzzing, adrenaline-filled vibe of a wrestling match. Not a mosh pit, not the most intense rock concert you've ever attended, not even the wildest, most exhilarating night of your life. It's downright contagious, the spirit of wrestling, the desire for good to triumph over evil, the howling from the fans at each setback, the screams of triumph when the babyface gets ahead. Even those who aren't wrestling fans get pulled into the spectacle, feeding off the energy, being sucked into the action on center stage. It's the classic good-versus-evil story everyone can relate to. Forever, people have loved to gather together to hiss and curse at the villain, to cheer for the hero, to hold their breath until the girl tied to the train tracks is rescued. It's a high that all wrestling fans know well.

In the mid-nineties, when wrestling in England was in its heyday and the halls were always chockablock with fans, it was my family's job to give them what they came for. And my job, even as an eight-year-old, was to help make the magic.

"Come on, kids. Up you go!" Dad called, slamming the double doors at the back of the family van closed, after boosting me and Zak into the family's big white cargo van, shoving me by the arse into the cramped space.

The van was loaded with all the parts needed to construct a full-size wrestling ring, packed Tetris-like in the back, and we crawled over the heap to find a space. The ride to the Corn Exchange wouldn't take long, but Dad worried we'd be late.

Mum came dashing from the house, nearly tumbling arse over tit, her dyed-tomato-red hair sticking up every which way, her tats on full display in a crop top despite the drizzling morning. She dragged a bag of wrestling gear and makeup behind her. Mum always did more than her fair share—driving everywhere, loading the van, herding the wrestlers and kids. She's a workhorse, a jill-of-all-trades.

"Careful there, love," Dad called to her. She was always getting hurt, mostly in the ring, and we all worried about her.

Trailing Mum was one or another of the wrestler/helpers who stayed with us, training with our family and generally adding to the blinding mayhem that seemed to surround us.

Zak and I found places on top of the heap of metal, foam pads, ropes, and canvas, and splayed ourselves out like starfish, keeping our heads as low as possible so as not to get smacked on the fucking head with every bump in the road. As the van puttered through the streets of Norwich, passing double-decker buses and the train station, Victorian homes and the university, we could hear Mum and Dad cursing and laughing, strategizing for the day's wrestling matches with their helpers, developing storylines to keep the punters entertained and screaming for more. Zak and I paid little attention, lost in our world in the back, but when Dad hit the occasional pothole, sometimes on purpose, Zak and I bounced around and laughed maniacally, screaming out curse words to his delight.

Once we arrived at our destination, the grunt work started. It was like we were the circus come to town, and now it was time to raise the big top—or at least the wrestling version of it.

The Ring. The Holy Grail. The Place Where All the Action Occurred.

First, we carried in the full-size iron posts we would use to make the ring's outer frame and pieced them together, all hands on deck. Then we laid bars of iron across that frame, like supports on a bunk bed, to create the foundation level. My hands smelled of WD-40 and iron from carrying the supports, an odor that soaked into my skin and never really went away. Once the support bars were in place, we heaved thick plywood boards, eight of them, each weighing what felt like a ton, across that foundation. The gym mats followed, and then finally the canvas, like a sheet stretched across the top of the mattress, the place where all the drama would unfold.

We had only one spare canvas, so if in the previous match a wrestler had bled on it or busted it or sweated all over it, you could never get it fully clean. We'd simply flip it over or switch it out with our only backup. Nine times out of ten, the canvas looked a bit dodgy.

We then tied all these layers down around the bottom of the ring with ropes before fabric—the skirt—encircled the rest of the ring. We weren't done, though.

The ropes went next, three tiers of them. Hooks connected the ropes to the posts and those connection points, the turnbuckles, needed to be covered in padding to protect the wrestlers. Sometimes we had big pads that covered all three points of connection, other times, smaller, individual pads did the job. My little fingers struggled, but I was able to tie the pads into place while Zak followed me, taping over the connection points.

That's one of the smells that really stick with you, the tape. There's the chemical smell of the adhesive part, but it's all mixed together with dirt and sweat and grime. Like us, that tape had been on the road for a while. It never got taken off. We just added another layer upon the coatings that already existed, creating a pungent odor without meaning to. Sticky stuff mixed with human perspiration, dust, and grunge, all with a heaping serving of the adrenaline that had soaked into the tape from the previous matches. The smell was sharp, and in some ways unpleasant, but will be forever tied in my mind with home and comfort and family and love.

Finally, once the ring was set up and ready to go, Zak and I got a little break. This was the moment I loved the most.

As Mum and Dad reviewed strategies with the other wrestlers, Zak and I tumbled our way through the empty seats of the venue, imagining the crowds that would soon fill the space until there wasn't room for even one extra body. Grandparents and great-grandparents, middle-aged folks, parents with their kids, teenagers with their friends. Today's venue, the Corn Exchange, was usually just a livestock auction house and reeked of cow manure. Soon, though, it would be transformed by all the crazy, wild energy of wrestling, the frenzied, hair-raising series of matches my family had come to present.

By the time I was eight, though, I was pretty sure I didn't want to become a wrestler myself. I'd seen too many of my family members hurt—my parents, my brothers, my uncles, and even Granddad. That was enough for me. But still, even from my place in the stands, I loved the energy of the ring. It's the rawest, most addicting drug I've ever encountered.

There was a time when I was smaller, when I didn't fully understand what was happening. Then, the whole scene fucking terrified me. When I was little, about four, I was seated with an older woman who'd been charged with keeping an eye on me. Once the venue had filled, my dad—Rowdy Ricky Knight, as he was known to fans—came roaring into the picture, circling the ring, talking trash about his opponent, beating his chest, showing his teeth, antagonizing the crowd, playing the heel. The whole auditorium went wild, booing him. Their screams echoed in my eardrums, drowning out everything else. I was terrified.

"No!" I screamed from the older woman's lap, squirming to try to get away from her and rescue Dad. People were so riled up at him, howling at the top of their lungs, even poking him with knitting needles they'd brought just for that purpose. I whimpered as the match began. Mum worked as Dad's manager, and though I tried like hell to wriggle out of the lady's arms to get to Mum, it was clear she was too busy to console me.

"They're hurting my dad!" I yelled at the lady restraining me, who only shushed me and tried to convince me it was all okay. I felt absolute terror. Blood dripped down my father's face, and I went frantic, trying to get to him, to protect him from the wrestler who was beating on him. Between the old woman and other helpers, along with a clump of fans, I was kept from flinging myself bodily into the ring. And then the match ended, and Dad was escorted backstage.

The lady brought me to him, and I ran into his massive arms, sobbing my eyes out.

"It's all right, princess." He wiped blood from his forehead before squatting to my level.

My dad was a straight shooter and he never lied to me. He never talked to me like I was a kid but as if I were an adult. He respected my ability to understand, even from a very young age.

"They were all yelling at you," I whined. "They said they hated you."

"It's okay. I'm just playing a character," he said. "*You* know I'm a good guy, but them out there? They all think I'm bad, and they enjoy shouting their lungs out at me. They think they're yelling at a bad guy."

"But you're hurt," I said, pointing to the thin line of blood that still dripped from his temple.

"This isn't real, you know?" he said. "It's fake blood."

I realized later that this was one exception to his honesty-is-the-best-policy rule. He was genuinely bleeding.

"See, princess, I'm fine." He dabbed the blood away.

From that day on, I started to get the picture. It's called kayfabe, the illusion that professional wrestling is not staged, that good really is brawling against evil before our very eyes. There's something so human about this, a chance to leave our daily chores, bullshit, and worries behind, to forget about complexity and shades of gray. This was a world where you fucking know good from bad right off the bat. And when good wins, we all scream and yell our fucking brains out, blowing off steam. And by the time we leave the arena, our shoulders are a little less heavy.

I came to see kayfabe like Santa Claus. When I was little, Mum would ring sleigh bells outside in the dark to convince us that Santa was on his way, and even after I was old enough to know the difference and to realize that Santa was really just Mum and Dad trying to give us a special experience, I wouldn't do anything to ruin the illusion. There's something mystical in continuing to believe.

And it's the same in the wrestling world. Belief is what makes the magic happen.

That day, we set up the ring twice; some days we did it as many as three times, bringing our family show on the road to multiple venues in a single day. And now I knew the secrets behind the acts. Zak and my big brother Roy taught me some moves. I knew to tuck my chin before I hit the ground and how to use the momentum of the person I was tussling with to make a more dramatic flip. I knew how to keep myself grounded so I couldn't be knocked over too easily. And I knew to wash or at least air out my stinky kneepads after training sessions. Those were foul pieces of equipment, and even with dryer sheets tucked into them and Febreze sprayed all over them, that god-awful smell haunted me. If a wrestling ring, just assembled, smells like home and love to me, then dirty kneepads were all the shit that came along with life, even when you were surrounded by love.

At the end of that long weekend, Zak and I hauled ourselves onto our perch in the back of the van as Mum drove toward our home in Norwich.

Most of the roads were made of cobblestone, and there were ruins everywhere, castles and buildings from years and years ago, all made of stone, and no one was allowed to touch them. The people in charge wanted to preserve the history and keep the ruins intact as long as possible, so it was illegal to mess with them in any way. There's a hill nearby—England's so flat, it's pretty special to have a hill—with Norwich Castle on top. Now it's a museum, mostly for history buffs and tourists. I totally loved history, especially after my mum pointed out one time when we were visiting that I had an ancestor in the castle! The castle had death masks—casts taken of criminals' faces after death to preserve their image, back in the days before photography—on display in the dungeon. One of the criminals was related to us. She was a woman, said to be a murderer, though I'm not sure who she supposedly killed. I think she was executed for her crimes.

The death masks were fucking terrifying, and yet I loved them, the way they captured the person's final expression. Some looked peaceful. Others in distress. Sometimes I could see a smirk or lack of remorse on the criminal's face. I noted wounds preserved in the cast, like the neck at a strange angle when a person had been hanged, or a jagged slice where a head had been severed from the body.

I dragged the few friends I had from school to the castle whenever I could to show them my ancestor's death mask. I was convinced she made me special somehow.

In addition to that castle and the freaky death masks, Norwich was known for having a church for every week of the year—though in our family, we weren't big churchgoers—and a pub in town for every day of the year. And eventually, my family would even own one.

The music in Norwich was also really good. We used to have a couple of venues where bands would pass through, and whenever I could, I'd go listen. There were a lot of buskers on the street, performing, singing, playing guitars and violins. And there was a staple I loved the most, the Norwich Market. It was gorgeous with colorful tents. Whenever I wasn't helping the family to set up rings, and if I had somehow earned a fiver, I'd be down at the market to buy what was advertised as "the cheapest chips in the UK."

*

When Mum finally pulled the van up back to our house, it was way past any normal kid's bedtime. But then again, we weren't a normal family. We were the Wrestling Knights of Norwich.

Dad woke me and Zak in the back, and we tumbled into the house, followed by our parents and the wrestling trainees. Mum and Dad hired out venues all over our part of England for wrestling matches, everything from grand halls to some pub car park. We needed to get a few hours of shut-eye because, too soon, it would be time to wake up and do it all over again.

RAISED BY WOLVES

Sink!" I demanded, standing next to the cooker in our little kitchen, staring up at Mum. I was really young, maybe three or four. She was running around like a chicken with her head cut off, trying to keep up with the chaos of our household, one that grew or shrank depending on the day of the week and which of the many different characters, mostly wrestlers, were staying with us at the moment. But whenever I asked for a bath, she caved. She adored me and would spoil the shit out of me all the time.

In that sink, I felt safe and loved, surrounded by sweet-smelling foam and my mother's warm attention. From that higher vantage point, I was able to see everything, the crazy-arse but wonderful mayhem of our house, and feel as if I were as tall as the others. I was still a lot smaller than Zak, who was fourteen months older, but I was gaining on him.

Mum gave me a cup so I could pour water over my head, and sometimes, I'd dump the entire cupful over the side of the sink just to see what would happen. I was a menace from my first breath, my love of mischief showing up early. Mum never got mad, though. She just laughed and fake-scolded me before cleaning up the mess.

After I was washed—Zak was often bathed before me—she wrapped us both in towels and took us to sit near the radiator to keep us warm, where we dug into the bowl of cornflakes with milk she'd placed there, just waiting for us. I always asked for more sugar, and she always gave it to me. It was the simple things Mum did that I just adored. She kept us toasty, wrapped up like that.

Once I was dry, I got dressed for the day and crawled under Daddio's legs. He sat on the settee watching the telly, a blanket thrown over his legs. I climbed under that cover, making a little fort for myself, protected from all the badness in the world. Sometimes Zak joined me, but other times I was alone and happy. I pretended I was an animal, usually Nala from *The Lion King*.

With Dad above and surrounding me, I felt secure. He was a big man—arms like Popeye's, thighs as big around as the tires on lorries, his hands the size of supper plates. I'd seen him pound the living daylights out of people, so I knew he could protect me better than anyone on this planet from anything. Under his legs, nothing bad could ever come near me. He was my world.

In our household, family was everything. I knew this from the time I could crawl. Zak was my best friend from the get-go. He kept close to me at all times, and at some point we started to feel as if we were twins, the age difference dissolving as I caught up to him in size, both of us glad to be in each other's company. Sure, we fought like all siblings do, tearing at the other's hair, raking nails across skin, and we got each other in trouble. In general, though, we were two peas in a pod.

We also had older siblings, Dad's kids from an earlier marriage. I've always hated the term "half siblings." We are brothers and sisters, blood related. There's nothing halfway about it to us. Roy and Nikki were a good bit older, and by the time Zak and I came along, they both had places of their own. Asa was only four years older, the closest in age to me and Zak, but he lived most of the time with his mother, Dad's ex-wife.

Meanwhile, a never-ending cast of characters showed up at our door whenever a big wrestling match was on TV or there was a tasty meal to be had. I never knew who'd be sitting at the table come dinnertime or sleeping over on any given night. This was just how family operated.

One time, an older woman was visiting us. She picked me up and was talking very close to my face. I squirmed, trying to get away from the stench coming from her mouth, a mix of onions, stale washcloths, and garlic. I kept pulling my face away from hers, but the odor flooded over me. When she wouldn't put me down, the words tumbled from my mouth.

"Your breath smells like dogshit!" I screamed at her.

I was only four, and Mum was mortified, though laughing under her breath.

"Saraya-Jade!" she scolded. "Apologize!"

And generally, no one scolded me for speaking the truth, a fact I appreciated. As I said, my parents were always honest with me and valued when I was honest with them. Maybe they should have thought twice about that, because speaking my mind got me into a shit ton of trouble. It still does. From a young age, I was like that: speaking my mind even if it got me into trouble. Of course, with that old woman I was rude, but my parents had told me it was okay to speak the truth. It took me years to realize that maybe I shouldn't do it all the time.

When I was little we struggled a lot financially, but since I was so well loved, I really didn't have a clue. Take Mickey, for example. Mickey was an old British gangster. He was my godfather and one of my dad's best mates; they'd met when they were both in prison. Mickey loved and doted on me. Whenever he came around, he always had presents for me, and sometimes a little something for Zak.

"Come here, Raya," Mickey called one Sunday, using the nickname my family favored. "I've got something special for you." Mickey had longish, wispy hair and reminded me of a rock star, slender and wiry.

I was only a small thing when he dragged into our living room the most gorgeous prezzie I'd ever laid eyes on. A rocking horse the size of a real pony! Made of wood that had been lovingly sanded and painted, she had genuine hair for a mane and a white glossy hide; her eyes were so realistic and captivating. Even eyelashes. She was a goddamn beauty! I was sure she would speak to me when everyone else went away and we were alone together. I couldn't believe how lucky I was.

For as long as I could remember I'd been pestering my parents for a horse, making an absolute nuisance of myself. They used it to their advantage. Whenever Dad wanted me to do something, he'd tease me.

"Be a good girl, and maybe we'll get you that horse you want."

Yeah, right!

But now, even though this wasn't a real horse, it was pretty fucking close. I needed help to pull myself onto the horse's back, she was so big. Mickey gave me a boost, and away I went in my imagination, riding this glorious animal all over England.

Mum and Dad looked at each other.

I paid zero attention. I was in heaven.

My parents were far from thrilled, since we could barely squeeze the rocking horse into the front room, behind the charity-shop couch and Dad's recliner. Certainly, there was no place else for it in our small home.

Hours went by, Mickey left, and I had to practically be pulled from the horse to have my tea. As soon as I finished, I climbed right back on and rode that horse until I almost fell asleep on her back. Mum finally carried me off to dreamland in the room I shared with Zak.

Our family was skint enough that dinner was sometimes mashed potato sandwiches (which, to be honest, I adore), and rent was always due. Bill collectors sometimes came to the door and we pretended we weren't home. Things were fucking tight, I get it now.

But I didn't then.

When I woke the next day and rushed from my bed to greet my horsey friend—ready to finally have the conversation I'd been dying to have with her, to hear about all the amazing places she'd been and the wisdom I knew she was just waiting to share with me—my beloved horse was gone. She'd been switched out with a tiny fucking plastic rocking horse suitable for a baby. I screamed like a banshee.

My parents tried to calm me. My beautiful creature, they explained, was half the size of our living room. It wasn't practical to keep it, and besides, they needed the money for bills. They sold my horse to buy groceries and to keep the heat on.

Did they think I was dense enough to believe this rinky-dink shit-looking plastic horse was the same as my dazzling girl?

I kicked the new horse and collapsed in tears. "Get her back!" I screamed. "Go buy her back!"

But that was impossible. The money had already been spent.

"We had to get food and pay bills," Mum said. "And it was taking up a lot of space. I tried to get you a replacement that's more your size and appropriate for our house."

I was fucking destroyed and cried for months. I am still not over it, though I can now see the truth. There's no way we could have kept her; she took up all the space in the front room, and there were more pressing needs. I understand fully why they got rid of her. But when I was younger, all I could think was *You evil, awful parents!*

It wasn't long after that that Mickey was murdered. At least, that's what my parents believed. The whole thing was kind of shady. He died in what the official record called a heroin overdose, but my parents were convinced that wasn't the case. First of all, Mickey had never been into heroin, and he'd been found dead with the syringe taken out of his arm. Given the amount of drugs found in his body during the autopsy, he would have nodded off right away, unable to remove the syringe himself. My parents didn't hide that they were certain his death was not accidental or of his own doing. He had not exactly lived an honest lifestyle.

My dad was crushed. . . . Mickey had been his best mate. And even though Daddio had mostly given up drinking when he met Mum and they had Zak and me, for a week or two following Mickey's death, he downed vodka like it was water, off somewhere in his own world. After a while, he pulled himself together.

This was the world I lived in. One in which rocking horses disappeared in order to keep bellies full, and where present-carrying gangsters like Mickey ended up murdered for no good reason. But as a kid, it was all just normal life. Nothing remarkable.

What saved me throughout that time and still does now is my love for animals. I don't know how I came to this understanding, but I think I had it from the day I shit my first nappy. I knew instinctively that people could be mean and nasty to one another hurtful and vicious in so many ways. Animals, though, were different. If you treated them well, they returned the favor. They could be trusted. So I surrounded myself with them whenever possible.

A few years post–rocking horse, I connected with an older lady and would go to her house after school. She was an animal hoarder, her house crammed with every kind of creature under the goddamn sun, even an aviary full of birds; she let me take home some of her pets as my own.

One day, I brought home a king python I called Zsa Zsa. My parents were into classic films, and I knew about the fancy woman Zsa Zsa Gabor. I thought that was such a classy name for a snake. I loved her and would talk to her at night. Her golden-and-black-scaled body was soft and dry to the touch, and she'd stick out her tongue for me. To feed her, I bought frozen dead mice from the pet store, defrosting them first—Zsa Zsa would never touch them frozen—and dangled them in front of her to convince Zsa Zsa they were moving. She was a very picky eater.

At one point, I convinced my mum to let me buy a pet mouse with a little cage, Bailey, named for Baileys Irish Cream. (Many things in our world were named for alcohol.)

I was worried Bailey was lonely all by herself, so I convinced Mum to let me get a second mouse I named Jameson, for Jameson Irish Whiskey, a male. Mum knew about mice and their tendency to breed, so why she let me do that, I don't know. As much as I wanted to be a veterinarian someday, I hadn't yet learned much about the reproductive habits of mice.

I was cleaning out their cage one day, and in their bed area I saw a bundle of pink stuff. I got closer and poked at the little pile. They'd had babies! I was so excited. I didn't tell my parents, just got more cages to house the little ones. But the space between the metal bars of those cages was way too big to hold back the mice babies. They were able to wiggle through the slats and get away.

I panicked, trying to collect them as fast as I could and shove them back into their cages. *Oh shit! Dad's gonna kill me!* For all his toughness, Dad was super squeamish about mice and hated them more than just about anything. He was annoyed Mum had let me get the two as pets in the first place. If he knew about the babies, he'd be pissed at me!

I ran to the cupboard and grabbed pillow cases to put around each of the cages to keep the babies from fleeing. There. That should do it.

But when I came home from school the next day, the mice had chewed through the pillowcases and were gone, scattered throughout the room. I found them in corners of my bedroom, hiding in my shoes, in drawers. I scrambled to get them all, but soon the babies were having babies and then the grandbabies were at it, too. Shit!

If Dad found out about this mice explosion, I would be in so much trouble.

The next night, people came to watch a wrestling match at our house. A neighbor screamed when she saw one of the mice scamper across the floor. The man who owned the pub down the road saw one in our bathroom. Dad, who hadn't noticed the mice until that moment, finally copped on and was now having a heart attack every five minutes. He's not a very agile kind of a guy, but to get away from the mice, he moved with the speed of a lightning bolt.

"Get these fuckers out of my house!"

That was it. Mum had had it. She took the cages from my room and brought them to the back garden, opening the cage doors. My adorable mice ran into the weedy yard and made their getaway. I was sad and cried, but I also celebrated their freedom. Imagine the adventures they might have!

Before we knew it, though, the entire fucking neighborhood was infested. Though the neighbors didn't complain, the critters got into other people's homes, could be seen darting in the alleyway. Even the church behind our house and the council house were overrun with them. Eventually, the council house people arranged for the entire area to be fumigated. My little mice had taken over everything, and that was the only option left. As I said, I was a menace from the get-go.

After that, my parents tried to stop me from bringing home pets, but I didn't listen. I just did what I wanted. Seemed a bit hypocritical to me as a kid, since my parents had always been the ones to teach me to ask forgiveness after the fact, if necessary, but to never wait for permission.

One time, I unknowingly stole the neighbor's dog. It was an Alsatian, a bigger version of a German shepherd, who'd been running around on her own. I thought she might be a stray, so I took her home. The dog was beautiful and regal, and for once, Daddio was on board with me bringing home strays.

"Maybe we'll keep this one," he said, though he quickly changed his tune when the dog took a shit in the living room.

It turned out the gorgeous creature belonged to Emily, the owner of the Chinese restaurant just down the road.

She knocked on our door and couldn't have been nicer. "Can I please have my dog back?" she asked.

I hadn't meant to steal her dog and would never have done anything to hurt Emily—I adored her. But to me, any animal on its own appeared available for adoption.

One night, a friend of Mum's came over with a dog. Her friends, a gay couple, were moving abroad and couldn't take the dog with them. She was all black and gorgeous. I managed to convince Dad to let me keep this one. Her named was Tari—short for Tarigan. We already had two dogs in our small house, and so it was mayhem after that. Zak had a turtle and a hamster I named Rowdy for my dad's wrestling name, Rowdy Ricky Knight. I had two rabbits, Peter and Pigsy, and two birds, Rocco and Roxie. After a while the house was too crowded, and Dad made me give Tari to his friend Joe.

"I can't deal with all these animals!" Dad said.

Zak was much the same with a love for animals. When we were younger, the two of us went to the little pond down by the park, a ten-minute walk, and caught toads and frogs we brought home. We dug a pond in our back garden, carrying buckets full of water from the kitchen, constructing a place for them to live. Of course, they escaped immediately.

I was always trying to make a safe place for my animal friends, and what better place for them than my house? Loved by me, protected by my family. That's the safest place there is.

All that started to change, though. My brother Asa came to live with us. I'd learn later that his mother basically abandoned him and had shown him nothing but neglect from his very first breath. My dad wasn't even his "real" father, but he had raised Asa as his own anyway. Asa joined our family as if he'd always been a part of it.

By the time I was too big to be bathed in the sink, I often took a bath with Zak and Asa, all of us throwing bubbles and water at one another in the tub. I should have known something was not quite right when Asa intentionally pooped in the bath. I don't know how, as a child, I knew that was wrong in a way that he, too, should have known. He and Zak thought it was hilarious. Me, not so much.

GYPSY

I was no more than an infant when the woman approached my mum as she pushed me in a pram over the cobblestone streets of Norwich. I was too young to remember, but the story was told and retold to me throughout my life.

The woman gestured for Mum to pause on her walk so she could take a good look at me. "Let's see that wee bundle you have there."

The woman was what we would call a gypsy, but some people think that's an outdated or offensive term. Many think of gypsies as Romani, but there are also migrant gypsy–type people from Ireland, like in my family. The correct term, I've been told, is "Irish Traveler" because of its traditionally nomadic culture, but it's never bothered us.

The woman was tiny and wore a full-length skirt with a blouse, a shawl draped over her shoulders, and a headscarf covering her hair.

After Mum stopped and chatted, the old woman peered into my pram. When she saw my face, her expression changed from one of mild interest to surprise bordering on astonishment.

"Oh my," she said. "This one is special. There's something about her." She studied me longer, then stood and addressed my mum.

"This girl is going to be something special. She's going to live in America one day. She's going to wear a uniform of some sort, and her name is going to be up in lights."

It was quite the wild-arse prophecy. Everyone told mothers of new-borns their kids were special, didn't they? And sure, at that time in the late nineties, everyone was dying to move to the States; that part was the most ordinary prediction one could make.

Some believe Irish Travelers have psychic abilities, though. Dad, despite being a descendent of Irish Travelers himself, was a skeptic. He does believe in Jesus and God but draws the line at ghosts and paranormal phenomena. But Mum has always been a bit mystical—she loved tarot cards and anything of a spiritual or supernatural nature. She used to take me to spiritual churches and ghost hunting at places like abandoned asylums—I loved it.

Over the years, Mum ran into that same lady over and over, at random places and times. On every occasion, whether I was present or not, the lady repeated her prediction and asked if it had come to pass yet.

During my teen years, Daddio was always bugging me to avoid drugs and for God's sake, don't get pregnant. I'm not sure he believed the woman, but he had it in his head that I was going to do something valuable someday, as long as I didn't fuck it up. Maybe I'd be a vet, which is what I initially wanted, and that was fine with him. And though we lived in a smaller house under pretty difficult conditions, he believed I was going to be exceptional somehow, someday.

He kept reminding me. It was up to me to make sure I didn't become a bum.

My parents were soulmates from the minute they found each other. They'd met at what's called a holiday camp in the UK, like a trailer park but with really nice trailers for families to come and have a getaway. People called bluecoats worked there like cruise directors, setting up entertainment and making sure everyone was having fun, encouraging folks to stay within the site boundaries. The bluecoats arranged shows and made sure all was well in the restaurant. Being at a holiday camp was basically like being at a resort, but you stayed in pretty nice trailers instead of villas or in a posh hotel.

Growing up, Dad had been a total pain in the ass and had done a lot of drugs. He has a bunch of tattoos he got when tripping on acid one time, all of them inked on that one occasion. Before he met my mum, his nickname had been Paddy the Bat. "Paddy" because his first name was Patrick and he was Irish, and "the Bat" for his weapon of choice. Watch out if he came at you wielding a baseball bat; he could be vicious with that thing.

Dad was a football hooligan and had very strong ties to British gangsters, like my godfather Mickey. Dad had gone to jail as a younger man because everything about his life was violent. He used violence to get money, and it was his go-to coping device whenever he was mad. That's how he solved everything. His family was made up of really proud people who fought stuff out. If you had a problem with someone, you fought it out, and everything was settled after that. Though he can get violent at the tip of a hat, he's also fiercely loyal. He never lost it with us, for example, but if anyone was to get mad at us, he'd blow a fucking gasket.

Dad had gotten out of jail before he met my mum and had been working as a bouncer in the eighties. He was a scary-looking dude, given his size, and people tended to give him wide berth. It was working as a bouncer that Dad met Uncle Jimmy, who's really not a blood relation but one of my dad's best mates.

"You ever wrestle?" Jimmy asked him after watching him pitch out a couple of rowdy blokes from a pub, tossing two full-grown men as easily as if they'd been sacks of potatoes. "I bet you'd be good at that."

That's when the family business started. Under Uncle Jimmy's direction, Dad learned the moves and then the two of them started tag-teaming it, earning a few bob here and there, performing at carnivals and other venues, a career move that allowed Dad to stay out of the more serious trouble that had long followed him. In prison, Dad had studied law and knew more than most solicitors did. People were always coming to our house to seek his legal advice. With what he knew about the law and how it could fuck him up, he didn't want to end up behind bars again.

He and Uncle Jimmy were booked to do wrestling shows for six weeks at this particular holiday camp, and—wouldn't you know it—my mum, Julia, twenty-one, was hired there as a chef in the restaurant.

She was basically homeless at the time, sleeping on friends' couches. She'd left her family home because her stepdad had sexually abused her when she was a kid. When she finally told her mum what had happened with her stepfather, her mum didn't believe her, so she ran. She felt as if she had no one in her corner and was at times suicidal after that trauma.

But then, here comes my dad, big and brawny, though inside he's a total sweetheart. Over those six weeks, they fell in love. He was twenty years older than her, and even though he told her a bunch of porkies at the outset—like that he drove a Mercedes and had a lot of money—she totally fell for him, and they became inseparable. Dad showed her that there were people in this world who would believe her, starting with him, and that was a big fucking deal to my mum. Though Dad had tried to make himself bigger than what he was when they first met, and my mum found out pretty quickly that he was none of the things he'd claimed, by then she was head over heels, and it didn't matter.

At that time, my dad had stopped using hard drugs though still had the occasional drink. He could see how the drugs were messing up his new girlfriend and suggested they both get and stay sober. She later told me how she'd come up with my name. She had gone to a Slayer concert in the eighties, and while high on acid, she misheard the band name as *Saraya*. She just knew that would be the name of her daughter, if she ever had one. Once they got together, they both straightened out their acts. To ask them about it, they'd tell you that finding each other and their wrestling business is what saved both of them.

He taught her the ins and outs of wrestling, and she was pretty good at it. She worked as the manager for him and Uncle Jimmy. She'd go out in the ring all done up in a dress and makeup, and then be ringside when the men wrestled. Anytime they had to play bad guys, she'd help them cheat to win. Soon, she was in the ring herself, running the ropes and doing slingshot catapults. She was known as Sweet Saraya.

They married, and Zak was born. Dad was still having the odd drink here and there, but at that point he decided to stop. They both wanted to make a better life for their kids than they'd had. I followed along quickly, and then we were a family, with our brothers and sisters from Dad's earlier marriage.

To say my life was formed by wrestling would be a massive fucking understatement. Dad watched *World of Sport* on the telly nonstop, old-school wrestling from the seventies and eighties rebroadcast. Then, every single weekend we'd be doing shows. During the week, we hosted training seminars, and a random assortment of wrestlers was always staying at our house. Mum constantly made wrestling merchandise and posters, and the phone rang off the hook with people wanting to arrange wrestling events.

Though it was the family business and you'd think he might get sick of it, wrestling was all Daddio ever talked about—his first love. He'd found himself and a feeling of worth in the wrestling world and absolutely nothing could dim its shine for him.

Zak, too, caught the wrestling bug the minute he popped out of Mum's uterus. He lived, breathed, and shit wrestling. He owned all the wrestling rings and action figures sold at the toy stores. Back then the premier professional wrestling organization was the World Wrestling Federation (WWF) before it became World Wrestling Entertainment (WWE) in 2002. We watched Jake the Snake and Stone Cold Steve Austin and Hulk Hogan on TV growing up, and Zak knew every storyline. The bedroom we shared had posters of these wrestlers on his side. He knew the world so inside and out, he could tell the identity of a given wrestler just by the boots he wore. He was a walking wrestling encyclopedia. Everyone we knew thought he would be a professional wrestler one day.

My half of our bedroom was different. I had animal and music posters, as well as ones from *South Park*. Sure, I had a few wrestling posters, a nod to the family dynasty—Scotty 2 Hotty and Rikishi and Lita—but I wasn't all that into it. My bed duvets featured Disney's Pocahontas, while Zak's were always wrestling related. He was the one in the family destined to go into that world. Not me.

Part of the reason I shied away from the business was that I was scarred from having seen people in my family, particularly my mum, hurt while in the ring.

Mum was a great wrestler but also very injury prone. I've never known someone who got hurt as much as she did. There was a period when I was little, in first school, that a wrestling injury blinded her for six months. That scared the shit out of me. She'd been hit in the head and one eye swelled shut and then a few days later, she lost most of her vision in both eyes. She didn't know if she'd ever see again.

For those months, Daddio had to cook for us because she couldn't see to operate the cooker, and in doing so, he nearly killed me. While he made a great cheesy mash, this one day he was making roasties—roasted cut-up chunks of potatoes.

I was still pretty small, and he'd cut the potatoes into pieces too large for a mouth the size of mine. And yes, I was a dumb dumb to put the whole thing in my mouth, but I'd always been able to eat the roasties Mum made without an issue. Of course, I choked on it, and he had to perform a Heimlich maneuver on me. So while he did almost kill me with the roasties, he also did save me. I couldn't wait until Mum was healed enough to cook again.

My mum is a badass bitch, though.

When I was about twelve years old, I hadn't started wrestling fully yet. My parents were away a lot, traveling to shows for work and taking my siblings along, too, since they were already wrestlers. On one particular trip, they went to Isle of Wight, which is a place in England that you have to take a ferry to, so it's quite difficult to get in and out of quickly.

I was staying with my friend Nevina and her mum, Sandra, who was a bartender at my parents' pub. We were running around the street, as you do at that age, when Nevina and I got into an argument. It was probably over something dumb, and I can't remember what it was about now, but it was enough for Nevina to go knock on a woman's door. I don't know how she knew this woman or what her relationship was with her, but her name was Ann. I would guess she was about forty but looked much older from the very obvious drug addiction. Ratty and unwashed long brown hair, facial features sunken and sagging. Gaps in her smoke-stained teeth.

Nevina started making stuff up, saying I was trying to fight her. I wasn't. All of a sudden, Ann comes out and grabs me by my hair and pulls me down to ground. She starts kicking, punching me, slapping me while having clumps of my hair in her hands. Clawing at me like a wild animal. I somehow fight my way out of her gross witchy hands and onto my feet.

"Go get Mummy!" she mocked as I made a run for it.

I ran straight to Nevina's house, grabbed the house phone, and called my mum.

"Mum, this lady just beat me up!" I said, sobbing. I told her everything that had just happened.

A reminder, reader, I'm only twelve years old, and I had just got my arse whooped by a rabid crackhead for no reason. My body was covered with bruises and scratches. Black-and-blue.

Mum said, "Stay there," and put down the phone.

Sandra, Nevina's mum, took care of my wounds. Within a few hours, we get a call from the police station. My mum was arrested.

How could that be? She's in the Isle of Wight working! You have to take the ferry to the mainland, then drive a few hours. But somehow my mum did that in record time.

She had hopped off the phone, walked out the door of where she was supposed to perform that night, and went straight to Ann's. When she knocked on her door, Ann answered by cracking it open just a little bit.

The moment she did, Mum Superhuman kicked the door in.

"Here's Mummy!" she said. "So let's do this one by one. What's the first thing you did to my daughter . . . ? Oh yeah, you grabbed her by her hair and dragged her to the ground."

So she did just that.

"What's next . . . ? Oh yeah, you started punching and kicking her like this." And she did that, too.

She threw that little crackhead around her shithole of a home, putting her through tables and cabinets. She picked her up and pinned her against the wall, pulling a knife from her sock and then proceeding to push it into her nose and say, "I dare you to sneeze, bitch."

Ann scrambled for the phone in her pocket, which had the police on speed dial. She clicked the number and put the phone to her ear. All the while, Mum still had the knife up her nose. My mum grabbed her phone and said, "You better come here quick before I really hurt her."

She threw Ann and her phone to the ground, walked out, and sat on the curb outside Ann's flat waiting for the police to come. She had shoved the knife back into her sock, accidentally stabbing herself, so then she had started bleeding too. We laugh about that part now.

The police did come, and both women were taken to the station. After a couple of hours, they were released. My mum got away with a slap on the wrist because of what Ann did to me, and Ann got away with it too—turns out, we learned she was an informant for the police.

Which is fucked-up, right? How is she allowed to beat up a child and get away with it just because she stooges on the other crackheads? Whatever.

My justice was already served because my mum beat the living fuck out of her and continued to harass her anytime she saw her in the street. She would scream, "I can smell a fucking rat!" and had told everyone Ann was an informant, so now she was not trusted around the area. She ended up disappearing somewhere, and we stopped seeing her around, thank God.

I went to school and told everyone that story. God, my mum is cool. There've been many times in my life when she was insanely protective, but that one always sticks out, because how the fuck did she get there so quickly?! My badass mother, ladies and gents. My hero. Mum, I love you so much, and I'll never forget that day.

Wrestling was different, though, and I hated when she would get hurt in the ring. All I could think was *Why do you keep doing this? You're constantly hurt!* Dad was injured a lot, too, but nothing like Mum. Why would I want to do something like that if it was getting them bruised and mangled all the time? It just didn't make sense. And since everyone was sure Zak was going to be the family superstar, I was excused from that calling. Sure, my stubbornness played a role as well. If the family thought I'd be a good wrestler, of course I wanted nothing to do with it. Whenever possible, I wanted to not be like the rest of them. I wanted to be unique. Besides, I loved animals so much and watched *Animal Planet* all the time and just wanted to be a zoologist or vet.

That said, growing up as I did, I had no choice but to learn a few wrestling moves. When I was just barely able to walk, my big brother Roy would put his hands, palms out, in front of my face and tell me to hit them. It was his version of self-defense training.

"Come on, Raya, you got more than that in you," he'd taunt until I whacked him with some power behind the hit.

"Good job! Again!"

I hit his palm, barely able to stand on my own two feet, and he'd move his hands about, teaching me to be agile and quick.

"Hit here. And here. And here," he'd say, the targets I needed to follow moving like blurry images in a kaleidoscope.

He'd praise me afterward, and I loved that.

Zak taught me the basic wrestling moves as I got a bit older—how to tuck my chin, how to take a fall, how to flip him and to execute spots—

choreographed series of moves. It was our way of playing. It might be serious stuff for Zak, but for me, it was just for fun.

My brothers always looked out for me.

Once, when I was in middle school, I wanted to get a haircut—long with those short, choppy emo layers on top that were popular at the time. I was dying for a professional haircut like the other girls' in my school. For the first time, I was figuring out what I wanted to look like—more alternative, more like myself—instead of just wearing my brothers' old hand-me-downs. Up until then, I had mostly dressed like a tomboy.

I had tucked away some money from my uncle Stanley and coins that I'd found in the couch cushions or on the pub floor. Even if I'd had the money sooner, I wouldn't have gone. Before that, I'd had a problem with head lice that had been a fucking nightmare. I was worried they'd see the lice and tell me to get the fuck out of there.

But once Mum and I got the situation under control, using skinny little combs and shampooing the shit out of me with eye-stinging chemicals, the first thing I wanted to do was get that haircut. Until that point, Mum had always cut and colored my hair—even when I was really small, she was always experimenting with my look. She once dyed my hair blond, and though I was tiny, people thought I looked like a young Britney Spears. Dad started calling me "Britney" after that.

My parents let me walk to the salon on my own, a stone's throw away from the house. I explained my vision to the hairstylist and showed her a photo I had printed out, nervous but excited to become a new, cooler version of myself. She went straight in, chopping one side off at the shoulder. Immediately, I started sweating all over. Things were going sideways fast, but I was too anxious to say anything. More and more hair landed in my lap and on the floor around me. I could hear my dad's warning echoing in my mind: *Just don't cut it too short.*

Fuck.

I don't know if I didn't explain what I wanted well enough to the stylist or she wasn't familiar with the newest emo hair trends. Whatever the reason, she really botched the job, and I looked *awful*. The cut was waaaaay too short and boyish. I looked like Lord Farquaad, straight out of *Shrek*. I had expected to walk out of the salon feeling like a badass. Instead, I rushed out with my tail between my legs, looking like I'd lost a fight with a pair of clippers.

I walked home, catching glimpses of myself in the shop windows I passed—the chemist, the butcher, the chippie—feeling myself shrink more each time I saw my reflection. It looked ridiculous. Daddio, who's very much into traditional standards of female beauty, was going to be pissed. It's funny, he thinks women should have long, natural hair and he hates tattoos, and yet he married my mum, who wears her hair dyed tomato red, her skin covered in tattoos. He would always say that a woman should look a certain way, and my mum would just do the complete opposite, which I loved. And secretly, my dad did, too.

Sure enough, the minute I walked in the door, Dad sucked in his breath at the sight of me. "What have you done?" he teased. "Wait until your brothers see this."

"Don't tell Roy." I was in tears, mad that my dad's reaction was exactly as embarrassing as I'd imagined all the way home.

Roy was like my second father, and it was bad enough that Daddio thought my haircut was awful. I'd have to hide from Roy for the next few months until it grew out. Thankfully, he lived seven miles away, so that wouldn't be too hard.

I ran up to my room, mortified. Meanwhile, Dad was downstairs on the antique rotary phone with my brother. He called me back downstairs so Roy could have a turn giving me a hard time over the phone.

"Raya, I'm so disappointed." He wasn't serious, but I was so upset I couldn't tell.

A few hours later, Roy was at the front door, having walked the seven miles to see me. When he got a good look at me, his whole body deflated. "Why'd you cut all your long hair off?"

I couldn't come up with words to answer him. . . . I was too humiliated. He tried to put on a stern face but failed. He wrapped his big arms around me.

"I think it looks good!" he said.

I realized he had just been giving me a hard time over the phone. He had walked all that way just to make me feel better about myself, and I did. Especially when I realized he still had a seven-mile walk to get back home. He'd done all that because he adored me. That's the kind of family I had. They would never judge me for something stupid like a haircut.

I was thirteen when my thoughts about the wrestling world changed. We were at a match and had just finished setting up the ring for the night's events. My part of the work was done for the next few hours until it was time to take it all down. Roy would be wrestling that night, as would Mum, Dad, and Zak. And I'd be screaming my head off for each and every one of them, with Asa, who also didn't wrestle, by my side.

That is, until Daddio pulled me aside. "Raya, we have a bit of a jam, and I need you to help out."

Zak and Mum crowded around me.

"There's a problem, and Sarah can't make it tonight."

Sarah was one of the female wrestlers in the gang Dad toured with. She was to be featured in a six-woman tag.

"I need you to go in and sub for her, okay?"

"What? I'm not a wrestler."

"Just for tonight, can you cover for us? You don't have to continue, but you know enough. We'll pair you with Zak. It'll be just like messing around in the training camps at home."

"How am I supposed to wrestle with Zak if it's a women's event?"

"He's always in that match, dressed like a girl. It'll be great!" Daddio said.

"I don't have any wrestling gear."

"We'll figure out something."

They pulled together a pair of my mum's beaten-up old boots that had holes in them. They were pretty awful, but the best we could do. I was wearing baggy black pants and just added on one of Mum's old wrestling T-shirts. Meanwhile, they got Zak dressed up like the Pink Power Ranger with a mask and a padded bra and we were good to go.

Fine. I'd do this thing this one time to help my family out, and that would be that.

"Ladies and gentlemen!" The voice of the announcer, Michael Mann, echoed over the PA system. He'd been the announcer for my dad since the very beginning. I called him "eyebrows" because he had these thick, bushy eyebrows that stuck out.

"Give it up for the amazing, incomparable Britani Knight!"

Just before that moment, we'd had a quick discussion about what my name would be. Ever since the blond dye job, Daddio had called me Britney, but we changed the spelling to make it an anagram of Britain. Our family ring name, the Knights, was also fabricated. In the wrestling world, people took on stage names. Dad had chosen "Knight" in homage to his favorite musician, Gladys Knight.

Upon hearing my name announced, my stomach hurt, and I felt like I was going to throw up; I was so nervous and terrified. To this day, that still occurs, and I always feel like I'm going to need to go to the bathroom beforehand, but it all changes the moment I step into the ring.

And that's what happened, even this first time. Despite the fact that the crowd was minuscule, and their cheers a little anemic, I was hooked. The adrenaline rush was amazing. I could feel the energy and excitement of every single person in the audience, cheering for me as I grappled with Zak, who laughed like a maniac as I tossed him, the Pink Power Ranger, around the ring. He and I joked with each other, and it was no different from when we did it for fun, only now people were hooting and hollering and appreciating our moves.

Now I got it. Finally. This was why Mum chanced injuries. Why Zak trained and lifted weights constantly. Why Roy had me hit his hands as a kid. Why Daddio spoke of little other than wrestling. There was no feeling like it. And maybe it hit me even harder because I wasn't expecting the rush. It took me off guard, in the best possible way. Whatever this amazing, joyous feeling was, I knew one thing for sure: I wanted more of it.

FADE TO BLACK

As a kid, did you ever have something so awful happen to you that you still work hard to not think about it, to try to forget it, to force it the fuck out of your brain? I wonder, sometimes, if those early experiences shaped me in ways I didn't fully realize at the time.

And shit, to be honest, I still don't fully understand their impact now.

Zak was there, too, and we never discussed what happened, not for nearly a quarter of a century. We were both really fucked-up by the experience, which is a warning to you, reader. If this sounds like something you know too well, if this sounds familiar in a way that makes the hair on the back of your neck stand up and your hands start to sweat, I'm so sorry that was your experience, too.

This is your out. Take it.

All I remembered for a long time was the smell, like unwashed arse. Unchanged underwear, someone who didn't wipe themselves well after using the toilet and who almost never showered. That smell is embedded in my brain. Plus, the image of dirty bitten-down fingernails, grime beneath the raw bleeding edges and all around the cuticles, the unwashed-arse smell seeming to seep from those hands.

I have to shake myself just writing those words, it messes with me that much.

It started when I was about six and still sharing a room with Zak. Until that time, everything about my life had been wonderful. I was surrounded by love. I had animals to play with and a best friend and brother in Zak, plus the adoration of my parents, and my older siblings, Roy, Asa, and Nikki. Nothing more for a girl to want.

Bedtime was my absolute favorite part of the day. Not because I was ready and willing to settle down—never!—but because Mum made those times so special. Instead of simply reading us bedtime stories, she acted out the whole thing. Goldilocks and the three bears. The troll under the bridge. Jack and the beanstalk.

"'Fee-fi-fo-fum!'" Her voice shook with fury as she looked for Jack—played by me and Zak—who'd stolen the giant's magic hen and golden coins. "I smell the blood of an Englishman!"

We dived under our duvets or ducked into the closet, trying to escape the giant's rage, laughing like fucking hyenas the whole time.

Zak and I ran from wardrobe to behind the bedroom door, jumped from bed to bed, following the stories, shrieking in pretend fear when she popped out as the troll, loving her dramatics. Seriously, I don't think this was the best way to settle down six- and seven-year-olds to sleep, but I adored every moment of it. Her love for us came through so strongly in those bedtime routines, the way she wanted joy and playfulness and laughter to be our inheritance—not the trauma she'd experienced.

That was important to our parents, to try to interrupt the generational traumas that had shaped both of them. But sometimes, in trying to get away from one reality, we don't recognize the way the fucking cycle is continuing on, all over again.

In my family, we always took in strays. If a wandering animal came within ten miles of our place, I'd find it in a heartbeat and bring it home. Mum and Dad were the same, but with people. They just always felt like they could fix the world.

As such, our house was constantly full of people who needed a place to live for a short period of time. Some were wrestler trainees who my folks took under their wing, and sometimes troubled youth who found a sense of self-worth in wrestling just as my father had. When people were having a hard time and needed a place to stay, they came to the Knight house. My parents always felt like they could help, like they could rescue people.

How could my parents not take them in, give them a place to stay, share a meal or two? My dad had grown up one of twelve kids, some of them foster children. Mum had been homeless for a time when she was younger. They didn't want to see other children suffer like they had.

That's how Todd came to live with us, though I don't remember him actually *arriving* there. Mum and Dad had known his parents and taken him in when he was small, thinking they might help save this kid. His father, apparently, had been sent to jail (later, my parents would hear that was because he was a pedophile, but that was not the story they were told at the time), and his mum didn't want anything to do with Todd.

He was about twelve years older than me—I was six when it started—so maybe he was eighteen? We were living on Morse Road. I remember that.

Zak and I shared a room at that stage, and my bed was along the wall on one side and Zak's was at an angle to mine, along another wall with a window in between so that we faced each other on a diagonal. We had a little TV with a VHS player attached to it, and we'd watch movies. Sometimes horror movies, which Mum would try to take out of the player, and I just popped them back in. The two-part miniseries *It* with Tim Curry, based on a Stephen King book, I adored. The thing was, horror movies didn't scare me much; it was in real life that things got really terrifying.

Our parents were looking to buy the local pub at the time. Soon, we'd move and live above that pub, so Mum wasn't around to do this bedtime make-believe routine with us anymore, busy getting things set up at the pub, working as a bartender and chef. She asked Todd to take her place, telling him about the stories and how to make them as fun as possible.

I don't know if he ever tried acting out the stories as she asked, because I have only a handful of memories from that time. But those I *do* have are like Technicolor, as sharp and stinging as an open wound. Did it start with me or with Zak? I'm not sure.

One memory is of Todd sitting on my bed, supposedly tucking me in for sleep. Rather than read me a story or act out a fairy tale, he introduced me to something I was not at all eager to learn about.

He pulled out his thing and started touching himself. I didn't know what to say or do. This felt very odd, and I was confused.

"I want you to touch it," he said, urging my hand toward his lap. "It's okay. You can touch it."

The whole episode felt wrong, and I most definitely didn't want to touch his thing, but he was older, and we were supposed to listen to him. He was in charge when our parents were out. I looked over at Zak's bed, and he looked like maybe he was asleep. I imagined him waking up, asking, "What's happening, Raya?"

Even if he had spoken, I wouldn't have known what to say. I felt gross inside and didn't know what was going on or how to stop it. I thought that if I did what Todd asked, maybe he'd go away. So at his urging, I touched his thing with one finger.

As soon as my skin touched his, though, he exploded all over me, covering me in a sticky mess that totally freaked me out. He tried to wipe it away but just managed to smear it on my pajamas, my sheets, and my Disney duvet.

From that day on, my bed became stained with his smell. I couldn't get the stench of him to leave.

The next night, the routine was much the same except this time he was sitting by Zak's bed, touching himself, urging Zak to participate as I watched from under the covers, wishing I was asleep. Zak and I said nothing to each other about what was happening.

In time, Todd was no longer just sitting on our beds but actually in our beds. I'm not 100 percent sure what he was doing with Zak, but he was touching me down there and making me feel sick. And I didn't know how to get him to stop.

Zak and I didn't talk about what was going on, and we certainly didn't tell our parents. If I'm dead honest, there was part of me that thought people wouldn't believe us. Mum hadn't been believed when she was molested by her stepfather. You would think that knowing that, I could be sure that she'd believe us. But I wasn't. And another part of me just felt sick that it had happened, and I didn't *want* to tell anyone. I didn't want it to be real.

The worst part, and I've only just begun to come to terms with this, was when Todd would initially come to my bed at night, and Zak intervened.

"Hey, Todd. Come over here." He'd pull back the side of his blanket and make a space for him.

I knew then, but didn't really understand until recently, in a way that now breaks my heart, that my brother was trying to take the abuse *for* me, to save me from this monster who was robbing us both of our childhoods.

Soon, our family moved into the apartment above the pub, and I hoped that maybe, with the change of places, the shit with Todd would stop. But it didn't. What made it even worse was that the music and chatter from the pub below seeped up through our floorboards. Our bedroom was right above one of the main rooms. People in England love their fucking sing-alongs, everyone out and screaming, having a good time. The sounds of their voices drifted up to us, making me feel even more alone and vulnerable. Or, if they weren't singing at the top of their voices, there'd be music, or a poker night, people laughing and having a good time, which made what we were going through that much more painful. I could picture Mum in the kitchen, cooking for everyone, a TV or two blasting as well, the sounds of hilarity surrounding them.

And there we were in our beds just above their heads, it felt like only inches away . . . screaming inside with pure, overwhelming frustration.

I just wanted someone to come upstairs. Someone to come rescue us.

Plus, on some nights when our house was filled with wrestlers staying with us, Todd would be told to simply share one of our beds—that was the absolute worst! Having that smell near me all night long was like torture. I'd crawl out of bed and sleep on the rug, freezing my ass off sometimes, just to be away from him.

Sometimes, I'd throw a tantrum, unable to really say what was happening.

"I don't want him in my room," I shouted at Mum. "I don't want people in my bed. It's meant to be *mine*!"

Mum didn't catch on. She thought, like most kids, I just didn't want to share my room.

One day, out of the blue, Zak couldn't handle it anymore and called me. This was the first time we had ever really talked about it, only now as adults in our thirties, finally confronting what we'd both been haunted by for nearly twenty-five years. He brought up his own three kids and how he'd never let an outsider into the house overnight, much less into his kids' beds.

"The difference is," he said, "if my son or daughters were saying to me, 'I don't want that person in my room,' that would send alarms off! Fire alarms. Red flags. But in our family growing up, it was simply, 'Well, we need these beds. You can just share.'"

It's not that our parents were insensitive. God no! They were the softest, kindest people in the world. They just couldn't see what was going on. They'd worked so hard to keep us safe from what they'd experienced, they couldn't imagine that the very evil they thought they'd escaped was living under the same roof, doing to their children what had been done to them.

Since Zak and I talked about what happened, he's spoken with our parents about it. I still haven't yet. I just don't want to because it's too hard. But after Zak spoke to them, I got a text from my mum.

I believe you, Saraya. I will ALWAYS believe you.

For now, that's enough. I don't need to hash it out any more. I'm just relieved that my parents believe us and support us.

44

I wonder sometimes if this experience fueled both Zak and me in the wrestling world, gave us access to a deep anger and a sense of having been wronged, a kind of energy we tried to work through with our wrestling. For me, I thought I just forgot about it all or buried it down under alcohol and drugs, but maybe it was working behind the scenes to provoke me. I asked Zak about it recently.

"I mean, at five, six, seven years old," he said, the pain evident on his face, "you understand that it's a willy, but you don't understand." He wanted to talk about what had happened to us, and like me, at the same time, he also didn't want to talk about it. "You don't know if this is normal. And that's the bit I really struggled with, wondering, *Does everyone do this?* But when I got older, like thirteen, fourteen, fifteen, Todd was still around but not touching us anymore. As soon as I started getting bigger and stronger, I became really nasty to that man. I hated him. And even later after he left—remember, Raya?—he would turn up and shower us with gifts, try to buy us stuff, and I'd be like, 'I don't fucking want that. Just leave us alone.'"

One of the worries Zak carried was that, once he realized that what Todd had done to us was wrong, he didn't want to admit that it had happened. After all, both our parents had been abused. Our older brother and sister had also been abused. He didn't want Todd to think it was a trend, that we *wanted* this to happen to fit in with our family.

"You know, sometimes I can wake up dreaming about this, or that smell can take me back to being that vulnerable little boy." His face cleared for a moment, and I could see his jaw twitch with tension. "I dread to think what I might do to this man if I ever saw him again."

We cried together, both of us fully grown now, him with a family of his own—and yet both of us still scarred from what we had tried to tell ourselves at the time was not a big deal.

"What breaks my heart," he said after blowing his nose, "is that the motherfucker managed to get his hands on *you*. That's what hurts the most."

And for me, what wounded me the most were those times Zak took the abuse so I would be spared. He later ended up having a nervous breakdown and needed to be hospitalized for a while. Sure, mental illness runs in the family, and we weren't exactly the most balanced lot. But what damage had it all caused? Did his efforts to save me harm him even more?

And the non-horror movies we used to watch? Two of them scared the bejesus out of me and it's only now I can see why. In *The Nutty Professor* with Eddie Murphy, the main character has a dream of kissing a girl on the beach, and she gets sucked into the sand. He's a big guy, and he suffocates her because he's on top of her. That's exactly what Todd felt like. Watching that scene would make me sick with terror.

And then—it sounds crazy, I know—I was terrified of the opening scene in *Look Who's Talking*, when the sperm is going into the egg. I used to scream, "I don't want to have tadpoles in my tummy!" I was paralyzed with panic. Mum would quiet me down and tell me that wouldn't happen, there wouldn't be any tadpoles in my tummy.

Those were the films that haunted me, even as Mum kept trying to keep me from watching supposedly genuine horror films. She had no way to know that I could watch the scary clown from *It*, no problem. That movie had nothing on these ones to scare the living shit out of me.

FIGHT FOR YOUR RIGHT TO PARTY

Chapter Five

Go to the top of the stairs!" Dad yelled at me. "Now!"

I knew he meant the metal stairs on the outside of the pub, and I ran like hell to scale those steps because when he spoke in that particular tone of voice, he fucking meant it.

We'd all been working in the pub our parents ran, everyone pitching in, pouring pints, grabbing plates of food from Mum in the kitchen to deliver to customers, emptying ashtrays, wiping up the spilled beer that seemed to be everywhere and made the rooms and floorboards smell like yeast and malt. Even at fifteen, I was put to work. It was just a normal afternoon for us in Norwich.

But now, from my vantage point up those stairs, I watched what was happening in the car park of the pub. I couldn't make out the exact words, but raised voices carried up to where I was perched. Before I knew what was what, a fight broke out. Best as I could tell, it was my dad, together with my brothers Roy and Zak, wailing against another father-son group, who'd come in asking for trouble. Before everyone started swinging on one another, they'd taken it outside. Our regulars were generally used to this kind of action and continued drinking as usual at the bar.

Meanwhile, outside, fists slammed against bodies, heads against ground, knees thrust into stomachs.

At some point, Roy must have gotten fed up, because he grabbed a baseball bat and smacked one of the sons in the head with it. I could hear the hollow sound of wood striking skull from where I was—all that force channeled through Roy's arms, into his hands, and then through to the bat. Holy shit. The coppers might show up any minute. I didn't want Roy to go to jail again. He'd already served time for violence, like my father had.

Still, I couldn't take my eyes off the guy who'd been hit. He was standing upright, just a dent in the side of his head from where Roy had pounded him. But then, all of a sudden, blood started spewing everywhere, a fucking geyser, his nose, his mouth, his face, maybe even from inside his ears, pouring out onto the ground. It was gory. The man fell to his knees before doubling over onto the concrete. His father and brother grabbed him by the arms as his eyes rolled back in his head. They pulled him, now limp as a fucking rag doll, into a car and got the fuck out of there.

Mum gathered everyone back inside the pub, checking for bruises and cuts she might need to sew up—which was a frequent occurrence. I went back down the stairs and got back to work, hoping to God the cops weren't going to show. And they didn't. The night wore on and no authorities came.

That was my family's motto: Never start it, but once it gets started, be damn sure you end it.

Only two days after that scrap, the father and sons who'd picked the fight in the first place returned. The one son had a hell of a bruise on the side of his head, his eyes still blackened from Roy's baseball bat; he looked a little dazed. He wore a beanie low over his forehead, as if that might make him appear halfway okay. I could feel Dad, Roy, and Zak eye them up as soon as they entered the pub. I continued pouring pints behind the bar.

"We're here to settle up." The father strode to the bar, which my dad was sitting at the end of.

Dad was unfazed. He glanced over at Roy and Zak near the kitchen, both of them ready to have at it again, if needed.

The father reached into his pocket and then slapped a tenner on the bar. "We're buying, lads. It's only fair," he said, then extended his hand for a shake. And with that gesture, all was forgiven. Dad and my brothers shared drinks with them; even the one with the dented-in head joined in. Everything was considered settled after that.

This value system, according to my dad, had come to us via his father's Irish Traveler lineage. They were really proud people, he told us, and loyal. But if there was ever a conflict, the way to settle it was to fight it out. Clearly, this father-son trio also believed in the same rules of conduct, because that's exactly what had happened, and now bygones could be bygones. There'd be no more trouble from that group.

That fight wasn't all that unusual. To be honest, fights broke out in that pub and others across Norwich every other night of the week, and my dad just told people to take it outside. Generally, they did. After the pubs closed for the night, those who had been hurt in such fights, as well as our wrestling friends who may have been injured in a proper match, inevitably ended up in our front room, where Mum stitched them back up. She was a kind of underground punk seamstress, medically untrained and unlicensed, but ready to go at your gaping wound with a barely sterilized needle and a little determination.

No one batted an eye at the violence and spilled blood—not to mention the spilled alcohol—around the place. It was the same at all the other pubs in town. Remember when I said there was a pub for every day of the year? That's just the way things were. Pubs and violence went hand in hand, and they were everywhere. I never thought anything of it.

My family were no strangers to backing each other up in a fight. One time, Dad had told me to sit outside of a dressing room at a show. Daniel Bryan, still an indie wrestler at the time (ex–WWE superstar, current All Elite Wrestling star, and included this story in *his* book a few years ago), walked past me, opening the dressing room door to see my dad and Roy holding a man out of the window, six stories above the pavement.

It was another wrestler who had been saying awful, disrespectful things about my mum. When Dad and Roy heard, they decided the best way to get him to stop was to have a chat with him while hanging him out the window until he pissed himself and agreed to apologize.

Daniel Bryan saw that and turned right around and walked the other way.

Most fights were like that—just looking after our own. I remember once, when we were all really young, Mum had piled me, my niece Terri, and my nephews Ricky and Patrick into the car. She had been taking care of all the kids while Dad coached Roy's footie match. After the game, Mum picked up my dad and took us all to meet my sister, Nikki, her husband, and the rest of the football team at the pub. Like most Sundays, when they won, everyone went there to celebrate afterward. That day, all of us kids stayed in the car while Mum went inside for a moment, and within seconds, some creepy, bald-headed man opened the car door and started talking to us, asking why we were alone and if we wanted to go home with him.

As he leaned over, leering into the car at us, something dropped from his pocket, and he reached down to grab it. In that instant, Terri and I jumped over the front seat and grabbed the car door, slamming it and locking it shut. He stared in the window at us, then turned around and went into the pub. I don't know exactly what he said in there, but I know it was about us, and clearly it was inappropriate, because almost immediately after he went in, he was being dragged back out. He was so covered in blood, you couldn't even see his bald head anymore. My sister, Nikki, was going crazy, kicking at him with her heels. You just didn't mess with our family like that.

One afternoon, when I was about fifteen, I was helping out in the pub and we ran out of whiskey, if you can believe that. I mean, come on. What's a pub without whiskey?

"Saraya," Dad said. "Pop in next door and get a bottle of Jameson, would you?"

It was broad daylight and no harm for me to be out on the streets alone, and though I was just a kid, the people who owned the shop next door knew I was helping out at the pub and would give me what we needed, no questions asked.

As I walked into the shop, though, a woman in there hissed at me, "Skank!"

What the fuck?

The woman was muttering under her breath, phrases I couldn't follow, but that one word showed up again and again in her weird-arse monologue. "Skank."

I didn't know if she was drunk or high or what, but she was clearly not okay. Next thing I knew, she grabbed a handful of chocolate bars and started chucking them at my head.

I got the Jameson from the clerk, who did nothing about the psycho woman, and marched up to her on my way out the door. She followed me outside. She looked really trashy, with paw prints tattooed on her boobs, which were spilling out of her top. We call them "chavs" in England, those overly aggressive, flashy, but cheap people.

"What's your problem?" I asked.

Out of nowhere, she started punching me.

Immediately, I started punching her back, and in between I screamed at the top of my lungs, "Dad! Dad!"

Her boyfriend hopped out of their car to hold me back.

She connected hard, giving me an instant black eye. At that point, they both got back into their car.

Just then, I see my dad and—I'm not kidding—the whole pub, every last person in it, come running with baseball bats, pool cues, and beer bottles, ready to defend me.

Afterward, we asked around town. Norwich was not a huge place, but no one seemed to know who she was or what her problem had been. The whole episode was just so insane and yet not so unusual. I had that huge black eye for weeks. It was a constant reminder: Out of nowhere, for no reason, you never know what might be coming at you. But if you were lucky, like me, you had some loyal backup.

There were always some interesting characters around. One night in the pub, we were hosting what my dad called pizza night. Though pizza was involved, that was not the real draw. Held upstairs maybe once a month, this was a scheduled night of totally illegal gambling, drugs, strippers, the works. We hosted these nights regularly, and I worked them, serving pints, sweeping the floors, clearing away glasses, whatever was needed. A few days earlier, I'd talked my parents into letting me get a kitten, this adorable ball of fluff that I loved from the moment I laid eyes on her. I carried her with me everywhere, still trying to suss out a good name for her.

The night wound down, and I left my kitten in the room where one of the strippers was dressing after her shift. Almost everyone else had already left. I had to bring a tray full of glasses and ashtrays downstairs to be washed. When I went back upstairs, the kitten was nowhere to be found.

I looked *everywhere*.

I ran downstairs in a total panic. "Mum! Dad! Did you see the stripper leaving?"

They shook their heads.

"That cunt stole my fucking kitten!"

I never did get her back. I was devastated for months.

Our pub was well known by the cops in town, and the SWAT team was always coming to harass us. One night, some woman showed up out-of-her-mind drunk and obnoxious. After taking a quick piss on the sidewalk outside the pub, she came in half-naked, trying to make out with anyone in arm's reach (half of them with their girlfriends right there, ready to tear her hair out). She was jumping on the bar with her trousers around her ankles and causing a scene. Mum tried to get her under control, but she took a swing on her. I saw red and ran straight at her like I was the Terminator, knocked her down, and started throwing punches at her on the ground.

All of a sudden, small red dots appeared through the window on the back wall of the pub. It took a second to register what was happening.

Holy shit. Is this a raid???

It was like something in a movie. Everyone froze as officers in tactical gear came storming into the pub while I was still on top of the deranged woman. Someone quickly pulled me off her.

They ordered everybody into a straight line while they searched the pub. They thought my dad was the leader of some kind of Mafia group, and that he had drugs and counterfeit clothes, jewelry and guns stashed all over the place. Every time they came looking, my dad would tell them the same thing: "You're out of your bleeding mind, mates. We don't have any guns."

He was telling the truth about the guns, though he never whispered a word about the other items they were looking for. The SWAT team never found them, but we did have drugs, counterfeit clothes, and jewelry hidden all over the place.

As they searched, they encountered our dogs. Our dogs were not aggressive and didn't give them any reason to feel threatened, but that didn't stop them from Tasering them. The dogs howled in pain, their cries so heartfelt, they'd break anyone with an ounce of humanity in their bones. They were the sweetest dogs ever and had meant the SWAT folks absolutely no harm.

"They didn't do anything to you!" I screamed at them.

They didn't care.

All this was just normal in our family, and you can imagine it made me stand out in school. I had very few friends, and people thought I was weird. By this time, I was dyeing my hair black and wearing black all the time, a little goth girl, and the other kids at school, especially the girls, seemed a bit afraid of me. I was also starting to wrestle professionally, which made me a further outcast, a freak. I would have really liked to have had a friend, but no one wanted to get near me.

During the days, Dad and Zak ran a wrestling training facility. Zak was really good working with the kids in the neighborhood, getting them to learn the moves. He even worked with a blind kid and taught him to wrestle, who later went on to become a professional. Zak knew there was so much trouble outside the door—drugs, prison, alcoholism, criminal activity—and maybe he thought it could all be avoided by simply getting into the ring. Hadn't Mum and Dad both been saved by wrestling?

One of the people who'd joined our family during that time was another lost boy, Isak, from Norway. My dad had a close relationship with a promoter in Norway who brought over trainees for him to work with. When Isak joined us in Norwich, he found a genuine and deep connection with our family. He moved in with us, and, for years, he became my brother, one of my favorite people. My dad never formally adopted him, but as far as I was concerned, Isak was absolutely kin. We spent holidays together and treated each other as family. I always considered him family. When I was thirteen, he went back to Norway to give living there a chance, and I missed him every single fucking day.

A few weeks later, I woke up to Mum running up the stairs, hysterical.

"Isak is dead! Isak is dead!" she screamed. I was half-asleep and didn't comprehend what she was telling me at first.

Isak had woken on the morning of his twenty-second birthday and was rushing to get to work on a snowy day. In his haste, he didn't properly clean the car's windscreen. He lived on a mountain and was going around a bend when his car skidded and hit a tree. He broke his neck and died instantly.

I stayed in my room for a whole week, utterly gutted. Isak had become so bloody special to me. By this time, Roy had his own family, and my sister, Nikki, wasn't around much, so we weren't as close. Asa kept getting sent off to mental hospitals because he wasn't really right in the head. So Isak had been, like Zak, a true brother to me. He had a heart of gold and was really creative with making videos. In fact, he made his own memorial video, though I don't know if that's what he thought he was doing at the time. In the days before he died, he put together a black-and-white video with slow-motion clips of him: smoking cigarettes, hugging our family members, relishing the love he'd found with us. As a soundtrack, he used the Johnny Cash rendition of "If You Could Read My Mind." After he died, I watched that video on nonstop repeat, bawling at the sadness of the song, the sadness of my loss. He was so young. And gone. Forever.

The creepy thing is that that Johnny Cash song almost never comes on the radio. But one time, years later, when I was traveling with the WWE, I had a very long drive down this road called Alligator Alley, a highway that spans the Florida Everglades between Miami and Orlando. Its name is due to the scads of alligators in the area; they sometimes come walking out on the route. There are no gas stations, nothing commercial for miles. I was alone and getting so tired. The road was not illuminated like a freeway; in fact there weren't many streetlights, and I had been warned that alligators might wander onto the road at any time, so it was important to drive at a speed where I might see them before slamming into one. The last thing I wanted to do was kill an alligator. Or myself. I was so exhausted, though. As WWE wrestlers, we were always going and going and not getting much rest. I started to drift off at the wheel. And just at that moment, that song came on the radio, the Johnny Cash version.

It was a message from Isak. I'm not a religious person at all, and not particularly spiritual, either. But I just felt like he was there with me. And he helped me stay awake, my eyes scanning the blacktop for alligators. He didn't want me to die in a manner similar to how he'd left us. I miss Isak to this very day, and after that drive, I got the lyrics from that song tattooed on me, in his honor. "If you could read my mind, love."

Looking back, it seems all the really weird shit started to happen in my thirteenth year. For a lot of girls, I think that's when how they're treated by the rest of the world begins to change. This time was particularly strange for me because, yes, I'm a girl and I was going through all the regular girl stuff, but I'm also a wrestler surrounded by brothers, and pretty much a tomboy, so I didn't really have a script to follow. I wore Adidas tracksuits almost all the time, not sexy outfits, and still my brothers were forever beating the shit out of anyone who looked at me sideways.

As I got a bit older, I would go to the shows less frequently. I didn't have many friends, so when my entire family was going to be out late on Friday for a wrestling match, that usually meant I would be home alone for the night. So I thought up a great idea. *I'll have a house party!*

I was in year eight and had just started high school. I was making a few new friends for the first time and I wanted them all to like me. I went to the off-license and bought a bunch of wine. They knew me from the pub and didn't bat an eye. I invited all the cool kids, including Charlie, one of Zak's friends. I'd had a crush on him when I was younger—you know how little sisters are about their big brother's friends.

We all started drinking heavily, and when I went to the bathroom, Charlie followed me.

I was really uncomfortable with him there, but I didn't know what to do. He kept trying to shove his hands down the front of my underwear.

I grabbed his hands and pulled them out. "I'm not interested in that."

He persisted. I think he was really drunk, though that's not an excuse.

"Leave me alone!" I screamed in his face to get away from him. I went upstairs to my bedroom because I was a little drunk and everything started spinning.

I was just getting my bearings again when Charlie burst through the door. Straightaway, he was lying on top of me on my bed, holding me down, doing stuff that I used to have nightmares about after Todd. I got mad and pushed him off.

My friend Chelsea was downstairs, and when I told her what Charlie had done, she let loose. She's the smallest thing, and yet she went fucking nuts on him. "Get the fuck out of this house!"

He left, but then my family all turned up. Their show ended earlier than I'd expected, and they were not happy to come home and find that the house was an absolute disaster and filled with teenagers who had spilled wine everywhere.

"What the fuck?" Dad said before throwing everyone out and grounding me.

It was the first and only time I was grounded, and by the next day, after having me underfoot for the morning, Dad got sick of it and I wasn't grounded anymore. But I ended up telling Zak about what had happened with Charlie, because I tell Zak everything.

Zak is like all my brothers, super protective of me, so I guess I shouldn't have been surprised to get a call from him the next afternoon.

"You need to come down to the mall, Raya," he said.

"Why?" I asked.

"I've got Charlie on his knees right now and he needs to make things right."

Oh. My. God! Why did I tell Zak? But he wasn't going to let it go— I know Zak. I had no choice but to meet him at the mall. He wanted to embarrass Charlie in front of everyone because he wanted the message clear: *You're not going to fucking do that to my sister!*

Charlie was sweating and squirming when I got there, and Zak popped him in the face and told him to kiss my feet. I was totally embarrassed, everyone looking at me knowing what was going on.

Soon, the gathered kids started chanting, "Kiss. Her. Feet! Kiss. Her. Feet!"

In my head, I was thinking, *Please don't!* but I knew none of us were going to get out of there until Zak was satisfied, so Charlie kissed my feet, and Zak yanked him up by the collar. "Don't you ever fucking touch my sister again."

There was no doubt Charlie got the message. *Loud and fucking clear, mate.*

Though the whole scene embarrassed me, Zak's motivation to protect me makes more sense now when I consider what he and I had been through as little kids with Todd. I only wish he'd been with me the day I went to a friend's house.

His family was really fucked-up, but I didn't know it at the time. I came over, and his mum and mum's boyfriend gave us weed and liquor. We were all just hanging out, drinking and partying. I thought it was pretty cool. I was finally starting to have friends.

When I got up to use the bathroom, though, his mum followed me in. What the fuck? A minute later, her boyfriend came in, too, and he locked the door. He started trying to kiss me. The bathroom was tiny and felt claustrophobic. I got scared. They were in their thirties and I was barely a teenager. They were trying to get me into a threesome with them. I was terrified.

Thank God for my friend. He knew something was up and started banging on the bathroom door. The boyfriend opened it a crack to tell him to get lost, but he grabbed me by the hand and pulled me out of there.

I realized later that he knew he needed to act, likely from hard-won experience. I hate to think about it, but he had probably been stuck in the same situation before. I never went back there again—I had learned my lesson—and never told anyone until now, writing this. Years later, I heard my friend's mum hung herself. I hope my friend from back then is in a better place now.

Around that time, my family would sometimes travel up to Scotland for a wrestling company. That's eight long hours in a car, and my dad believed wrestling etiquette meant you were not allowed to fall asleep on car journeys because it's not fair to the designated driver. It was *brutal*. I was young and wanted to nap. Back then we didn't have iPads or iPhones to keep us busy (or to look up maps—once we arrived, we would have to pull over and ask strangers where the building was that we were wrestling in that night).

This one time I went up to Scotland with just my mum. My brothers and dad had not come along.

There was this wrestler named Jay based there who would message me on MySpace. He was a lot older than me, in his twenties. He somehow got my number and would text me very flirtatiously, sending me the odd shirtless pic, which I never asked for. Looking back, I should've thought that a grown man texting me, a young girl, was absolutely disgusting and insane. But I was fourteen, and at the time I was thinking only, *Wow, this man thinks I'm so "mature" for my age*, and *Wow, he keeps telling me how beautiful I am*. At that age, I hadn't had sex; I hadn't even done anything with a boy. (Minus Todd when I was younger, but that wasn't something I had consented to, either.)

Mum and I finally made it to Scotland. Jay was chatty with me straightaway. He wasn't shy about conversing with me, that's for sure. He followed me around everywhere. We were in the ring training, and then he rolled in and started getting playful. I just thought it was funny. He chased me around the building, trying to tickle me. Well, he caught me and grabbed me. Turned me upside down and shoved his face in between my legs.

At that point, I stopped laughing, and it made me feel uncomfortable. My mum saw him from across the hall and bolted toward him, grabbing a fire extinguisher on the way. She came in swinging, trying to hit him with it. All the wrestlers—including Drew McIntyre, who had not yet signed to WWE—only saw my mum flying at him like a bat out of hell. Drew intercepted her and tried to talk her down. Jay attempted to convince her he didn't mean anything by it, but my mum wasn't having any of it. She snarled at him to stay the fuck away from me. The promoter had to take her to the pub next door to calm down.

At the time, I was so mad. . . . *Why is my mum embarrassing me in front of everyone like this? He said it wasn't anything, we should just believe him, right?*

Later on that night, I sat in the corner, trying to cool down after my match. Jay found me right away.

"Wow . . . you look like you just had sex. It's so sexy."

This time, though, Drew heard. "What the fuck did you just say to her?"

Jay had gained some undeserved confidence from what he had gotten away with earlier. With a creepy smile that I'll never forget, he gave the same half-assed excuse, sure he would be let off the hook again. It didn't work. Drew looked furious.

"Let's go talk." Drew grabbed him by the back of his neck and pulled him away. Even through the walls, I could hear the muffled yelling from Drew as he lost it on Jay in the other room.

Whatever Drew said, it worked. From that day on, Jay did not make eye contact with me. Didn't try to talk to me. Didn't send me inappropriate messages. Didn't chase me around and shove his face in between my fourteen-year-old legs as a "joke."

Jay would later be convicted of a number of sex offenses involving children. At fourteen, even after Todd, I had no idea what was really happening at the time. I still couldn't always tell who was safe and who wasn't, only when I suddenly felt uncomfortable. It was like there was an invisible line that became glaringly obvious to me only once someone had already crossed it. Later on, I felt bad for not listening to my mum, but I was so thankful that Drew McIntyre was there to scare Jay off. He stopped a pedophile from trying to groom and have sex with me. He saved me from what could've been an even more awful situation. I'm forever grateful to Drew for that night.

If somehow Drew sees this: Thank you, forever.

Isn't it crazy, looking back on it all, how much women deal with? How much *girls* have to deal with? I know I'm not the only one. There are a lot of good guys out there, but man, are there also a lot of really shit ones. It's something we almost just assume is normal.

Other than that, though, Zak was always there whenever I found myself in a fucked-up situation. Once, I was outside my mum and dad's house, and my grandma was visiting. She had this big SUV. Zak and I were playing outside; he was tossing the ball around as I rode around on a bike with no brakes—you know, just being kids. And this car came barreling down the road just as I popped out from behind my grandma's SUV. I didn't see the car coming at first, and when I finally did, I couldn't brake. She hit me head-on, and I rolled over the hood, landing flat in the road, gravel in my knees and stinging my face. I was in total shock. *Ouch.*

I could faintly hear Zak yelling at the lady, and his voice must have been what got Mum and Dad to come outside. By that point, I'd jumped up to a standing position, almost ashamed to say I was hurt, needing to prove it was all okay. I looked down at myself and was covered in blood. When my dad got to me, I collapsed in his arms, the reality of what had just happened sinking in.

The lady, too, was in shock, worried she'd hurt a child.

Dad held me up and felt for broken bones. "Can you wiggle your toes?" he asked.

I could.

And with that, Dad told the lady she could leave. I was fine.

He brought out a pair of crutches from the house—we always had stuff like that hanging around because of all the wrestling injuries. I was starting to feel woozy and would go on to have a headache for the next three weeks. . . . I definitely had a concussion. But all that mattered was that I seemed okay.

Dad helped me on the crutches into the house. "Good thing you weren't injured," he said. "We have a show tonight."

Typical Mum, she cleaned up all my cuts and bruises. And stubborn as I was, determined to prove I was tough and not hurt, I wrestled in that show. I was wrestling regularly by then, and injuries weren't exactly a big deal, even if they came from a car. Just a normal day in our family.

It was around this time that my older brother Asa was causing some issues. I adored him, and he always loved and protected me. But his mother, my dad's ex-wife, was a total disaster. She had raised Nikki and Roy and treated them really badly, and she'd basically just given Asa to my dad when she decided she didn't want to care for him anymore. Now, as a young teenager, he was becoming a handful for my parents. I was never scared of Asa, but others were.

I have in my head a picture of Asa as a little kid, eating strawberries. His face was aglow with happiness and he kept saying, "I'm gonna eat all the strawberries!" His voice was filled with absolute fucking glee. He looked so normal, like an average kid.

But things changed. There was a brightness behind his eyes that started to get wilder. He got paranoid. He'd barricade himself in the caravan he lived in in the yard (it was kind of like a little camper), or he'd barricade us all in the house. "There's something in the streetlight!" he warned us. He was convinced the CIA had put cameras in there to watch him.

If someone drove past the house twice, he was sure they were coming to off him.

. One time, he randomly said to me, "I don't want anyone to think I'm a pedophile."

"Why would they think that?" I asked.

"The CIA is just trying to get me arrested for something. Maybe they'll think I'm a pedophile and come get me."

"Asa, you're fine," I tried to convince him. Over and over. "No one's chasing you," I had to reassure him. "No one thinks you're a pedophile."

He didn't believe me.

"The CIA wants to put a microchip behind my eye."

He'd already been "sectioned" a number of times. That's a British phrase for when a person is detained under the Mental Health Act and taken to a hospital for assessment or treatment and not allowed to leave until they have permission from a doctor. It's usually done when the person is considered a risk to themselves or to others, or is unable to make decisions about their mental well-being. He got sectioned a lot, but he kept coming home to us and only getting worse. The more severe his behaviors, the longer he would stay in the hospital, but it's not a permanent solution.

Eventually, over the course of a few years, he became convinced that just about everyone in the world was out to kill him, except me. Even when he thought the entire population of Britain was against him, he always knew I was on his side.

In his mind, my mum was the biggest killer of them all. She did nothing but care for him with kindness and compassion, but he burned with fury whenever she was around, certain she wished him lethal harm. He was a big guy and got physical with her one time. My dad had to pin him against the wall to get him to stop. That terrified me. It was one thing to be rough with other people, but never within the family. Something was going on with Asa that I didn't understand.

As he got worse, I started to get more worried. Once, I saw Asa running circles, naked, around his caravan in the back. Something was definitely off. And though he was protective like my other brothers when it came to me and guys, Asa took it a step too far.

I was at the park one winter evening with a bunch of kids from my high school, all of us drinking this cheap-arse cider that tasted like shit but would still give you a buzz. It was awful, and we loved it. Then Asa showed up. A boy in the group was flirting with me, and I liked it. I sat on his lap for a moment, and he teased me in that young teenager way, making me melt inside. In no time, I lost track of Asa's presence. Asa, though, hadn't lost track of me.

It was the dead of winter, and in that park there was a pond where we'd catch frogs in the summer. Asa apparently didn't like the boy flirting with me. He went to the pond and extracted a huge chunk of ice.

The boy tickled me, and I squirmed away from him, slapping his arm and jokingly telling him no.

That's when I was just far enough away from him to give Asa his shot.

Asa raised the huge chunk of ice high over his head and slammed it onto the boy's skull, acting with all the fury I'd witnessed when Roy had slammed that baseball bat into the guy's head in the pub brawl. But this was my friend, the guy I liked.

He fell to the ground, knocked out cold—just for flirting with me. I tried to wake him, and eventually he came around, but after that, he wanted nothing to do with me and my family ever again.

I pulled Asa aside. "You can't do that to people!"

His eyes were huge with terror; he hated if I got mad at him. I was the only person on earth who, he was sure, had never tried to kill him.

"I was only trying to help."

I thought he understood. I didn't yet know that mental illness has a way of making people unable to understand, sometimes in ways that are incredibly damaging. I was about to learn that with a very painful lesson.

RUNAWAY

The minute we entered the house something felt off. It was well into the summer, August or so, and we had just come home from doing a wrestling show. Being home was usually such a relief, but it didn't feel that way now. Over the past few days, tension at home had been stretching thinner, but I was fourteen and wrapped up in my own stuff—getting ready for school to start, not paying that much attention to the world around me. This day, I felt as if something grabbed me by the jaw and turned me to look squarely at my parents. Something was not right.

They were arguing. That had become more of a thing recently, but not something I was used to. They usually got along smashingly. Zak and I went to the landing on the stairs, where the lower part of the house with the front room, kitchen, and bathroom connected to the upper part with the bedrooms. We were trying to stay out of it, huddled together. Whatever it was they were arguing about—I still can't remember—the conflict escalated quickly. They bolted from room to room, yelling and screaming at each other, getting ever closer to where Zak and I crouched, possibly unaware we were there. And that's when it happened.

Mum picked up a mug and hurled it straight at Dad's head. Mum plays a heel when wrestling, and you would think she was a total menace to see her in the ring, but normally—apart from fiercely protecting her kids—she's the most gentle, nonviolent person I know. A complete teddy bear. So this was really fucking out of the blue. Dad ducked to miss the mug, and it shattered against the wall.

What the hell was going on? Zak and I looked at each other. Something was seriously wrong.

"She threw a fucking mug at me!" Dad bellowed. "Did you both see that?"

"Fuck this," Zak said. "I'm not sitting here and watching this." He pulled me by the sleeve and tugged me upstairs, away from the chaos.

Whatever was happening hadn't started that day. It had been building for some time. Over the past few weeks, there had been all kinds of interventions. Roy had come over and tried to talk sense into my mum, who'd been acting weird and threatening to leave. Nikki came over and pleaded with her; even Uncle Stanley came. It was a massive ordeal, a riot of opinions being offered, so many people trying to have their say on what needed to happen to restore peace in our family. And all that had really done was add fuel to the fire.

But now, back in the house, they were really going at each other, calling the other every name under the sun. Zak and I tried to get away from them, not wanting to see or hear any of this, but their argument spread through the house like a virus.

"I'm done," Mum said. "I'm going. I'm out of here."

"What do you mean?" Dad said. "There's no 'done' here! We're in this together. Like always."

"I can't do this anymore," she said. "Not any longer." Mum went upstairs to pack.

You know, my dad is a man's man, very old-school. Rough and tough. Nothing touches him. I've seen him in the ring countless times as massive, scary men run up to him and punch him, try to take him out. He doesn't budge an inch. He's fucking impenetrable. But now, it was as if Mum's words had pierced through to his very core, letting all the air out of him, releasing whatever force had kept him upright in the world. He slumped next to the fridge, looking like he was about to have a stroke or a heart attack. He literally put his hands to his heart as he slid to the linoleum.

"You can't," he muttered. "I'll give my right arm to make sure you stay." He was still talking to her though she'd left the room. "What have I done wrong? Can we talk about it?"

Clearly, Mum was way past talking. When she came downstairs a bit later with her bag packed, Dad barely lifted his head.

"If you go, you have to take Saraya with you," he said.

"Fine," she agreed.

I'm not sure of Dad's rationale, only that if I was with Mum, maybe she couldn't do anything too crazy. Next thing I knew, Mum and I were in the car driving to Aunt Louise's house an hour away in Yarmouth.

"Don't worry," she reassured me. "We're coming back. Just not right now. I need to get away for a bit."

I don't remember much of the drive, but everything felt weird and off. When we got to Aunt Louise's, we ended up going to a pub late that night. But here's the thing: My mum doesn't really drink. When she was younger, she'd done a lot of drugs, but she's never been a drinker. It's just not her thing. A cup of tea, yes, but hard liquor? Never. I mean, we owned pubs. Mum worked in them as a bartender and cook, so to go hang out at a pub would be like going to work for her.

But not that night. We went from pub to pub, and Mum became someone I didn't recognize. She was drinking and partying, dancing. Throughout the night, Aunt Louise and Mum kept having what seemed to be side conversations, and I was kept occupied by my cousins Jake, Holly, and Amber so I wouldn't overhear—which was also really fucking weird because, in our family, pretty much everything was on the table. Nothing was normal that night.

When we got back to Aunt Louise's house at whatever god-awful hour of the morning, Mum and I shared a twin bed.

"Good night," she mumbled before drifting off.

I stayed awake for a while, looking at the ceiling, wondering what the fuck was happening. She wasn't acting like Mum. I wanted to be home with Dad and the rest of the family. Maybe in the morning, we'd go home and everything would be back to normal. I drifted off to sleep hoping that would be the case.

But sometime in the middle of the night, a feeling came over me, the weirdest ever. I would have sworn I'd just been smacked in the face, but when I opened my eyes, nothing was there, only this gloomy feeling. It felt like a warning. I struggled to consciousness and sat up in bed.

Mum was gone.

Oh shit. I went through the house, looking for her, calling her name. I couldn't find her anywhere. I started screaming, "Where's my mum?"

Aunt Louise came out of her room to calm me. And that's when I knew. Whatever Louise and Mum had been discussing last night, it had led to this. Mum was gone, and Louise had helped orchestrate her departure.

"Where is she?" I kept asking. "Where the fuck did she go? I need to bring her home."

Louise said she didn't know, but it was clear to me she was lying.

I was fucking devastated. My mum had abandoned me, snuck out of the bed we shared to leave me behind. I would never get over this.

I don't know how I got back home after that, but my next memory is of my dad, who by then was a total fucking mess.

Zak told me later that the minute Mum and I had left the house, Dad had sent Zak to the Fiveways Garage gas station to buy Dad a bottle of vodka. After being sober pretty much all of our lives, he was ready to tumble himself off the fucking wagon, all responsibilities be damned.

Since the store didn't know my family, it took Zak three hours to get that bottle—he'd had to wait outside the garage until he could talk some-one into buying the liquor for him—and by the time he got home, Dad was raging. He proceeded to get as shit-faced as possible.

And from that point on, Zak and I had to take care of Dad while we looked for and heard nothing from our mother for four months.

I remember the first week really clearly. I was reclusive, staying in my bedroom, my safe place, and because of that I missed a lot of the weight Zak carried for our dad. It was the same routine, day after day. Dad ordered Zak to the store to buy him four bottles of Lambrini—a pear cider favored by chav girls, advertised with the slogan "Lambrini girls just wanna have fun"—along with a two-liter bottle of vodka for getting the business done. When Zak got home with the booze, Dad put the Stylistics on the stereo and cried, the songs playing on a loop the entire fucking day, seeping up through the floorboards and drifting to my room, where I tried my best to pretend none of this was happening. To this day, if the radio plays "You Make Me Feel Brand New," or "Na-Na Is the Saddest Word," I'm pitched back into that dark time.

Dad sat in that damn recliner and cried, getting drunker by the minute. "I'd give my right arm for Mum to come home," he mumbled.

And every bloody day that followed was a fucking repeat of the one before, listening to Dad cry and tell us how much he missed our mum. Didn't he think we missed her, too? This wasn't only about him, but he was in so much agony he couldn't see that.

Dad wouldn't eat breakfast or lunch, focused solely on the alcohol, so Zak and I would sweet-talk him around four or five in the afternoon into eating a few bites of tuna salad that we'd made for him, and then he'd nap from six till about ten. That was when Zak and I took turns staying with him because during the night he'd often projectile vomit while lying on his back. We'd have to get our fingers into his mouth to clear out the vomit and turn him on his side.

He was a mess and not getting any better. Meanwhile, Zak and I asked around town, begging shopkeepers and Mum's friends to see if anyone had info on her whereabouts. We got nowhere.

School resumed, and I went that first week and ran into a mean girl. She followed me into the girls' toilet and went into a stall while I washed my face and checked my makeup. From inside the stall, she started talking shit.

"I heard your mum left you. I don't blame her," she taunted.

I was so sad about my mum being missing, and worried I'd caused it somehow. And so exhausted from dealing with my dad and his melt-down. Watching my father, whom I'd always adored, fall apart like that had been scraping me raw inside. I still wanted to adore him, but I was quickly losing respect for him. Zak and I were trying to hold everything together, but it was far too much for fourteen- and fifteen-year-olds to fucking deal with.

In that moment, this girl talking like that filled me with absolute fucking rage. Her words lit the flame that had been smoldering inside me. I kicked down the toilet door and she was sat there with her trousers down to her ankles, and I didn't fucking care. I started swinging on her while she was still sitting on the toilet.

"Don't you ever fucking let me hear you talk about my mum again!" I dragged her off the toilet and around the bathroom, her bottom ex-posed, spitting on her, beating the shit out of her. I was so furious, and it felt so good to let fly with all the upset, rage, and sadness that had surrounded me since the moment I'd woken up in Aunt Louise's bed to find Mum gone.

Obviously, I got kicked out of school, but I didn't care. I wasn't going to go back anyhow. There was too much to take care of at home. Zak and I both missed out on school for that entire year, and it really set him back. He was then in year nine, going into ten, getting ready for his mock exams. That year cost us so much.

In the meantime, we still needed to pay the household bills and to run Dad's company. To access electricity at that time and place, we had a little key thing that we had to plug into a meter. For it to work, though, we had to run around to the shops in town and make sure the bill was paid or our electricity wouldn't come on. And then, of course, there was the wrestling company. Shows had been booked, trainees were coming into town. Zak took it upon himself to start running the events as the promoter, taking Dad's place. He made sure the people who owed us money paid it. He'd get on the phone and sound all tough. "Look, we need this money. If you don't pay, we're not going to wrestle."

To make ends meet, we needed to come up with a thousand pounds a month. We worked our arses off to make sure the wrestling shows didn't lose money, because when they did, Zak and I didn't eat for a week.

It was so awful, and the pressure on us so intense, that Zak started to drink himself as a way to numb the pain. Soon, he was matching Dad drink for drink. He was only fifteen. One night, Zak took off, blind drunk, and we didn't know where he'd gone. I told Asa, who was still living in his little caravan in the back. This whole time, he'd been there but always in his own strange paranoid world and mostly of no help to me and Zak. But that night, Asa was a hero. He found Zak in the middle of the night in the park, passed out. He called for help. The paramedics came and took Zak to the hospital, telling us later that if he'd been in that park another hour or two, he would have died of hypothermia.

I was pissed. I needed Zak to help me. I couldn't do this shit by myself, and if he was going to get shit-faced with Dad, I was fucked. When he came home from the hospital, he passed out in bed, and I got my revenge. I took a condom and wrote "dickhead" on it and laid it across his face so it would be the first thing he saw when he woke up. *Quit fucking around!* was the message, and he got it.

After that, we had a good chat. "We're going to need each other, here," I told him.

"Right, Raya," he said. "I'm sorry. I'll be on your team. We'll get through this together."

Which we did, starting by watering down Dad's vodka, trying to get him to stop drinking himself away each night.

Our older sister, Nikki, was living a distance away at that time, and she came round to see how we were doing every so often. She saw that we were sleep-deprived and struggling, and decided to get involved. She arranged for Dad to be sectioned off for thirty days with the hopes that he'd straighten himself out so Zak and I could get a break. It wasn't hard to get him sectioned. By then, he was a total mess. He had cut himself all over his body with the little razor blades he used in the ring. His blood might as well have been straight alcohol. He had lost nearly a hundred pounds, as if he had a terminal illness, which he must have felt he had—how could he possibly keep living without Mum? He wouldn't eat the food on offer in the hospital. He looked terrible and was disappearing before our very eyes.

So Zak and I—mostly Zak—had to see to it that he was fed. Zak wasn't yet old enough to drive, so he'd take a bike six miles to spend an hour or two with him, bring him food. Sometimes, I'd hop on the back and we'd ride together, bringing Dad food in Tupperware containers—a roast dinner we'd made at home or a breakfast fry-up—along with things he could snack on like bananas and crisps.

We were ragged and worn-out from all this, but Dad seemed to be having the time of his life now that he'd sobered up a bit. He was convinced all the ladies were after him there, that he was a big catch.

"Dad," I wanted to say. "You're in the loony bin. All those girls? They're loony, too."

He didn't care. He felt like a right playboy.

But as the days became weeks, we started to see our old dad again, and when he came out of there, he had stopped drinking.

"I promise you guys, I'm not going to drink," he told me and Zak, and he was true to his word. He even did things he wouldn't have before, like take us for a walk in the park or play football. He made an effort. Before, he'd always say, "My back's bad. I can't walk," which was true, but now he tried anyway.

Once, he suggested we walk together into the city, and I couldn't believe it. At first, I offered to get the car keys or suggested we could take the bus.

"No," he said, "we'll walk." As usual, he would call me princess. We didn't do much on that outing, just looked around and shopped, maybe had breakfast, but what I remember most was that he made the three-mile walk with me. That was unheard of.

By then, Mum had been gone for months.

Zak and I kept looking for our mum, and we weren't getting anywhere. England is not that big a place. Where could she have gone? The police, I think, were starting to get suspicious, too. Here was my dad, a criminal known for violent behavior, and his wife was suddenly missing.

One day, about thirty police officers, basically a riot squad, turned up at our house. Apparently, someone had told them my dad had killed my mum and buried her under the patio. Zak had gone to open the door in his boxer shorts, not knowing who was pounding like that, and ten fully grown men pinned him down.

"Where's your father?" they demanded.

They stormed past him, into the front room, where Dad was in his chair.

"Where'd you do it, mate?" they demanded. "She buried right back there?"

Eventually, Dad was able to convince them that she had left on her own. Still, no one knew where she'd gone.

Later, we learned a bit about what sent Mum fleeing. We didn't know it at the time, not me and Zak, not Roy and Nikki, not even Dad, but Asa had been threatening her. He was deeply unwell. By this time, Asa had been given all kinds of diagnoses, basically covering every letter of the alphabet: paranoid schizophrenia, psychosis, psychopathic tendencies, autism. What I later learned is that people with this combination of mental challenges can often zone in on one person as the cause of all their issues. And Asa had decided that was Mum. When none of us were around, he tormented her. He drew pictures displaying how he'd kill her. One time he put a knife to her throat while she was cooking and said, "Dad won't even know if I killed you right now."

It got to the point where she felt there was no one who could protect her.

It was too much for her. As a younger person, she'd not only been sexually abused by her stepfather, but at one point she'd been drugged and gang-raped. But when she told her family, they didn't believe her. They abandoned her. . . . She couldn't go through that again. She'd struggled with PTSD and had spent her own time in the hospital, suffering with anorexia and was eventually down to seventy pounds and had to be sectioned off. Now, though, we had no idea the extent of what was going on. It would take us a long time to realize that she'd simply shattered mentally, after all Asa had put her through.

Even with Mum gone, the wrestling matches went on as before, and there was a group of wrestlers we worked with from Colchester. I don't know what tipped Roy off, but he got a sense that these blokes knew something about Mum.

"You're not telling me something," he said. He didn't get physical with them, but he did threaten a bit.

And finally, they blurted it out. "Julia. Your mum. She's in Colchester, mate."

Dad caught wind of that news, and together we went down to Colchester looking for her. The first time, we found her white Honda Civic parked on the street, with her purse and phone on the front seat. Zak and I had called that very phone how many times over the six months she'd been missing. I can still recite the voicemail message.

*Hello, this is Julia, I can't be with you right now. Whoever this
is, please leave your name and number and I'll get back to you.*

Zak and I had played that message over and over again, just to hear her voice. We missed her so much, it made my stomach hurt with wanting her back. And now, there was that very phone, sitting on the seat right in front of us. But no Mum.

In all, we made five trips to Colchester with Dad looking for her. One time, Dad and Roy and a bunch of Dad's buddies, including Uncle Stanley, went there with baseball bats, planning to kick the arse of anyone who got in their way, and steal her. But they didn't find her.

Finally, Zak and I decided on our own we'd go there ourselves. She adored us. There was no way she could hide from *us*, right?

We took a train and headed straight to the police station. "We're looking for our mum, Julia Hamer," we explained to the copper at the front desk.

"Hang on," the officer said.

Finally, someone was going to help us! In Norwich, the police had been anything but helpful. He took us behind the counter to a small, freezing-cold room that was empty except for a table and a couple of chairs. We waited for hours. Hopefulness slowly turned into boredom. Occasionally, someone at the station would bring us water and packets of crisps. We waited some more.

Eventually, the officer came back.

"You want to go see your mum?"

Did we want to see her? Yes! We both broke down. "You found our mum?!"

We couldn't believe it. Suddenly, there she was in the doorway.

Except she wasn't, not really. Normally, Mum dressed like a goth. Dr. Martens with jeans tucked into them, hair piled up on her head and no makeup—a bit disheveled and punk, in a low-maintenance sort of way. But now she stood there, every hair in place, makeup perfectly done, a feminine outfit.

It wasn't just that, though. Her faced showed no emotion, no excitement to see us. Our mum was warm, loving, bubbly. But now she was cold and distant. Her energy felt completely foreign. We had finally found her, and she still felt a million miles away. Zak and I looked at each other. This wasn't our mum.

"If you want to come with me, you can't tell your dad where I am." That's all she said. No *I love you*, no *I missed you*, not even a *How are you?* But we were desperate to just to be with her, so we went, hoping she'd snap out of it.

She took us back to her apartment to show us the life she'd built. Mum had filled our house with antiques and knickknacks. Now she had a whole other flat, but it was simple and plain-looking. It didn't feel like her, either, impersonal and uninviting. She even had a new dog named Keyser, after Keyser Söze, the elusive bad guy from the movie *The Usual Suspects.*

So, you're just having this whole new life without us? It was a very weird feeling. But apparently, she hadn't completely forgotten about us.

"Zak and Raya, I've been thinking about you this whole time." She showed us the room she'd made for us, a bedroom with a little TV. All this time we'd been going out of our minds, missing her, wondering if she was missing us at all. This was the only sign so far that she had.

It was surreal. We didn't recognize this new person. Before this, we'd always known our mother loved us. Now we weren't so sure.

We stayed there with her for a while. Zak would go back home sometimes to check on Dad, and I always stayed behind, scared she would disappear again. We kept out promise to our mum, though, and didn't tell him specifically where in Colchester we were staying.

We tried to think up fun things for us all to do. She'd always been very playful and up for anything, with more ideas than we could keep up with. But not now.

"No, I'm not doing that," was her ongoing reply, no matter what we suggested.

So it was even more odd to us when one night she took us to a pub nearby to drink Guinness and black currant with some woman Zak and I had never met before. Mum ran the pub at home but was never a drinker. By the end of the night, a fight had broken out and Mum's new friend was grinding a pool cue into someone else's head.

"You can stay here as long as you want," she said.

"But what about Dad?" Zak pressed. "He's a mess without you. He really wants to talk to you."

"I can't do that. And if you tell him where I am, that'll mean I can't trust you, and I'll have to move again."

We were between a rock and a hard place, with a father who was just barely back on the wagon and dying to have his wife home, and a mother we hardly recognized.

It took ages, but over time, there were subtle changes that kept us going. Our mum was always a feeder, and she loved to cook our favorite meals for us. One day, out of the blue, she did just that. She made Zak pork chops and peas, and rice pudding for me. She makes an incredible rice pudding, and the fact she was doing so now meant, maybe, that she was coming back. She even gave me a little tickle on the head as she passed by me. That was more like it.

I was so excited. I called Dad. "Mum's cooking for us!"

It took a while to break down the walls she'd put up to protect herself, and in many ways, Zak and I had to kind of baby Mum into returning to the woman she'd been. We'd bring up memories and show her photos. *Remember this? Remember that?*

We called Dad all the time. Eventually, we convinced Mum to talk to him. We didn't listen in, but she seemed happier. Giddy. We knew they were reconnecting, talking through some of the issues they had been having.

Slowly, she began to return to herself, but the price it cost me and Zak was steep. We were teenagers and having to parent both our parents, who were unwell and having a hard time coping. That's a huge thing for kids to have to deal with. In many ways, Zak and I had to grow up very quickly. We had always had to fend for ourselves to some degree, cooking our own meals, washing our clothes, caring for the animals when Dad and Mum were working. But now the circumstances were different—we weren't caring just for ourselves, we were caring for them, trying everything we could to get them healthy and back together again.

When Mum and Dad started talking to each other, they remembered why they'd been together in the first place. After Zak and I had asked a million times, she agreed to see him in person.

Mum and I pulled into the McDonald's car park at the same time as Zak and Dad were walking toward the entrance.

"Why is Roy here?" she asked me.

He wasn't. My dad had lost so much weight while she'd been away, he was almost unrecognizable. It felt like, in that moment, it dawned on her how much my dad truly needed her. Not just her cooking—he couldn't function without her.

We sat down at the table, and, instantly, everything was normal. Mum snapped back to her old self, like nothing had happened. She was the same Mum from before all of this. She told us there and then she was coming home. Dad was so happy. We all were.

That first month with Mum home, they hardly slept, staying up all night talking. It took a little while for them to talk through everything that had happened, but soon they were closer and happier than they'd ever been before. By this time, Asa had been sectioned off again and wasn't there to threaten her. And while I adore Asa and think the world of him, it was really better that he was elsewhere. Even after Mum came back home, she continued to advocate for him, to worry about him, to make sure he was getting the best care possible. These days, he's in a kind of permanent section, cared for in a facility that can safely deal with his outbursts and help him.

It was a huge relief for me and Zak, but it took longer for us to move on. We loved her and were so happy to have her back, but sometimes it was hard not to feel a bit of resentment for everything our family had been through. My dad forgave her instantly, but it took me longer to adjust. She was my best friend, and I was struggling to stomach how she could just up and leave in the middle of the night like that. Still, though, she was my mum, and she was home again. That's all that mattered.

After that, life got back to normal. Or, as normal as our lives ever were. One thing stuck with me, though. One night, Dad called a family meeting.

"We need to put all our cards on the table. It took us seven months to work this through, but now we'll finally close the books on this ordeal. Let's talk about what went wrong, why it went wrong, and get all the pent-up resentments out."

It may have been a good idea, but I wasn't really ready to say my piece. I was still just trying to keep my feet under me. Dad, though, wanted it all behind us.

"Anything you want to say, you say it now," he said. "And once it's been said, you don't need to ever mention it again."

I was still hurt and angry. I was years, if not a decade away from processing what had happened, and not yet brave enough to say, "Well, hold on a minute. . . ."

Zak and I lived with those unspoken fears, resentments, and complicated feelings throughout our teen years while Mum and Dad reverted to the way things were, as if nothing out of the ordinary had happened, as if we hadn't paid a huge price for that nightmare.

I've learned that mental health challenges afflict not only the person suffering but also all those around them, especially the children. Mum had been suffering from bipolar disorder, exacerbated by Asa's outbursts. But once the episode had passed, it was as if it had never occurred.

Did it affect us long term? Yeah, I'm afraid it did. And for Zak, it also took a toll. Six years ago, when he was in his later twenties, he met his own match with the vagaries of mental health and ended up in the hospital himself. When we talked about this time recently, he put it this way: "You can only run away for so long."

I'd have to learn that lesson eventually, too, the hard way.

GIRLS, GIRLS, GIRLS

I sat on my bed, scissors in hand, and went to town, tearing whole pages from the new glossy magazines I'd swiped from the store, along with old issues I'd gathered from around the house and neighborhood. I clipped photos of beautiful dark-haired women, followed by bottles of expensive perfume and luxury jewelry. I collected pictures of fancy houses and gorgeous animals—horses and dogs especially—as well as sports cars, pop stars, and female wrestlers. The smell of the pages filled my nose, and my hands were stained from the ink. I tore pages in full sheets from the magazines until I was nearly buried in photos.

Next, I trimmed around each to focus clearly on the part that appealed to me, cutting out the elements I didn't give a shit about. Soon, I had more glossy pictures than would fit on my poster board. I'd have to do some editing. I pasted my favorite brunette models on the board, covering every inch, and then selected the items that meant the most to me to be featured on top.

One was a photo of a CD. I loved to sing and wanted to be surrounded by music. My voice was not half-bad. I sang whenever I could, as long as it wasn't in front of many people—in the shower, in the van on the way to matches, by myself in the bedroom. So that would have to be on the board.

With the scissors, I carefully rounded the edges of a photo from a fashion magazine, the paper crisp and heavy. The image was of a lipstick, huge, almost as big as the page itself and in the brightest, in-your-face red I could find. One day, I'd like to have a makeup line of my very own.

And in the middle of all the pictures I pasted onto my vision board, I slapped on top a for-real American dollar bill. One day, I promised myself, I'd make a lot of money and live in America—that was everyone's dream in our neighborhood, and besides, the fortune-telling lady had said I would.

Those were my dreams. And though every single one of them felt completely out of the realm of possibility, didn't I first have to imagine something before it came to life? You have to hum a tune before you can write a song. You have to imagine the wrestling choreography before you can execute it. I could envision it. Though I was mostly convinced I was a silly girl with oversize dreams, still, a small part of me believed.

The craziest dream of all, it seemed to me at the time, was represented by the gorgeous women whose photos I'd used as the backdrop. No one in my life thought I was attractive, myself the least of all. The boys at school called me ugly and teased me about my looks. Living in a family of mostly boys and men, there was never much time or focus for hair and makeup, and, being a wrestler, not a lot of energy for being a girly-girl. But still, all girls dream of being ravishing and a knockout one day. Maybe I'd grow into that?

Truth be told, I didn't have a lot of hope. When I was younger, my granddad on my mum's side wanted to be in our lives for about half a second. He was a total con man, even featured on the TV show *Crimewatch* as one of England's most wanted criminals, and pretty much absent my entire life. But during this short period of time when he showed up, he couldn't help but point out the many ways I was far from beautiful. I was hairy, he said, like a fucking chimpanzee. Even as a young girl, I'd shave my arms all the time to keep the other kids at school from noticing, though they always did. At the time, I was also a bit chubby, and Grand-dad came up with a nickname for me, one he used all the time: "dump truck." What little girl wants to be called a bloody dump truck?

Even if he hadn't given me that name, I still would have felt the gaping fucking distance between me and the pretty girls. The ones the boys paid attention to all seemed to have blond hair and blue gentle-doe eyes and slender tan legs. They spoke quietly and kept their opinions to themselves.

In every fucking way possible, I was the exact opposite. Dark-haired with skin so pale it pretty well glowed in the dark and a mouth that got me in trouble all the time. Everything in the world around me said I needed to be an attractive girl in a very particular way, to achieve the Barbie ideal.

I was not a fucking Barbie.

Not conventionally pretty. Too hairy. A minger. A fucking sight.

At least I could wrestle, and that gave me confidence in a weird fuck-you-world kind of way. Okay, so I might not be a guy's first choice to take out for a pint, but so what? I'd sure as hell be the one you'd want in your corner when the shit hit the fan. I leaned into my goth look. You think blond hair is nice? Fine, I'll dye my hair black. Tan legs the ideal? In that case, I'll keep my bright whiteness as untouched by the sun as possible. I should be demure and gentle? Go fuck yourself.

I was also hypersensitive to what I saw as unfairness in life. There were so many challenges people struggled with, as I'd already experienced at home. Coping with mental illness, addiction, struggling to make ends meet. Even an abandoned animal wandering the streets. I felt so deeply over these fucking grim situations. I felt everything so acutely. I was like my parents—I wanted to rescue everyone and everything. I couldn't ignore it. I would stand up for the underdog, getting involved in school when people were being bullied, find ways to try to even the playing field. This got me into trouble at school all the time, but I couldn't seem to help myself.

I was about fifteen and wrestling regularly, starting to make a name for myself on the independent European circuit, missing school a bunch and generally having a blast. Britani Knight was booked, sometimes even headlining, in venues all over the place—in Norway and Spain, Switzerland and Italy. I was flying cheap-arse airlines like Ryanair pretty much every weekend. Though, at first, I'd been a little nervous about traveling alone and going through airports in different countries, soon I became a genius at navigating air travel and taxis, sometimes staying in cheap hotels, other times at people's houses. This one weekend, I was back in England wrestling for a promoter at home, Brian Dixon. I was there, hanging out with Zak; Roy; my boyfriend at the time, Eirik; and a few of the other wrestlers. One in particular was Klondyke Kate, a well-known performer from the eighties and nineties, the original Hell in Boots. She was a middle-aged, plus-size wrestler with burgundy-red short spiky hair whose character was threatening and mean. To see her, most people would be intimidated, but she's the sweetest person on this planet, and I adored her.

The show had just ended, and we were getting ready for the journey back home, leaving by the side door. As we opened it, instantly, there was this group of three girls who'd been out partying. It was a Friday or Saturday night, and they were dressed to the nines, probably heading back to their cars after clubbing. We were off the main road and in an area of small side streets and car parks, everything cobblestoned.

The girls were a little drunk, and right off, Zak and Roy started teasing them, half flirting and half just giving them a hard time. I have to blame my brothers for starting it. The girls probably would have kept right on walking if my brothers hadn't been such menaces.

Our family's van was just a short distance away, but when Zak and Roy started being jerks, the girls got rowdy. Actually, to be fair, they were rowdy to begin with . . . talking too loudly, laughing and weaving, clearly fucking wasted, but the boys did not go unnoticed.

"I have a cousin who fights for the UFC, and I'm calling him now. He's gonna come down and kick your fucking arses," one of the girls yelled at full voice, digging her phone out of her purse and making a scene of dialing this cousin.

Zak and Roy started laughing like fucking idiots.

"Oh, we're so in trouble now, mate!" Zak said to Roy.

"Shaking in me boots!" Roy responded.

"Cut it out, lads," Kate said. "Let's just get home." She moved past the boys and toward the van, trying to get them to follow her.

By then, the girls were riled up, and the minute Kate spoke, they seemed to notice her for the first time. Immediately, they lasered in on her.

"Who's this fat bitch?" one girl asked.

"Oh my God! She's so gross!" another said.

That's when I had it. The boys deserved anything those girls could have thrown at them, even the supposed UFC fighting cousin, but Kate? She'd done nothing wrong. She was a total fucking sweetheart and meant the girls zero harm. She was always getting booed in the ring—she played a heel—but what really annoyed me was how she was regularly fat-shamed. And in this case, if anything, she was trying to defuse the situation. Still, the minute they noticed Kate, they turned all their venom toward her. As if just being a larger-size woman was offensive to them. I was not going to put up with this shit.

I handed my bag to Eirik. "Hold this."

I ran toward the girls and punched the first one with a vicious right hook. She flew back from the force of my hit and fell into her friend, who in turn collapsed into the third girl. It was like a domino effect, all three tumbling tits over arse and now lying in a pile of heels and purses and limbs on the ground.

At just that very moment, the promoter, Brian Dixon, came walking out. He'd missed the punch but saw the pile of girls and looked to me for an explanation.

"I don't know what happened," I lied. "They were all on the ground, and I'm just making sure they're okay."

I don't think he believed me. He walked in the opposite direction, as if to say, *Whatever you're doing, I don't want to know.*

"This is what you fuckers get for starting shit," I said to my brothers once Brian was out of earshot, as I pulled them to the van. The girls were starting to untangle themselves, and I wanted to get the hell out of there as quickly as possible.

On the ride home, Roy started calling me "Rocky" and Kate dubbed me "Chinner." (It's what we say in England for someone who's got a nasty right-cross to the chin.)

It wasn't like I was going out of my way to prove I was a badass. It was the unfairness of the situation that got to me. I couldn't stand to see Kate bad-mouthed like that. If I wasn't going to be able to impress people with my looks and sophistication, at least I'd make them think twice before they fucked with me and my friends.

Despite my fierce loyalty to the people willing to be close to me, at school during the week, I became a complete outcast. If I thought I hadn't be-longed when I was younger and only wrestling around England, now that I was getting famous in Europe and jetting off all the time, I was ridiculed relentlessly. The boys in high school were mean to me constantly, I guess because I was a total tomboy. There I'd be, dressed in my brothers' clothes and wearing baggy sweatpants and jumpers. I was a kind of chav, too. Thankfully, I wasn't there enough for it to get under my skin.

I didn't want to be in school in the first place. . . . I was going to be a wrestler. What did I need this shit for? I wasn't a very good student, for sure. As a result, I got sent out of class a lot to a place called "isolation," where all the poor students were sent to sit all day long, doing nothing.

It was so stupid. The teacher there was always on a power trip and known for being a bitch. I don't know what happened this one day, but she and I got into it verbally. Out of nowhere, this stupid guy in class joined in, calling me names, throwing shit at me, saying I had hairy arms. He was sitting next to where a fire extinguisher was mounted on the wall, so I just grabbed his head and went—bam!—

smashing his skull right into that fire extinguisher. That shut him the fuck up.

My mum was, of course, summoned to the school. Her only question was, "Did he deserve it?"

When I said yes, she was ready to defend me to the death. (To be fair, he definitely didn't deserve the physical part, but I love that she was willing to defend me anyway.)

Thankfully, by this point, the school was aware of my wrestling career and how often I was gone. As punishment for the fire extinguisher event, I was excluded from school for a few weeks—*Oh no, anything but that*—and then sent to anger-management classes, which were sort of like therapy sessions. It felt like a waste of time to me. I wasn't mature enough yet to really benefit anything from them. Eventually, though, we hit on a proper solution. Mr. Hawthorn, a teacher I liked, who was understanding of my situation, also happened to be married to the headmistress. He was one of the few people who made my life in school easier, and he understood the pressure I was under. He suggested maybe I could do a part-time schedule, and that's what we did. From that point on, school was not an issue.

"Not good enough yet," Drew McDonald said. He was one of the old-school wrestlers who knew my dad and had been hired as a talent scout for WWE. He'd come to a lot of my matches since I was sixteen and had the same feedback for me every time. "Not yet. But keep at it."

He made it clear he wasn't in the business of setting up tryouts if you weren't going to shine. He had his credibility to maintain. I got it. I didn't want to blow my shot, either, by being seen by them when I wasn't yet ready.

I had finished school and turned eighteen when, out of the blue—or so it seemed to me—Drew changed his tune.

"Okay," he said after one of my matches, talking to me in the locker room. "This is it. You're finally ready. Don't let me down. I'm giving you this chance because I think you have something special."

Holy shit.

"I swear, Drew. I'll make you proud." And though he was a huge man, I hugged the stuffing out of him.

Thanks to Drew's report to WWE, both Zak and I were invited to Manchester in November for their semiannual tryouts. Because we were still pretty young, we were allowed to bring our mum along. Drew reassured us he'd be there as well, cheering us on.

I was so excited. This was finally my chance, everything I'd been working toward. My life was going to all make sense now.

But I knew there was a problem. Sure, female wrestlers were still a kind of rare breed, but the few who were in the WWE at that time all looked the same: blond, gorgeous in that Barbie doll way. Nothing about them looked like me.

I'd need to look more like them if I wanted to be accepted. I convinced myself of that, and instead of spending every second preparing for what I'd do in the ring when I finally made it to the tryouts, I started obsessing about my looks. To be chosen by the WWE, I needed to look like a Diva, and they all looked the same: huge fake boobs, a big toned arse, golden tans, and showing lots of skin.

I looked in the mirror. I saw an emo girl in a ripped black T-shirt with all these piercings and a poorly managed comb-over. . . . I was fucked.

I couldn't go in there like that. So I got to work. First, I removed all my piercings. Then my sister, Nikki, gave me a spray tan and helped whiten my teeth. (She worked as an esthetician.) I changed out of the all-black clothes I usually wore and chose instead a tan-colored top that was frilly and paired it with a black skirt and heels. That would be perfect for the interview part and was just about all the color I could handle. I sometimes think I'm allergic to wearing colors.

I dyed my hair a natural-looking brown rather than the pitch black I favored. When I got it all together, I looked in the mirror, knowing exactly what I was aiming for. The Divas all displayed unattainable levels of fitness, glamour, and beauty.

The mirror didn't lie. I had failed miserably.

Well, at least it was a step or two closer to the Diva look. Maybe the WWE would help me get the rest of the way there.

I was super nervous on the drive to Manchester and feeling like I needed to take a shit the whole time. Just before a match, that same feeling always came over me, even when I knew I didn't need to use the toilet. When it was my turn, I was paired with a wrestler I knew, Lisa Fury from Liverpool. She was stunningly beautiful. That discrepancy between her looking the part and how far short I fell of it was all I could think about as we put together a match to showcase ourselves and what we could do. Thankfully, I liked Lisa, and we worked well together.

When it was our turn to go, man, I fucked it up. I'm not sure how I did it, but I managed to cut Lisa's lip and make her bleed. That's like the biggest no-no in the business. Lisa, of course, was an angel about it, which only made her look better. Here I was, trying to showcase my skills, and I fucking hurt someone. I wanted to die of shame. When it was over, I was called into an office.

"You're lacking things the other girls have," the man behind the desk told me. "Things we're looking for."

I said nothing, waiting for him to make more sense. Sure, I'd made Lisa bleed, but still, I'd wrestled well. Did they have an issue with my skills? I could deal with that. Then I'd know what I needed to work on. But what he was telling me was too vague.

"The way you look, you know?" he said, stumbling to explain why the WWE was going to reject me.

"You're just not there yet," he continued. "If you know what I mean."

Just spit it out, dude. Say it: I'm not pretty enough!

I was mad and sad all at once and just wanted to cry. I was overthinking it, focused on the wrong things. Was he telling me I wasn't glamorous enough, that if I wanted a career in the WWE, I needed to get fake boobs? What the fuck was this? Sure, the WWE had a certain look for their Divas, I got it, and I supposed that was okay, it's their business. I mean, those women became superstars. Whatever they went through to get there, it paid off for them.

But as I sat in that office, one thing became clear. Yes, I *did* want to be a Diva. But not a copycat one. I didn't want to look like the rest of them, to not be myself. I sank into the chair and wished it would simply swallow me up.

I felt so stupid. I'd thought they'd be able to look past my appearance to notice what I could really do. And I had tried to help them do so, dressing the way I thought they wanted, plus trying so fucking hard in the ring. I could read between the lines: *You are simply not pretty enough.*

I got up to leave.

"If you want, we'll have another look at you in six months," he said.

I nodded and shut the door.

Was he giving me time to get plastic surgery? I didn't even know what to say. Even more time in the gym wouldn't change the baby fat in my face. I felt so defeated.

Leaving, I ran into Drew in the hallway. He tried to spin what I'd just been told.

"Look, they want you back in six months. That's a positive!" he said.

I cried all the way home. Zak, too, had been rejected, but he'd been given specific instructions: to bulk up and develop more defined muscles, really carve his body. At least he had a plan on how to go forward. I just felt like a loser.

During the six months between that initial November tryout and the next one in April, I wrestled a lot. At that time, in addition to wrestling on the European circuit, I was doing a little wrestling in America, which only increased my appetite to join the WWE and move abroad. I loved the size of America, the way there seemed to be room for everyone.

My mum and I were hired as a tag team for Shimmer, an all-female wrestling organization out of Chicago. Created to give female wrestling talent from North America and beyond a platform to display their skills, Shimmer Women Athletes was a great fit for me. Shimmer focused on only female wrestlers. I liked that.

Mum and I traveled twice to Chicago to do Shimmer events, and in between, we made a stop in Florida. There, Lexie Fyfe, one of the Shimmer wrestlers, hosted what was called "customs" in a shed in her backyard.

Shimmer fans requested special matches just for them, and paid extra to get what they wanted. One request might be: "I want to see Saraya wrestle her mom with no shoes on." (It turns out there's this thing on the internet called wikiFeet. Apparently, I have five-star feet. I always get people writing to buy my shoes and socks or to photograph my feet. If I take a picture out by the pool or if my feet are in the picture in any way, shape, or form, people take a screenshot and post it. It's a little weird. I don't want to knock anyone else's kink, but that's one I just never got.)

Or they might request, "I want them to have a normal wrestling match, but they have to be in one-piece bathing suits." Or "I want her to pull this other girl's hair the whole time." There were never any outright sexual requests allowed, but it was still kind of creepy. There would be no audience for these matches, just Lexie's husband with a camcorder. Once the tape had been made, it would be shipped to the fan, and Mum and I would pocket thousands for our effort. The things people will do for money, am I right?

I focused on my wrestling skills. I was never going to look like one of those Diva girls, so why even try? I was just going to be me. Sure, I'd go back to that second tryout in April, but I was no longer determined to make them love and want me. I was not capable of making anyone love me, I realized, just as I hadn't been able to make my mum come home when she'd left us. I was not capable of making Asa suddenly not mentally ill. And when Mum had left and Dad was drinking night, noon, and morning, I had not been capable of stopping his drinking. I knew by that point that some shit is just not yours to control, no matter how bad you want it.

Despite all that, there was still one thing I *could* do. Wrestle.

So that was the plan. When I returned in April, I'd give the WWE a taste of the real me. The goth wrestler girl from Norwich. And if that worked, great.

And if not, fuck 'em.

The second WWE tryout was in London, and both Zak and I attended again. This time, the lip ring and gauges stayed in, the inky black hair stayed dark but with a sassy blond streak underneath that my mum called a skunk. I dressed in my all-black goth look, wearing my black Converse—no fucking heels this time. My skin was as glow-in-the-dark white as ever.

If the other Diva wrestlers were Barbie dolls, I was a Bratz doll. If WWE was going to reject me again, it was going to be the actual *me* they rejected this time. And if so, then we'd be clear with each other. They would have made their intentions known: They had no need or desire for a wrestler like me. And I would be free to make my own path elsewhere.

When I got into the ring that day, I realized I was the only woman there. The rest were all men. And they had changed things around this time. Instead of doing matches, like singles tag matches on the fly, we had to all stand around the side of the ring and tag ourselves in and out. With this new setup, we couldn't plan anything in advance. I guess they wanted to see how we managed.

The tryouts were being held the day before *SmackDown* and as a result, all the talent for that show was gathered now around the ring, watching us, including Hunter, a.k.a. Triple H, the chief content officer for WWE and spouse of Stephanie McMahon, daughter of WWE founder Vince McMahon. It was so fucking intimidating. Mum was in the seats, too, behind a barricade, watching. Goldust, an iconic nineties wrestler and son of the legendary Dusty Rhodes, ran the tryout along with another legendary wrestler, Jamie Noble, one of the producers, and Ty Bailey, who worked talent relations for the WWE.

It was me and all these men, and they were tagging in and out, trying to show off for the gathered talent and the coaches. There was this one giant, jacked-up wrestler who I guarantee was on steroids. He was so huge, it was intimidating, and I thought, *This motherfucker is gonna pop!*

I stood quietly on the sidelines, noting which wrestlers seemed the best, when Jamie Noble came up to me from behind.

"Tag yourself in," he said.

Clearly, I was being way too nice, standing on the sidelines, awaiting my turn, the moment when someone would tag me in.

But tagging myself in? That was not a great idea. I might steal someone else's moment to shine. Everyone there was trying to get signed by the company, and tagging yourself in felt kind of selfish. But Jamie was the boss.

Just as he said that to me, the really big guy had another guy in a headlock, and they were coming toward the ropes. I tagged myself in, and the big wrestler looked at me like I was complete dogshit. His look said it all. *What the fuck?*

I whispered a quiet "sorry" and jumped in and started hitting this guy. Soon, Zak tagged himself in, and it was the two of us.

Goldust told Zak, as he took the ring, to "beat the shit out of her, but, like, in a wrestling way."

And so that's what we did. Zak was punching me, throwing me, body-slamming me. Then we started to just run spots. Zak and I had done these together so many times, they were basically memorized.

Zak whispered to me, "RVD?" This was shorthand for our favorite spot, named for an old-school wrestler, Rob Van Dam.

"Yes!" I nodded. Soon we were both flying around and doing all this crazy shit.

"All right, Saraya, cut your brother off," Goldust instructed from the sidelines, and so I did.

Zak and I were at it for about 70 percent of the allotted time, which was pissing off the other wrestlers, but Goldust and the other organizers wouldn't let us tag out. And besides, it felt so good to be in the ring with my brother. I knew I was going to be safe with him, and he was going to make me look like a million bucks, and vice versa. We were having the time of our lives. Everyone around was getting impatient, and I wanted to say, "Look, we're only doing what we've been asked to do." But inside, it was as if a switch had been flipped. This was my time, too, and I was going to fucking take it! I was the only fucking female there, and I needed to not be scared.

And I wasn't.

"All right, you guys, go get cleaned up and come back when you're done," the WWE representative instructed.

The tryouts were over. I was still getting my wind back and felt good about what I'd done.

"Hey, Saraya."

I was just about to hit the locker room when Goldust and the others stopped me. "Can you stay for a second?"

"Sure."

"That was just really great wrestling," Goldust said.

He went on to show me things I could tweak to make my moves even better. Like, when I had someone in a headlock, he showed me a better way of doing it.

"Roll all the way back to make it look as real as possible," he said.

I ate up every word, wanting to get better. Fucking Goldust was coaching me!

"You did a really good job. I'm proud of you," he said.

My head was spinning.

"And you got some balls," he added.

Being recognized by someone I had looked up to for so long took my fucking breath away. I was nearly shaking.

"Thank you." I ducked my head so they wouldn't see the tears in my eyes and headed to the locker room to change.

Like before, we were called into the office, one by one.

"Not this time," Zak said when he came out. "They said I need to be bigger."

"Oh shit. I'm sorry, bro." I gave him a huge hug. Hearing that, I was all ready to be turned down again, too. If they said no to Zak after that amazing display we'd put on, they certainly weren't gonna pick me.

Walking down the hallway to meet my fate, I passed Kelly Kelly, a wrestler they say is "so nice, they named her twice." She was the epitome of a Diva: gorgeous, blond hair, and an amazing body. She had her hair up in rollers when I saw her, and I thought she was still so glamorous. It was like spotting Marilyn Monroe or something. I passed all these wrestlers I had grown up watching, like Edge. This might be the closest I'd ever get to this world, and so I soaked up every minute. It was just surreal, seeing all those famous people. I was so happy to be there in the first place.

When I got into my one-on-one meeting with Ty Bailey, I started to sweat. This was it. My do-or-die moment. I had given them my everything. I had shown them what I could do. I hadn't hurt anyone this time, and I had given a fair representation of my skills. If they didn't want me after all that, then it would be their loss. I steeled myself, terrified I'd have to repeat that phrase "their loss" for the rest of my goddamned life.

The first thing he said, though, blew my mind.

"We love the way you look. Do not change anything."

Well, shit. Guess it worked.

The bottom line was that I was so much more confident simply being myself than I had been when I'd tried to be someone else. I stood out.

"We're going to sign you. You'll get an email soon to get your visa started."

Inside, I was screaming: *Oh my God! Oh my God!* Outside, I just started crying. I felt like a thousand things were all happening at once.

When I came out, my mum and brother were there. The minute they saw my face, they knew. And bless Zak's heart. Even though inside he was dying because he wanted to be signed, he gave me the biggest hug ever.

"I'm so proud of you. Even if I stay here and you go there, I'll be with you every step of the way. Go out there and fucking kill it."

Before we left for the day, after I'd gathered my things, I found myself out by the stage area, looking around. *Holy shit. One day, I might be wrestling here!*

Just then, Triple H, my new boss, came walking by. He looked at me, and I was intimidated as shit.

"Welcome aboard," he said, putting his hand out to shake mine.

That was the moment I'd never forget. I was there, beside the ring, and Triple H knew who I was. He knew I was signed and that I was going to be working with him. I wasn't just dreaming this shit. It was real.

That vision board I'd made was coming true. I'd always wanted to be in America, working for the WWE, and now it was happening. I had worked so hard for this moment. And I had fucking made it. I was finally here.

PART Two

LOSE YOURSELF

Saraya!" Lexie, the Shimmer wrestler who'd hosted the customs in Florida, wrapped me in a big hug when she met me at baggage claim. She was older and maternal, nurturing, and I melted into her arms. I was exhausted from the flight from London to Tampa. I was used to traveling, but this was different. At least Lexie was there, and I knew she would make sure I was okay.

But first, I had to pee.

I went into the toilet and saw myself in the mirror. I looked a mess: makeup all down my face, my hair a total rat's nest. I'd slept or cried the whole flight over. I rinsed off my face and looked hard at myself, allowing the reality to hit.

I'd left home in the early hours of New Year's Day in a puddle of tears, Mum and I hanging on to each other for dear life at the check-in desk, all the wrestlers from home escorting me to the security line in the predawn darkness. Dad was bawling his eyes out. It took all the strength I had to extract myself from their embrace. I pulled the hoodie over my head, snug under my leather jacket, and turned away from everything and everyone I'd ever known. As I walked toward security, I was fully and uncontrollably sobbing.

By the time I made that flight, eight months had passed since I'd been signed by the WWE, and I'd turned nineteen. I hadn't been able to pick up and leave for the States immediately upon signing because there were visas to straighten out. And when my visa arrived, my dad had to show it to everyone because it listed my employer as World Wrestling Entertainment. He was so fucking excited. Plus, I had already been contracted to wrestle on the European independent circuit, with dates to finish up in Norway, Spain, Italy, and Switzerland before I could start my new life in America. I almost messed up my transition to the WWE by finishing out those dates. I did an event in Switzerland where I was to wrestle a girl named Amy.

"Can you do a cross-body off the second?" I asked her before the show as we sorted out our moves.

"Yes, I can," she said.

"Have you done it before?" I asked.

"Yes, I have."

I don't know why, but my intuition kicked in, and I didn't believe her. She'd be jumping onto me from the second rope, and I needed to be sure I'd be safe.

"Let's practice it before the match," I suggested.

She clambered onto the second rope, and I stood there with my arms out, providing a base for her to land on. I was to catch her when she flew from that height. But when it was time to launch, instead of coming straight at me as she should have, she leaped off to one side, and in doing so slammed right into my nose. Fucking hard.

The pain was immediate, startling in intensity. Instantly, I started gushing blood. My hands flew to my face. I was so mad.

"If you've never done this before, why not tell me?!"

"I thought it would be easy and that we'd figure it out by trying it."

"Amy! I'm signed by the fucking WWE. I can't go there with a busted face!" I was so upset. The bleeding wouldn't stop, so I asked the promoter to take me to the hospital. We still had a couple of hours before the show.

On the ride to the hospital, I called my mum in tears. "I can't believe this!" I yelled down the phone. "My nose is totally fucked-up. It's swelling! She said she could do a cross-body, and she couldn't fucking do it! And now my face is all busted."

"Just calm down. Get to the hospital," Mum said.

The promoter left me at the ER doors, where a clerk checked me in, but hours went by, and no doctor came out to see me. Time was ticking away. Finally, I called the promoter back. "Just come back and get me. The show's going to start soon, and no one here is taking care of me."

By the time he arrived to retrieve me, the nurses had just figured out I'd been overlooked. "Oh, we're so sorry about that."

Like, how do you forget a patient? But it didn't matter by then; it was too late. I wrestled that night's match against Amy with my nose totally fucked-up, all swollen. I couldn't breathe through it and had to pant like a dog to get oxygen. And then, during the actual match, she fucking managed to clobber me in the nose again. Oh my God, this bitch!

I was mad. So fucking furious. I took it out on her, yanking her by the hair with such force that when I finally let her go, a chunk of blond curls was wound around my fingers. Oh fuck! I hadn't meant to do that!

I came back to reality in that moment. Amy was a sweet girl and didn't mean me real harm, but fuck, she'd popped me in the nose twice in the same day! All I could think about was that I was going to America for my big break and now my face was fucked-up.

"I'm so sorry," I told her after we left the ring. And I really was; it was unprofessional of me to have behaved that way. "I was afraid the injury would mess up my contract."

"It's okay," she said. "I understand." She was such a sweetheart, which only made me feel worse for having been so rough with her. Her skull must have stung like crazy. To be fair, so did my nose.

But here's the funny thing: That second hit to my nose seemed to have straightened it out. When I got back to the UK, Mum took a look, going at my nostrils with swabs, examining my nasal ridge carefully. She was always the one to patch up people after matches, to bang dislocated joints back into place, whatever was needed.

"Your nose looks totally fine," she said. "And you're breathing through it, no problem. I think Amy managed to pop that shit back into place, even if she did it by accident."

It took another month for the bruising and swelling to go away, but I looked pretty much normal by the time I landed in Florida.

I was here! I'd finally made it. I was in America, not as a visitor for a week or two but to stay, signed as a wrestler with WWE. Well, technically, with Florida Championship Wrestling, the developmental system for the WWE, but basically the same thing. This was what I had been asking for. I needed to wake up and see that being in Florida was a good thing.

Making my way back to the baggage claim and Lexie, I took it all in—the heat and humidity, the American accents that were everywhere, just about everyone tanned, wearing flip-flops. Everything was so different from in the UK. As I walked, I felt adrenaline make my chest tight. The whole flight I'd been filled with nothing but dread and sadness over leaving everyone behind, but now a 180-degree shift was occurring in real time inside me. Just seeing the bright Florida sun filling the airport gave me hope. There was so damn much to look forward to. If I worked hard, I might do well and prove myself, make my family proud, build a life beyond my wildest dreams. And it all started now at nineteen years old.

At the very moment I had that thought, Lexie's arm resting over my shoulder protectively, my luggage appeared on the conveyer belt and moved toward me as if by magic, finding me amid all these people, making me feel as if all I'd ever fantasized and wished for in life was on its way to me at this very moment.

That said, I was also completely fucking knackered. The day had been such a roller coaster of emotions. I just wanted to collapse.

✳

For the next few hours, my emotions ping-ponged all over the fucking place, nearly giving me vertigo. I was swept up one moment in everything that lay ahead, and then plummeted the next into the deepest despair. I'd left everything I knew behind. What was my life going to look like now? It was a complete blank slate, and I had no family with me. No backup.

But this was what I'd wanted. I was in America and hired by the WWE.

These two forces, excitement and regret, thrills and second-guessing, battled in my head and heart for hours. By the time I collapsed into the bed Lexie had prepared for me, I cried myself to sleep.

A few days later I stood at the address in Tampa I'd been given for Florida Championship Wrestling, FCW. Even though it was the early days of January, the sun overhead was brutal and I was already sweating from the heat and clamminess. It would take a while to adjust to this new climate.

On my first day, Lexie drove me. We pulled up to a large black building, with huge yellow letters looming over me: "FCW."

I nervously entered through the side door, but no one seemed to notice me. It was the first day back after the holidays, so everyone was busy catching up with one another, which gave me a chance to have a look around. There were locker rooms and a small office for the trainers to work, a wrestling ring (where later we'd do promo classes and sometimes put on mini shows for an audience of about a hundred), and two more practice rings, one behind the other. In those rings, wrestlers were running through spots. The noise of bodies hitting mats, coaches bellowing, and whistles blowing mixed with the smell of wrestling-ring tape and body odor. I was sort of surprised. This place looked almost identical to every training facility I'd ever been in. I'm not sure what I had expected, but it brought me some comfort. It sounded and smelled exactly right.

This was the first thing in America that made me feel at home.

Windham Rotunda, later known as Bray Wyatt in WWE, was the first person to talk to me as I stood at the entrance. He welcomed me in, making me feel more comfortable right away. Not far behind him, Summer Rae came over to say hi. She was the only girl who did. A super-muscly, friendly guy introduced himself as "Big E." They were all very welcoming.

A few men walked by me into an office, among them Dusty Rhodes, Joey Mercury, and Steve Keirn, all of whom I recognized. I ducked my head a bit and raised a hand in a shy greeting.

I heard my name being called from the office. I walked over to join them, as well as a man I didn't recognize who was sitting behind a desk. Judging by his physique, he was clearly a retired wrestler, but I had no idea who.

After he'd told me about the training schedule and how it would all work, he looked at me for a second.

"Do you know who Dr. Tom is?" he asked.

"I've heard of him, but I've never met him."

"That's me, but that's okay," he said, unfazed.

Shit.

"I'm really sorry." I had already fucked up on the first day. I felt humiliated and wanted to die. Not a great first impression in front of my new boss.

In my defense, I knew practically every British wrestler. Here I was, the new female wrestler who supposedly knew so much about wrestling, but I was off to a pretty shit fucking start. Thankfully, though, I didn't end up holding on to that feeling long. Dr. Tom turned out to be the sweetest person, someone who tried to make me feel at home there.

Before I left that day, I met the other girls in my group. They'd all been hired well before me and had been at it a while, hoping to be called up to the main roster any day now. The first thing I noticed was that they were all wearing makeup. I was used to training a lot, hair in my face and sweat on my skin. As far as I had been concerned, training was the last place on this planet for wearing makeup, but there they were, looking the part even at training. Everyone was so pretty and put together. I realized maybe I should start showing up a bit more presentable. I knew I wanted to keep my look, but I could learn to clean it up a bit and still put my head down and get to work.

The next day, I dove in. I quickly realized that our training would be mostly in the ring, often doing blowup drills, which were these horrible nonstop drills literally designed to blow us up, work us until we couldn't move. We'd run the ropes, then do lots of wrestling drills. We did drop-down tackles, and leapfrogs, and man-in-the-middle, where you have to stay in the ring as one by one, the other wrestlers come in to run a spot with you and you have to do that spot with everyone in the room. By the end of it, you were exhausted and would still have to keep going and going. We needed this kind of training for the cardio, obviously, but I hated the blowup drills. I just wanted to fucking die afterward.

About a week after I got there, the WWE asked me to come up with a list of potential names. I'd been thinking about the question for a while. Since I was thirteen, I'd wrestled as Britani Knight, but upon joining the WWE, I'd been told there was already a female wrestler with that first name, so I needed to choose another. We'd narrow it down to three options. Two of theirs: Mara, like Rooney Mara from *The Girl with the Dragon Tattoo*, and Echo. And one of mine.

"I was thinking Paige," I answered his question. "Like the witch on the TV show *Charmed*."

I'd watched that show since I was a kid and always loved the actress who played Paige. She was pale with dark hair and a butt chin, just like me. They liked it, too.

Just like that, I was Paige.

One day, we showed up and Dr. Tom had been fired. We didn't know why. Everyone was shocked—he was so well loved by everyone. But it got even worse when we met his replacement.

This new guy was hated by everyone, even his favorite trainees. Unlike Dr. Tom, he didn't care about any of us. He'd make people train until they threw up just because he could. In no time, I got frustrated because I didn't think I was learning anything new. Sure, my cardio was improving, but my wrestling wasn't getting any better because we weren't doing much of it.

Another trainer, though, Norman Smiley, was this old-school British wrestler who had moved to America in the seventies and long since lost his accent. He was a legend, and the complete opposite of the new trainer: extremely nice, liked by all, and a force of positivity at the gym.

We had promo classes with Dusty Rhodes, too, and I was finally learning something. Dusty genuinely wanted to help the next generation grow and be a success. We worked on our microphone skills in his class, doing promos against one another or just introducing ourselves. Sometimes, we'd do little skits we made up by ourselves or with a partner, something from a movie or whatever we liked. Dusty let us do anything we wanted as long as we were talking and acting and getting used to entertaining people.

The first time I did a promo, I was so nervous. I was totally intimidated because I was still new and now standing in front of all my peers who still looked at me as the new girl. They'd all been here much longer than me and knew one another. I was the odd woman out.

I took the microphone, and though my hands were sweaty and shaky, I postured, trying to look tough, saying the bit I had planned.

"Paige, baby. Loosen up a bit." Dusty was unimpressed.

I tried, but the second attempt was no better.

"How's this?" Dusty said. "Your boyfriend just dumped you and stole your toaster. Go!"

I did a promo with that prompt and made a royal fucking mess of it.

Among the other trainees in the room was a wrestler who went by Leakee. Fast-forward to now, and he's one of the biggest WWE stars, known as Roman Reigns, a huge Samoan guy, but that's not what he was called back in the day.

"Leakee, baby," Dusty called him from the back. "Go up there and sit next to her."

"Okay." Dusty turned his attention to me, giving me another shot. "He just dumped you"—he motioned at Leakee—"and stole your toaster. Go!"

I muddled through the promo, and though I loved Dusty and his class, I always felt so stupid. I made a total arse of myself on a regular basis, but over time, I got better. Dusty training me to think on the fly became invaluable.

At the same time, I was getting to know the other women. Summer Rae had come from the Lingerie Football League. At the time, she was the only one who was really nice to me. Shaul Guerrero, daughter of the legendary wrestler Eddie Guerrero, had, like me, come from the wrestling world. She got hurt sometimes, but she was great on the microphone and coming up with gimmicks, a real character. I loved whenever she took the mic.

Audrey Marie was like a Southern belle with huge boobs and red hair; I think she came from the modeling world. Caylee Turner, who was the sister of Alicia Fox from the main roster, had also come from modeling. And then there was Ivelisse, who came from wrestling and was a bit feisty.

All the girls were absolute tens in looks, with perfectly styled hair and flawless makeup. And there I was, plain face, goth looks, not in their league at all when it came to appearances. But I knew I could wrestle, and that's what this was all about, wasn't it?

I mostly kept to myself.

One of the girls there was always giving her uninvited criticism of my hair and makeup. If she wasn't making fun of my looks, she'd repeat whatever I'd just said in a really awful British accent, laughing her head off. She even moved my stuff out of the locker room. Typical mean-girl shit. I did what I could to ignore her; there was no point in engaging. Eventually she'd grow bored with poking at me like a trapped insect and leave me alone. But before that could happen, something in me snapped.

I had been at FCW maybe a couple of weeks and putting up with her taunting. That was piled on top of the physical exhaustion I felt all the time, thanks to the nonstop blowup drills. Plus, I was missing the daylights out of my family. I'd gotten my first apartment and was settled in, only to find myself so lonely in Tampa—no friends, no Mum and Dad keeping an eye on me, no Zak to decompress with, no Roy and Nikki to visit. I was eating shit meals every night and missed everything about home. The heaviness of what I'd signed on to had gotten far too real.

This one day, this girl was up to her normal shit, making fun of how I talked and really rubbing it in. That was it. I exploded.

Before she knew what was going on, I spun on my heel and then kicked in the locker room door. I got in her face and practically screamed at the top of my voice, "I'm fucking sick of this shit! I'm going to beat your fucking arse if you keep doing this." My hands were shaking, and my voice cracked with emotion. I fucking meant it.

The girl looked at me, her eyes widening in what may have been shock—or fear. I didn't give a shit what she felt. But whatever had motivated her to torture the new girl in that way, she never ridiculed me like that again.

But even after her insults stopped, I still had no real friends, and the loneliness that surrounded me felt itchy and sharp. It reminded me of high school, but worse. I had spent my entire life encircled by people who loved me, being doted on and adored. Now I was either invisible or actively disliked.

The schedule stayed much the same day after day, week after week. After training in the ring or doing our promo class, we'd all head to the gym, thirty minutes away, for strength training. I'd catch a ride with Big E Langston because he lived in my apartment building and always let me tag along. I was settling in, though not really finding my place.

There had been a quick romance, started a month before I moved to the United States. At the time, we told each other that once I left, that would be that. But the night before I left, he changed his mind.

"I love you, and I think we can make this work."

I wasn't so sure, but I liked him, and we said we'd try. Still, I was realistic. "You realize I'm not coming back, right?"

He said he did. And it felt good to have someone to text and stay in touch with amid all the changes in my life that were unfolding.

A month after I left, he flew over to see me and to hang out for a week. Almost as soon as he landed, he saw what was coming. "I just don't think this is going to work," he said.

Of course he was right, but the breakup left me feeling even more sad and alone.

Meanwhile, everything was so different in America. The cars were bigger; the roads were bigger. The food was different. The food in England wasn't pumped full of the artificial crap we eat over here, some of which I found really delicious. There were fast-food restaurants on every corner—Wendy's, McDonald's, Burger King, Chick-fil-A—and the portions were huge! Even though I'd grown up with my mum, who was known for her massive portions, they were nothing like what I was getting in America. When I'd stayed at Lexie's house, I couldn't believe the size of her refrigerator. It was the kind you might see in a restaurant in the UK but not in someone's house. And all the swimming pools! In the UK, you'd have to be super rich to have a pool, but here, even the smallest house might have a huge swimming pool in the backyard. It was just so different.

During those early weeks, Lexie took me to dinner one night at a Cheesecake Factory. I'd never seen a menu like it; it was crazy. Chinese food, Mexican food, Italian. Everything. It still blows my mind, over ten years later, every time I go there. I'm just like, *This is too much!*

And though mac and cheese wasn't big in the UK, I ordered their crispy crumb-coated mac-and-cheese balls served over a creamy marinara sauce that night and was totally hooked. For dessert, I obviously had to order cheesecake, right? Though we had it in the UK, I'd never eaten it before. Oh my God: so delicious! I became obsessed with cheesecake after that.

In my little apartment, most of my meals were microwavable things I bought at Walmart because I didn't know how to cook. Despite my mum being a chef, I hadn't picked up her talents. And now, whenever I shopped, I picked up one of the cheesecakes you have to defrost. I gained fifteen pounds in the first couple of months, every one of which I attribute to that delicious cheesecake and those mac-and-cheese balls.

We all had weigh-ins at FCW every Monday. In my head, I started to feel insecure about the effect it was all having.

But that wasn't the only part of training that sucked. I mean, *really sucked.*

The trainers got switched out a lot, so Norman wasn't working with the girls anymore, which was disappointing. He was replaced by another trainer who was super nice to the other girls with no previous wrestling experience but not so nice to the ones who did. I tried to cut them some slack; they had to basically train the others in wrestling moves I already knew, but at a certain point, I got frustrated. I had to do the same fucking drills with them over and over, a lot of arm drags every single training session, like: arm drag, arm drag, hip toss, hip toss—the same stuff every single time—and I wanted to scream: *I'm not learning anything!* How was I going to get to the main roster this way?

I was miserable and lonely, so much so that I occasionally wanted to quit. This was not what I thought I had signed up for. I hated going into training every day and was deeply unhappy.

Then, during our gym workouts—we had two hours in a gym each day, thirty minutes away, after we'd finished the wrestling training—they replaced another trainer everyone loved, John Cena's personal trainer Rob, with a guy who was a piece of shit and a complete creep to women. He took pictures of us girls working out when we didn't realize he was photographing us. We'd be bent over or in other compromised positions, and then he'd post the photos on Facebook with the caption "I love my job!" It was so fucking creepy.

When I complained about the trainer who was taking the photos to the other trainer that no one liked, he simply asked why I felt it was okay to be looking at his Facebook page.

"What do you mean? He's taking pictures of us bent over like that and it's okay?"

I didn't get much of an answer. I fucking hated that. He eventually did get fired, though, maybe when WWE caught wind of it in the main office in Connecticut.

At my first match on *FCW*, I walked out to the ring for a battle royale—a single match to showcase a large number of wrestlers or to determine a championship title. Another old-school British wrestler, William Regal, was on commentary.

"The mysterious raven-haired lady, Paige, all the way from Norwich, England," they announced as I got into the ring just as I had done a million times before.

Regal was the one who would give me the moniker "Hell in Boots," while he was on commentary during my very first match. He said it was because I wrestled like one of the guys, and always in my Doc Marten boots: the iconic British combat boots of punks and goths everywhere. By the seventies, they had become popular with the alternative crowd, practically part of the uniform of rock stars and punk bands—and now part of my uniform, too. I immediately liked the name because it reminded me of Klondyke Kate back in the UK; it's what she had been called. It helped me to feel connected to home. And it fit me—I wanted to raise hell.

But I was going through it.

I called home a lot during that period and talked to my mum. It was all overwhelming at times, so I was having panic attacks and she was great at calming me down. Dad was a little more tough love—he knew this was a huge opportunity and didn't want me to waste it. He told me I had to pull myself together and not let them see me cry.

So I stopped calling. I tried to follow Dad's advice and just push through it.

I had a roommate, Jose—not a wrestler—and he was really helpful, giving me rides to work all the time and cooking me really incredible mac and cheese. Mostly, when not working out, I stayed in my room, sad and alone and in over my head.

Eventually, I adopted a dog to help me through it, Sooki. She was a rescue, a whippet mixed with maybe a Chihuahua. Having a dog always helped. I was a fan of the show *True Blood*, and the main girl was called Sookie Stackhouse. My Sooki was a light blondie color, and I adored her, cuddling with her, crying into her fur.

She seemed to be the only living creature around who liked me.

"Want to go to the beach with us?" one of the male wrestlers, Maddox, asked one afternoon as we were leaving the gym after training.

I was surprised because for the most part, I'd kept to myself, and all the others had let me. They all got together for drinks or whatever regularly, but no one ever invited me. I was tired of being by myself all the time, still sad over my recent breakup, and really wanting to make some friends.

"Yeah," I answered. "I'd like that."

Maddox came over to pick me up and took me to Clearwater Beach, where a bunch of our fellow wrestlers were having a day off. A volleyball court was set up, and everyone was hanging out, playing in the water, tanning. I tried to stay covered up a bit—I'm so fair-skinned—but joined in, and for the first time since I'd moved to Florida, I felt part of the gang.

After the beach day, Maddox drove me home. He'd been super sweet to me the entire day, and honestly I was so starved for a little love and attention by then, I ate that shit up. . . . I'd been so fucking lonely.

We sat in his car for hours, talking. Then he leaned over and started kissing me. He was about eight years older, so that felt a little strange. He wasn't my usual type, either, but it was nice to have someone be so nice to me.

The minute I was out of his sight, he was texting me all the time. It felt so good to be invited out with people and finally accepted here in Florida. We didn't broadcast that we were talking, it was just lighthearted and casual—nothing serious. Still, though, he was always checking in on me, making sure I was okay.

But then, of course, things got complicated.

We'd been hanging out for a month or so when a bunch of wrestlers and I were at the gym, getting ready for the next two hours of lifting weights, running, going through our training routine. As usual, we all gathered up before we started to go over the routine for the day. I had been texting Maddox all morning, and he hadn't been responding, which was really weird for him. But then the trainer gave me some insight.

"So, it looks like Maddox won't be joining us today." They always let us know when someone would be missing.

"Make sure you say congratulations when you see him! He's at the hospital right now with his wife, who's currently in labor."

I kept my face neutral as the trainer's words ran through me. Oh shit. Maddox was married. Not only married, but having a kid.

What the fuck?

THIS IS ME

You're in the hospital?" I texted Maddox when I could get away from the others. "With your WIFE?" I was completely blown away. I didn't think of myself as his girlfriend, but I didn't think he was married and expecting a baby, either.

"Yeah," he texted back straightaway.

"This is definitely a conversation we should have had."

He explained that he and his wife had broken up. I thought it over and reasoned that his story had to be legit because, come on, there was no way he could have gotten away with the stuff he'd been doing, like staying at my house all night. I asked some of the other wrestlers about him, and they all confirmed the breakup story.

Looking back, I just wonder at myself. Why did I believe that shit?

The whole time we hung out was kind of messed up, and I didn't see it. Things escalated quickly. Naive is an understatement. He wanted to film, photograph, or in some way record everything sexual we did. He asked me to send him erotic pictures all the time. Every time we had sex, he was videotaping it. I never wanted to, but somehow it always ended up happening anyway.

"Let's do a threesome with Woods," he suggested later on, wanting us to be with one of his best friends, Xavier Woods, a wrestler with WWE.

I wasn't entirely comfortable with that. So to get through it, I drank a ton. Of course, the whole thing was filmed. After, I did feel gross with myself.

Honestly, my discomfort had nothing to do with Woods. He treated me well and is genuinely a friend of mine. Of course he just wanted to have a good time, and he never knew how I was feeling because I never let on. I just wanted to be accepted and liked. At that point in my life, I was young, I was alone, and I would've done anything for that.

The news came down from above about a year and a half after I first landed in Florida. Florida Championship Wrestling, where I was employed, would be no more. A new entity, NXT, an innovative new version of the developmental system, would take its place. By June 2012 we all needed to move to Orlando, a two-hour drive away, where the new NXT facility awaited us.

This had all come about because Triple H had taken over FCW with the plan to make it bigger and better than ever, and to turn it into a proper academy. He bought this big, massive warehouse as the training facility and called the new organization NXT—which really doesn't stand for anything, just means the next generation. He planned to make NXT the *American Idol* of wrestling. As it was explained to me, just like American Major League Baseball had a farm system for up-and-coming players, now so would the WWE. And like those emerging baseball players had their own stadiums, we would have an amazing new facility of our own, the Performance Center in Orlando. There, NXT would provide live events and TV tapings for pay-per-view. It was a way to monetize and get more attention for the wrestlers coming up through the ranks to the WWE.

To make the move, all the other wrestlers and I had to get out of our leases and say goodbye to any non-wrestling friends we'd made in Tampa. The WWE was helpful by covering the costs involved with the move, and by then, I'd become friends with two other female wrestlers, Bayley and Emma, and we all helped one another pack up our lives, taking turns driving the truck from Tampa to Orlando.

When NXT was announced, Stephanie McMahon had told the world about an exciting new eight-woman single-elimination tournament, featuring four women from NXT and four from WWE's main roster. The winner of that event would be crowned the inaugural NXT Women's Champion. Every single one of us wanted that championship belt.

Though the training sessions had improved over time, and I was finally getting to work on my skills, I was regularly annoyed with how we were treated as female wrestlers. For instance, we were made to do bikini contests in the middle of wrestling matches. At first, it hadn't bothered me. It was just the way things were, but over time, I got really fed up with it. We'd have to come into the ring wearing some kind of cover-up, and then take it off to reveal ourselves in a bikini while the crowd voted on who was the sexiest.

I found myself in Hot Topic one day, looking for oversized band T-shirts I could use as my cover-up, and I thought, *Why am I doing this? I don't want to parade around in a bikini.* All I wanted to do was wrestle. I played the grumpy emo girl because I hated the contests. In truth, just about all the other girls hated it, too.

"I don't want to do these fucking bikini contests anymore," I said to Dr. Tom when I got really fed up before he was let go. "They're fucking gross, and we don't want to take our clothes off in front of kids in the crowd. We want to wrestle. That's why we're here."

Though the other girls felt the same, most were too scared to speak up, afraid they might lose their jobs. When any of us challenged management too much, they let us know how they felt about it by cutting our time in the ring or not putting us into a show.

And this is why I love Dr. Tom. He was totally receptive to what I had to say, and after that, the bikini contests were eliminated.

He and the other trainers also let us get away with stuff that was banned for women on the main roster. At the time, Vince McMahon didn't want women to wrestle like men and do the more acrobatic moves the crowds loved. He wanted us to "look like women and fight like women." That was the style of the time.

"What does that even mean?" I asked.

"A lot of scratching and pulling hair."

"I don't want to do that," I said. I wanted the fun athletic stuff the guys got to do. So while the women on the main roster were prohibited from doing those moves, management for NXT turned a blind eye, since Vince McMahon wasn't paying close attention to what we were actually doing.

Dr. Tom, who knew we wanted to do more athletics and less hair pulling, gave us these crazy matches, like one called "Money in the Bank," where there's a briefcase hanging from the ceiling. We had to climb up to the top rope to even get it. It was great. And he allowed us to do all the crazy moves the men were allowed. Dr. Tom's attitude seemed to be *You want to do this? Okay. Show me!*

So we worked on things like the Tower of Doom and the German Suplex. The Tower of Doom is impressive, involving multiple wrestlers in a high-risk sequence—usually used in a tag team, or a multi-person ladder match. It often begins with one wrestler positioned on the top rope at the turnbuckle (where the rope is connected at the corner). That wrestler is considered the anchor. The other wrestlers position themselves at the middle ropes or at the corner opposite the anchor. For the "dive," one of those wrestlers grabs the anchor and they proceed to execute a simultaneous suplex or powerbomb maneuver, lifting the anchor off the top turnbuckle. The anchor is sent crashing down to the mat, and the other wrestlers crash down on that wrestler in a kind of chain reaction. The audience usually goes bananas, and we had so much fun working on it. It's a visually stunning move, often used in a climactic moment, and such a blast to execute.

Emma and I had been working together for a while, and with the silent approval of the trainers, perfecting our versions of these complex, generally male-only moves.

As soon as I made the move to Orlando, though, I had to contend with a health issue. Earlier, when I'd first started with FCW, I had been talking to my trainer Rob. He was so intelligent and would give us spontaneous little lessons about anything, physiology, history, art, theater, whatever subject caught his attention. Over the weekend, he'd write up notes on whatever he'd become interested in, and at the start of all our training sessions, he'd share with us what he'd learned, writing cool stuff all over the whiteboard. I loved him, and we were all invested in what he had to teach us.

This one day, early on, I had been doing bent-over rows after his lecture, and he'd been watching.

"Do you have scoliosis?" he asked. I had no idea what he was talking about. Had I missed a key lesson from his earlier lecture?

"Excuse me, sir?" I pretended to be morally offended, having no idea what scoliosis was.

"I can see it, your spine. It's curved. See: Your shoulder blade on one side comes up more than the other." He showed me in the mirror. "Stand up straight for me."

I did.

He looked at my back, feeling my spine. "You definitely have scoliosis."

I ran my hand along my spine as far as I could reach. This was so weird. Growing up, I'd always hated my back and felt it looked weird. If there were pictures or video of me from behind, I didn't like how my back looked in them. And I thought I was just strange, because, how do you not like your back? But my book bags had always looked weird on me when I was in school. And now I finally knew why.

"You should go see a doctor about this," Rob said. And since he was always so nice and smart and I loved learning from him, I did.

The scoliosis turned out to be no big deal, but the doctor ran a full scan of my spine to see what was what, and that led to the discovery of what's called a dermoid cyst on my ovary.

The doctor tried to explain to me what this was, the words scrambling in my brain. "It's a fluid-filled sac containing tissue of hair, skin, teeth, or other body parts."

"So it's my demon baby?" I asked, fascinated by the freakishness of having this sac with skin and teeth.

"I wouldn't call it that," the doctor said. "Yours is about the size of a grapefruit. It's not cancerous but can cause complications. We will need to do surgery to remove it."

"It's not a good time for that." When you're a professional wrestler, there's no good time to have surgery.

"Well, you can leave it for a while, if you like. But if it starts to cause pain, you'll need to have it removed."

I had put off dealing with it back in Tampa, but now in Orlando, as everything for the NXT inaugural championship was ramping up, suddenly I was in excruciating pain. I saw a doctor there who confirmed what I feared. I couldn't wrestle under these conditions because the cyst could rupture. I needed to have it out. Immediately.

As all the other wrestlers were preparing for the fast-approaching championship I was dying to participate in, I was scheduled for surgery to deal with what I still lovingly called my "demon baby." The recovery time, according to the doctor, would be more than a month. God, I wanted to wrestle as part of that championship so badly. I had been working nearly two years toward this moment and now, because of the fucking surgery, I didn't even know if they'd let me in the ring.

If they did, I just had to hope I was in good enough shape to compete when the medical shit was all taken care of because I wouldn't have a chance to prepare any further. Either the skills and fitness were good enough, or they weren't. Still, I worried I might have to drop out of the match—my first big shot, my debut. It all depended on how the surgery went.

My mum came from England to help me through the ordeal, and when I was rolled into the recovery room, instead of finding the two tiny incisions the doctor had described for me in advance, I had a massive incision in my lower abdomen as if I'd just had a C-section. It turned out that in order to fully extract the cyst, which was larger than they expected, they'd had to cut into me like that.

I kept complaining to Mum. "Why this? Why now?" I didn't know if

I'd be okay to wrestle in time. Shaul Guerrero came over with flowers and a balloon to make sure I was okay. That was so sweet.

Still, if I couldn't wrestle in time, I would definitely not be okay.

I rested as much as I could over that month and a half. Eventually, the stitches dissolved. According to the doctor, the very first day I *might* be cleared to wrestle again was the day of the championship match. That was cutting it way too fucking close.

That day, I got to the venue early, determined. Triple H was there as well as the team doctor.

"Okay, let's see how you do. Start by running the ropes," Triple H said.

I did that, sprinting backward and forward into the ropes, both of them watching me carefully.

"Now, let's take a few bumps," Triple H said.

I did.

"Do you think you're okay to wrestle?" they asked. "Because you look good to us."

"Yeah, I'm ready." It was about time.

I was so fortunate to have been cleared for that particular match, because it was the start of everything for me.

I knew I would be wrestling Emma, but we hadn't yet been told who was going to win. We practiced our match with two different finishes, one in which she won, and the other where I triumphed. We were ready for whatever the powers that be had in mind.

"This could totally make your career," I told Emma. "I hope it's you."

"No, Paige, it could be you!"

We were both really excited.

Because the organization didn't want anything to leak out, they didn't tell us what they had in mind for our match outcome, which I appreciated because otherwise I would have had butterflies all day. As it was, my nerves were shot. The event was held at Full Sail University and there was a Starbucks there where I'd been downing caffeine all day—not a smart move. That, plus having been unable to wrestle for the past month and a half, had me on edge.

Soon, the men's matches started, and the energy was really ramping up. As per usual before a big match, I felt like I had to take a shit so badly. Just nerves. Nerves and too much coffee.

And then, minutes before it was our turn, Emma and I got word. I was to win the match.

Emma hugged me. She was one of my good friends who I'd met during training at FCW, and really happy for me, but I'm sure she was also a bit disappointed. Who wouldn't be? She worked hard, though, not to give off that vibe.

"Just being part of this match is so cool," she said.

We had some amazing shit in store for the audience and couldn't wait to present what we'd been working on.

When they announced our names, we took the ring, acting like we hated each other with every ounce of our beings. At that moment, all the stage fright I'd been feeling disappeared, and, in no time, we moved in sync with each other. It quickly became clear the entire crowd was also split on who should win.

Chants of "Let's go, Emma!" alternated with "Let's go, Paige!" and so it went, back and forth, adding to the excitement and tension.

We went through our moves, and it all unfolded perfectly. I nodded at Emma toward the end of our choreographed match.

You ready?

She was.

And then we prepared for our big finale, the suplex from the top rope, something that wasn't being done in women's wrestling at all at that time. I climbed up the ropes as the crowd went bananas. The minute we landed, both of us flat on our backs, the crowd fucking lost it.

There's a chant wrestling fans do only when they're super impressed: "This. Is. Awesome! This. Is. Awesome!" Before, I'd only ever heard that chant at men's matches, never for the women.

But now the auditorium filled with it, my ears ringing with the words. They were shouting their heads off, seeing us as wrestlers first—like the men—not as objects or only as women.

We were professional wrestlers doing the best wrestling of our young lives, and the audience felt it, saw it, celebrated it. It was fucking amazing. And before I knew what was happening, I was standing in the middle of the ring, my arm held above my head by the ref, being given the belt I had lusted for: I was the inaugural women's NXT champ! My breath came in gasps. I was still recovering from the surgery, and this match had wiped me out. But I was on top of the world. I wasn't just a professional wrestler for the WWE—I was a *champion*.

GET THE PARTY STARTED

Chapter Ten

Don't put your stuff in there yet," a voice called to me backstage.

I turned to find Vickie Guerrero, who played a manager for the live events on the main roster, mother to Shaul Guerrero from NXT and the widow of wrestling legend Eddie Guerrero. I'd just come out of the larger of two women's locker rooms at this massive arena where I'd be wrestling that evening. Even though Vickie played a bad guy on TV, she's really a total sweetheart. There she was, jumping in to save me some embarrassment. I was happy to take her advice.

There's an etiquette to wrestling that I was still learning. I didn't want to fuck up right off the bat and piss off the other, more senior wrestlers. I wasn't even on the main roster yet.

This was to be my first live event with wrestlers from the main roster, and I was super nervous. After I'd won the first-ever NXT Women's Championship, I kept hearing rumors I would be called up to the main roster. My win was amazing, but now it was back to life as usual. I was still doing NXT live events, still doing their training and promo classes. Not much had changed—and wouldn't change for some time.

The one thing that *was* different was that I had been asked to do some live events on the main show. It wasn't official yet, but I was asked to participate in these non-televised events with some of the bigger WWE wrestlers. It was basically a test run, to see how I'd do on the road, traveling, working with the seasoned wrestlers. I needed to prove myself before I'd be given the chance to be bumped up.

To show respect, I had arrived at the arena super early that day. If you're a trainee, you needed to get there before any of the other wrestlers to demonstrate your commitment and how hard you were going to work. It didn't matter one ounce that I'd just won the NXT inaugural championship; I still had to pay my dues. When I'd arrived, no one else was around except the producers and referees.

Everything about the day made me nervous. That night, I'd be wrestling in front of something like six thousand fans, the biggest live audience of my career. My stomach hurt just thinking about it. I was full of butterflies wandering around backstage. Unlike the televised events when all the wrestlers and crew members were present, only the people involved in this particular live event had come, so there weren't as many people backstage; it was mostly a skeleton crew. But soon the wrestlers started to arrive, like John Cena, the biggest star in the company. *Oh shit. That's him!* I was totally starstruck. Luckily, some of the people I'd trained with in FCW and NXT who had been called up before me were also arriving. Just seeing their familiar faces helped me stay calm.

I was still carrying my gear around backstage when the current female champ, Kaitlyn, swept into the arena. I introduced myself and she was so sweet.

"Why are you carrying that around? Here, come put your stuff down. You can share this room with me," she suggested, going into the smaller of the two locker rooms. Maybe it wouldn't have been a big deal, but I took that as a sign that waiting had been the right move, thanks to Vickie.

I had been told I'd be wrestling that night with AJ Lee, and when she arrived, I went up to her and introduced myself. I was surprised to finally meet her in person and realized with shock that she was way shorter than me, a tiny little thing, actually. In the ring, she plays a nerdy character, sure, but in a really alluring and crazed way. She's like a manic pixie chick you want to be super careful around because she might lose her shit at any minute, as if she's mentally unstable. But the tiny woman before me was nothing like that. She wore glasses, along with an anime T-shirt, jeans, and Chucks, and shouldered a backpack with something cartoon-ish on it. She was geeky and carried around comic books.

"Welcome aboard," she said right off the bat. "Want to get in the ring and figure out what we'll do?"

"Absolutely." I was so excited.

While we figured out our moves, AJ introduced me to Tamina Snuka, who's the Rock's cousin and played AJ's bodyguard. She, too, was super welcoming. Later, when we were filming together in a bar for *Total Divas* this guy tried to spin-kick us in the air. Tamina just went—boom!—and fucking clocked him. If I was ever in a fight for real, I would 100 percent want Tamina in it; she was such a badass.

Those two made me feel like I belonged. Which was such a fucking relief because I'd heard horror stories from the main roster about how the girls all bullied one another. They'd throw your stuff out of the locker room or put it in the shower and turn on the water. I had been expecting just the most intimidating, awful experience. But the only really weird moment had already occurred, when Vickie told me not to leave my shit in the locker room. Other than that, everything was good.

I'd later hear one of the female wrestlers say that the girls' locker room was like a vagina. It cleans itself out once a month. I took that to mean that all the bad women were cleaned out or pushed out in a natural process, and I loved that analogy because it was true. Sure, there was always one person who came in and tried ruffling stuff, but she never lasted very long. Unless, of course, she was making the company a lot of money.

AJ instantly took a shine to me and took me under her wing. We worked on our plan together. The nice thing about wrestling at a live event, rather than for TV, is that you see the person you're going to wrestle that day, and then you start planning what you're going to do in your match. With these live events, everything was a lot easier because you're not in front of a camera. You can be a bit goofier and talk to the crowd more rather than focus all your energy on not messing up your moves on TV. When it came time to wrestle, we moved together seamlessly. Until I fucked up. She got me in a choke hold on the mat, and I accidently headbutted her. She looked at me like I had rung her bell a little bit.

"I'm so sorry!" I tried to tell her as we continued to grapple with each other. I was nervous and not totally on my game. That little blip aside, we got along so well from the outset, maybe because we're both outsiders—she's a geek, and I'm a goth freak.

For whatever reason, we meshed well, in the ring and outside, and later, after I finally made my way to the main roster, we traveled together every single week. It was funny because we portrayed mortal enemies in the ring, and then we'd leave the arena together and she'd hide in the footwell of the passenger seat while I drove so the fans wouldn't see us together—we had to keep the kayfabe going. In reality, we were good buddies. Once, trying to get to our hotel late at night, we nearly got run off the road by a drunk driver. It was crazy the kinds of things we encountered together.

When you're on the main roster, though the organization books your flights for you, it's up to you to book your hotel and to get to the places you'll wrestle once you land, so you have to rent a car. But that was difficult for me because I wasn't yet twenty-five. There was one car company, Avis, I think, that would rent a car to me, but coming from a different country, I often didn't have the kind of credit card they wanted. AJ helped me figure all that stuff out, and we drove thousands of miles together, getting to the venues. I was initially daunted on those outings because I hadn't traveled around America much or been to all these different states, but she helped me figure my way around. In no time, I came to love the travel because it made me feel so fiercely independent.

But at this time, before I was called up to the main roster, I occasionally wrestled with AJ or others from the WWE while I continued doing all my NXT work. I kept hearing rumors that my time might be coming soon, that I'd get the call any day now.

Still, almost a year passed.

It's been called by all kinds of fancy names. The Grandest Stage of Them All. The Showcase of the Immortals. The Super Bowl of Sports Entertainment. As usual, everyone who's anyone connected to wrestling was in New Orleans that April 2014 for WrestleMania. The annual event, in addition to showcasing headline wrestlers via pay-per-view or in-person before an audience of more than seventy-five thousand, was also where many soon-to-be-famous wrestlers made their breakthroughs. Plus, at other WrestleManias, celebrities often made special appearances, some even participating in a match, folks like Muhammad Ali, Mr. T, Mike Tyson, Bad Bunny, and Shaquille O'Neal.

Of course, all us trainees from NXT were brought to New Orleans for the event. I would even get to stay after many of the others headed home to see the filming of *Monday Night RAW* that would follow, broadcast from the same arena.

As WrestleMania unfolded, I wandered around backstage, gawking outright at the many famous wrestlers parading about, athletes I had looked up to for years. I had absolutely no shame about how much I loved and admired them; these people were my fucking heroes. At one point, Dwayne Johnson approached me. I tried to act cool when he asked if his daughter could take a picture with me. His daughter Simone was one of my fans; she'd been following me on Instagram, and I was thrilled to be asked to take a selfie with her. Sure, compared to so many of the wrestlers there, I was small potatoes, but that moment made me feel part of the bigger wrestling world.

From the catering area backstage, I watched the matches on huge monitors. Brock Lesnar defeated the Undertaker to end his undefeated streak. I saw John Cena face off with Bray Wyatt. Even my buddies AJ Lee and Tamina Snuka were part of the action, and AJ triumphed over and over again to keep her title as the Divas Champion. It was so exciting, and I was caught up with the crowd, inspired by the amazing wrestling going on all around me.

Everyone was rushing around backstage. It was a very chaotic atmosphere—but fun to be a part of. The energy was fresh and exciting. And then my phone buzzed. It was a text from a number I didn't recognize.

> Hey, Saraya. It's DJ. I would love to speak to you at some point today if you have time. I'm available. I'll have someone come grab you.

I didn't know who the fuck this was and why they were texting in the middle of WrestleMania. Clearly, they had the right number because they knew my name. I turned to Dean Malenko, an old-school wrestler who'd been big through the eighties, nineties, and early 2000s, and who mentored me.

"Who the fuck is DJ?" I asked. "And why is he texting my phone?"

"That's fucking Dwayne Johnson, you idiot!"

OMG! I was getting a text from the Rock! This couldn't be real, could it? I'd looked up to this man throughout my wrestling career.

I just needed to stay cool, be chill. I texted back, my hands trembling just a tiny bit, trying to keep it together.

> Oh, hey DJ.

(I didn't even know we had a nickname for him!)

> Just free as a bird out here. I'm on your time.

In minutes, one of his assistants was at my side, ready to escort me to see the Rock. I was led down a series of hallways, and then the assistant opened a door, standing back for me to walk in, alone.

The Rock was on the other side of the luxury suite, allocated just for him. A few other people were in there, too, but I didn't know who they were. The minute I walked in, he asked them to step away for a moment and turned to me, giving me his undivided attention.

"Hey, I'm Dwayne," he said, crossing the room and extending a hand, as if I didn't know who in the world he was. Sure, we'd met briefly earlier, but this time felt more intense and focused. I hadn't been nervous before because we'd just sort of passed each other when I took that photo with his daughter. But this was different. WWE wasn't going to let me go while I was at WrestleMania, were they? I didn't think so. Still, I stumbled over my words, saying hello, not sure what was expected of me.

"So, I was just in the UK, filming *Fast and Furious*," he said.

I nodded, mmm-hmmming, trying to figure out where this conversation was going.

"And I came across this documentary: *The Wrestlers: Fighting with My Family*."

Holy shit, he'd seen the 2012 documentary about my family and my efforts to become a professional wrestler. That was wild to me.

"I loved it," he said. "It was the most beautiful story. It reminded me of my own family. You guys are all so close."

His grandmother was one of the first female pro wrestling promoters— she'd taken over Polynesian Pacific Pro Wrestling after her husband's death. A big portion of his family wrestled professionally.

"I just related so much," he said.

"That's so cool," I responded, still unsure of what I was supposed to say but flattered.

"So, if you don't mind, I'm going to make a movie on it," he said.

"What?!" In my head, I thought, *Are you shitting me, dude?* I didn't have words and didn't know how to respond. . . . Was this for real? He didn't look like he was messing with me. Before I could come up with something intelligent or gracious to say, I was crying and had snot bubbles everywhere. He handed me tissues. It was a totally crazy moment and insane thoughts crossed my mind, like *You can't make a movie of my life. I'm not even dead yet.*

Meanwhile, some seventy-five fans were just upstairs, outside this door, down the hall, screaming their heads off, on top of hundreds of wrestlers and crew members running around backstage. Despite that, I couldn't hear a thing over my heart racing. It felt as if we were in a sound-proof bubble together, separate from the rest of the world, and that time had slowed to a crawl.

"It's just going to be a project with my production company, Seven Bucks," he clarified.

That was cool with me. Of course, neither of us knew at the time how big it would become—the script was loved so much that MGM would pick it up, as well as production partners Lionsgate and Film4. Still, I couldn't have been more thrilled. After he gave me a few details, the conversation started to die, and I figured maybe it was time for me to leave. I turned to go when he stopped me.

"I've got something else to tell you," he said, leaning in closer. "And this cannot leave this room."

All I could think was, *What the fuck are you going to tell me next? How do you follow up on making a film about my life?*

"So, I was in the writers' room," he said, his voice low so the others in the room wouldn't overhear. "And they said that you're going to debut on *RAW* tomorrow."

"Tomorrow?" I asked. "*RAW*?"

"And you're going to win the Divas Championship."

"What?!" I just started sobbing even harder. This was all too much to take in, in the space of five minutes. I was only twenty-one and being told I was having a movie made about my life. *And* I was going to be the youngest Divas Champion in history. Since I was from a completely different country, that meant I'd be making history for my country as well.

I felt like a child in that moment and could not stop bawling. Everything felt messed up, but in a good way.

I asked again to be sure I'd heard right. "I'm debuting tomorrow?"

"Yup. Congratulations."

What the fuck just happened?! I felt so extremely fortunate to have someone of Dwayne's caliber telling me this. Eventually, I got the tears under control and thanked him for his time as he once again reminded me not to say anything.

The minute I opened the door, I found Tamina Snuka directly on the other side of it. The roar and clamor of WrestleMania hit me hard in the chest, filling my ears with a blast, nearly stunning me.

She looked at me a little weird. To be fair, it *was* weird for me to be coming out of her very famous cousin's dressing room sobbing.

"I'm just really a big fan of Dwayne's," I blubbered, and ran away.

I found a stairwell to hide out and gather myself. When I felt I could talk without bawling, I dialed my family in the UK and told them about the movie. I didn't mention the debut because he'd sworn me to secrecy, but I thought it was okay to share the film news. They didn't believe me. I kept telling them I wasn't bullshitting them, but I don't think they fully got it.

"Do me a favor," I said before we hung up. "Watch *Monday Night RAW* tomorrow night."

"Why?" they asked.

"Just watch."

That night, when I got back to the hotel, I went down to the bar with Maddox, where everyone was hanging out. In the back of my mind, I resolved to not drink too much because, what if the Rock's words actually did come true the next day? I'd want to be in the best shape. Still, I had my doubts. I'd been told before that I would be debuting soon, and nothing had come of it, so I also didn't want to get my hopes up. I kept my promise to Dwayne and didn't breathe a word to a soul, but I still wondered if it was really going to happen.

The next day, I got to the arena at noon, super early. Sure, the Rock had told me I'd debut and win, but no one else had confirmed it. Had he just been messing with me? I even left my gear in the car in case it was all a mistake.

I wandered around backstage, trying to look occupied, but all I could think about was that maybe this had all been a dream. Perhaps my old NXT life would continue, and maybe I'd never be called up to the main roster. Then again, they loved to keep these things a secret, and they wouldn't have told many others. Maybe I was one of the people it was supposed to be a secret from.

As the backstage area got busier, a number of the girls from the main roster ran past me into the office for the head of talent relations, Mark Carrano, looking really pissed. The day before, no one had been able to take out the female champ, AJ Lee. During WrestleMania, there'd been a battle royale to unseat her. The previous day, every one of the WWE female main-roster wrestlers had entered the ring, one by one, until all were present. The match then unfolded and continued until only one wrestler remained. AJ Lee.

It was about ten minutes to when the doors would open for the general audience, and I still didn't know what was happening. Fit Finlay, an old-school Irish wrestler I adored, approached. He was a friend of my father's, and I had watched him, growing up, when he'd been on *World of Sport*.

"Hey, can I talk to you real quick?" he asked.

"Absolutely." In my head thinking, *Is he about to say what I think he's about to say?*

"So, you're going to debut and you're going to win the Divas Championship," he said.

Oh fuck! It wasn't a dream. I started crying again.

Fit Finlay glared. "Yes, but you've got to keep it together, you can't tell anyone."

But how were we to keep this a secret if he was about to take me out there to talk with the champ, AJ Lee, and her bodyguard, Tamina? Surely, the others would figure out in a split second what was happening.

Many of them had been on the main roster for some time, just waiting for their chance, and here I was, about to step out of my trainee world and onto the main stage to be the champ. Nobody was more surprised than me.

"Congratulations," AJ said when we met in the ring to figure things out. "I'm so glad it's you."

I thanked her.

"So, what do you want to do?" AJ asked.

I shook my head. I hadn't thought that far in advance.

"I think you should beat me with a three-count rather than a submission," she suggested.

"You okay with the Paige-turner?" I asked, referencing one of my finishing moves.

"Absolutely. This is going to be super quick and surprise the shit out of everyone. We'll do our promo and then it'll be a very fast match," she said.

"Okay." I was getting my head wrapped around what I needed to do.

AJ steered me to makeup next. There was also a hierarchy of who was supposed to get their makeup done in what order. This time, though, the girls let me jump the line. Thankfully, it was AJ helping me figure out this new role, a person I trusted. While I was in the makeup chair, she and I worked out our promo. She and the producers wanted me to be a little timid.

"But that's not my character in NXT," I said.

"That's okay, we'll figure it out."

Meanwhile, my voice went all wonky. When I get nervous, that happens sometimes, and now it was almost down to a whisper. Mum always said it was polyps, but I don't know about that. AJ calmed me again, and we went over our promo a few times. We both felt good about our plan.

It was then I remembered I'd left my gear in the car. I rushed out to get it. Previously, word had come down from Vince McMahon that I needed to wear purple and black rather than the all-black I'd always worn. When I got my bag from the car, I had a black-and-purple outfit all ready to go.

As I went to get changed, AJ pulled me aside. "Listen, this is going to be so easy and so good," she said. "We're going to have this awesome storyline, you know?" She got me focused on the job at hand.

Then it was showtime.

AJ's music came on and the crowd went nuts. Even though she always played a bad guy, the people loved her. She did her whole spiel about being the one Diva no one could beat.

As I prepared to make my entrance, I hoped some people in the audience might recognize me and cheer. A lot of people from the UK and Europe, where I'm more well-known, came over every year for WrestleMania. I didn't want it to be totally one-sided, but I wasn't sure if anyone would even give a shit I was there. But I certainly didn't expect what happened next.

My theme music came on and the crowd went fucking ballistic. I walked down the ramp to the ring thinking in my head, *Holy shit, holy shit.* Tens of thousands of fans were on their feet screaming. Their voices seemed to bounce off my sternum with every step I took. I couldn't believe I was here.

I got in the ring and it was fucking amazing. AJ and I didn't even have to say anything to each other. The crowd just started chanting. "This. Is. Awesome. This. Is. Awesome."

Did they know the champ was about to be unseated? Something was clearly in the air.

AJ and I came face-to-face for the first time in front of the camera and I looked at her, like, *Holy shit, what's happening?!* And she gave me this look: *It's all good. Go with it.*

We started our crowd work with a premise: that I had come to simply congratulate AJ on her fabulous battle royale win the day before. She played her role as an absolute shit, telling me to go "running back to NXT because the champ doesn't like being interrupted." It was all part of the storyline we'd been given, and in that moment, I was so grateful to Dusty Rhodes and his promo classes because I wasn't freezing up on the mic and could pull off the character.

Then AJ put down her challenge: "Since you're here, maybe I should do to you what I did to every single Diva last night. Why don't I beat *you*?"

"But I'm not ready," I replied, trying to play nervous and shy. With that, she slapped me.

In no time, the crowd started chanting, "Paige! Paige! Paige!"

"I think we should have a match right now, and for a special post-WrestleMania treat, I will put my title on the line," AJ shouted to the crowd. The space was electric, and now they were all chanting to me, "You fucked up. You fucked up."

"This is *my* house," AJ screamed, then she barked at the ref: "Ring the bell!"

We literally did only five moves, nothing too crazy. Then AJ hit the ropes and went to give me her Black Widow Submission, which the crowd recognized and they amped up the screaming until I could hear nothing else—not my own heartbeat, not AJ's breath, just the loudness of the fans hollering their throats raw. I waved my hand around, indicating I wasn't going to tap. And the crowd clamor, which I thought was as loud as humanly possible, ratcheted up yet another level.

Then, as planned, I swung all the way around and hit my finisher out of nowhere. But my Paige-turner didn't go quite as well as I wanted; the timing was a bit fucked-up, so it looked like I just swept her off her feet. But still, we accomplished what was needed.

The ref's voice on the mic penetrated the uproar. "One, two, three!"

I jumped up and realized I'd won.

Before I'd gone into the ring, one of the trainers, Sara Del Rey, had told me to act happy when I won, and I'd wondered, *Why would I need to act? I'm going to be very happy.* But now I was not only overjoyed, but acting extra happy to make sure I did it right. In fact, I was so genuinely over the moon that I rolled out of the ring, completely forgetting to grab the championship! The ref, Jason, had to roll out after me to hand it to me.

"Congratulations," he said.

I ran up the ramp, lifting the championship, absolutely freaking out. Meanwhile, AJ was losing her shit in the ring, playing her character, and Tamina was jumping around like she was going to attack me. All the while, the crowd was losing its fucking mind. What had happened was just too huge.

I held the championship belt over my head and screamed and cried on the ramp, panting and gathering my breath. The crowd was still shouting their heads off and my stage name echoed in my ears.

"Paige! Paige! Paige!"

Over and over until my head was ringing and I could hear nothing else.

Holy shit! This felt like the biggest moment of my life.

The minute I got backstage, cameras were instantly in my face and everyone was congratulating me. The few girls on the main roster I'd started to develop friendships with came up and hugged me: Rosa, Summer Rae, Alicia Fox, Lana.

Then came AJ. "You killed it," she said, hugging me. "I'm so proud of you!" This was historic. At the time, she was the longest-reigning Divas Champion in WWE history. No one, until now, had been able to dethrone her. She was so gracious with me.

Eventually, I started to come back to the real world. I walked through the backstage viewing area, where all the other wrestlers had been watching. I passed Randy Orton, one of the biggest names at WWE.

"So you beat her with a leg sweep?" he asked, mostly teasing, having noticed my fucked-up finisher.

"I know! I know! I'm so stupid. It wasn't the perfect move."

"No worries," he said. "Congratulations!" His voice carried his genuine well-wishes.

The cameras were still following me around, and now orders came flying at me.

"Okay, we need you to go take pictures right now with the championship."

"Next, you have to do some media really quick."

"We need you to do this and that. Welcome to being the champion."

It was awesome, but I also wanted two seconds of peace to let it all really sink in. I was having trouble processing what had happened. No matter, I was the Divas Champion and on cloud nine, certain no one and nothing could ever bring me down.

It wouldn't take long for me to realize just how wrong I was.

ALL I WANTED

"Congratulations," Maddox said as he side-hugged me backstage. None of the other wrestlers knew we were still hanging with each other except a select few, and it was definitely for the best.

I could feel his energy was off. It felt like he wasn't entirely happy for me, and we felt very disconnected from each other. Maybe I was over-thinking it? But at the same time, I honestly didn't really care.

I was too caught up in this huge moment for me, so I let it go. I gathered my things and made my way to the car.

I can't believe my dreams have just come true. Less than twenty-four hours after *the Rock* of all people—an icon, a legend—had told me my fate. I couldn't believe how my life had just changed over the course of one day. Everyone was celebrating me. After years of work, after having left my family and all I loved behind in the UK and being sick with missing them, I'd done what I'd come to do. I was being recognized in the US with the WWE. On this one special night, I was feeling every good feel there is.

I bloody did it.

As I drove back to my hotel, my phone had been blowing up ever since the win with countless people who loved me, and genuinely cared, sharing my joy and sending me texts. I wanted to write back to every single one, to thank them for their kindness; my thumbs flew across the screen, picking out emojis and pasting in tons of hearts.

"OMG, this is what they're saying on Twitter!" I read aloud to Maddox some of the kind words people had posted. "And my Instagram has gone bananas. People are so excited for me!"

I kept scrolling and scrolling. Blown away by the reaction.

It was the first time since the match I'd had a moment to soak up what had happened. So many people were rooting for me, were happy for me. I was touched deeply by their love. My parents and family were crazy happy, and all my friends from NXT. It was *my* night.

When we got to my hotel room, I rushed to change. There were plans for a few of us to meet up in the bar, and I was ready for the party to begin.

Maddox made zero effort to get ready to go out. He wanted to stay in, which was fine. By this time in our . . . I mean, again, I wouldn't say it was a *relationship* but . . . I had been getting fed up. I just felt like his energy was always off and that he wasn't genuinely happy for me and especially at this moment. For whatever reason that may be.

I had made a comment asking what his problem was, and it had turned into an argument. He was going off, saying the most hateful shit out of anger.

After the argument I just told him this had to end. It wasn't healthy for either of us to continue if it wasn't fun anymore. And it wasn't. It wasn't even close to fun anymore. So we parted ways and continued to work together but never uttered another word to each other.

Which was for the best.

The bottom line, though, was that on the biggest night of my life, a person I thought was in my corner . . . was not.

It was a lesson I wish I could say I learned on the first try, but in typical younger Saraya fashion, it wasn't.

I stayed in that night and just laid in bed, watching *Friends*, my comfort show, and took some time for myself.

I deserved that.

From that night on, my whole life changed. People may not fully understand this, knowing that who wins and who loses in these matches is essentially scripted, but the reality is, the fact they chose me to become the new champ said a lot about what they thought I could do. It meant the decision-makers at WWE trusted me to be the face of that division, and of the company. They had faith I could put butts in seats, and do media interviews, and sell merchandise. When you think of the WWE brand, one of the first things that comes to mind is the person who's the champ at the time. So the fact they chose me, especially since I didn't fit the mold—the blond, sexy girl—was huge.

I knew at least part of the reason was because of a shirt WWE had made for me while I was in NXT. Triple H came up to me, holding out a black T-shirt emblazoned with "Think Again" in pink and purple lettering on the front.

I just looked at him, confused. "'Think again'?" I asked.

"Yeah!" He was clearly excited.

"Is that mine?" I asked. I was not following.

"We designed it for you. What do you think?"

"I don't know what the fuck it means," I said.

"Think again!" he said, as if it should be obvious. "If you think you know what a Diva is, think again."

Ahhh. I got it then, and loved it. Yes! *Think again*, baby!

I was worried I might have to explain it to a bunch of people, but as it turned out, I didn't.

The shirt sold out in record time, which was amazing. When you're a kid following the WWE, you're buying all the T-shirts and action figures you can, asking for them for Christmas or your birthday, and now here was a WWE T-shirt in the world, representing me! And it was selling like crazy. It proved something.

Still, I was up against stiff competition on the main roster now. AJ Lee had been an amazing source of merchandise sales. Her T-shirt— "Love Bites"—had sold incredibly well. I had big shoes to fill.

Meanwhile, I had to adjust to life on the main roster, and that also meant relinquishing my NXT championship. At first, I held both NXT and Divas championships simultaneously, but to be fair to the others, I needed to let go of the NXT one. Still, no one ever took that title from me. I held it for 273 days.

Soon my life revolved around doing WWE events, and often AJ and I were on the road together. By now, the writers had really developed our storyline. We had this frenemies thing going on, where we kind of hated each other but also were kind of obsessed with each other.

She had always bellowed from the stage, "This is my house," but once I took the championship from her, I stole her line, too. "This is *my* house now!"

They gave us papers each day with a script on it, and thank goodness for Dusty, who'd long ago told me I'd have to stay flexible and be ready for change because day after day, the stuff they'd write for us would change on a dime, sometimes minutes before we got in the ring and I would have to remember we needed to pull it off.

One time, Vince came up with our promo. He wanted me to read a love letter to AJ; it may have been a Valentine's card. The words inside the card were a kind of poem.

> Roses are red, wood chips are beige
> I'm sorry I pushed you off this stage.
> It's not that I hate you. I like you a bunch.
> But you just have to face that I want to punch.
> I'll see you this Sunday, but this part is vital.

I'll be skipping my way out of SummerSlam
With my Divas title.
Love ya!

Immediately, I knew I needed to memorize the verse. Just in case for some reason I didn't have the card with me when the time came. That was what Dusty had taught me: always be prepared and know that *everything* is going to change. This was at a time after AJ had reclaimed the Divas title, but I was hoping it would be coming back my way soon.

And sure enough, just as I was about to go out into the ring, Vince was at my side.

"Wait, Paige," he called to me before I could make my entrance.

"Yeah?"

"Give me the card. You don't need it out there."

"What?" My heart skipped a few beats but I played it cool. "Okay, Vince, here you go."

I was scared and intimidated, and I made my way to the top of the ramp. But even without the card, I fucking remembered the verse. I had it down.

You never knew what Vince or the others were thinking or what they'd do to up the excitement level. Often, I had no idea what was going on and I'd be thrust into the ring to figure it out. But because of all the stuff Dusty had taught me, I had gotten good, rolling with whatever was happening. He'd helped train my brain to spontaneously react, and there I was, able to manage the storytelling between matches and making it all work.

We had so much fun working with each other, AJ and I, and the crowd could feel it.

One time, she brought me out a box of chocolates, and I ate one and then spat the chocolate at her in the ring. We were having a blast.

Every week, we traveled with each other, leaving the venue together with her ducked in the front seat, covering her up with a jacket. And

I'd yell at the fans, "AJ sucks!" and she'd be laughing hysterically next to me. We were traveling so much, I could never keep straight what city we were in. And now I had to keep all these storylines clear in my head as well.

There were weird fans, too, something I hadn't expected. Sometimes fans would follow us home. It was scary at times. There was a Facebook group that tracked where we were at all times.

One time, I was with another female wrestler, Alicia Fox (Foxy), and we were in some tiny little town in the middle of fucking no-where, like a dusty old town with just one hotel and a huge parking lot. There was a dive bar down the street, so we went to have a drink before bed, needing to relax a bit after our long drive. When we got back to the hotel, a cop car was parked in the lot, its red and blue lights spinning.

"Can you come over here for a second?" the lady who worked at the front desk asked me when we came in.

I walked over to her.

"Are you a wrestler?"

"Yeah."

"Do you or your friend"—she nodded toward Foxy, who was waiting for me—"wrestle under the name Paige?"

"Yeah. I do."

"There's some guy who's been running around the hotel, knocking on all the doors, trying to break some of them down, screaming, 'I need to find Paige!'"

He must have followed our car all the way from our previous match to this hotel in the middle of fucking nowhere.

"So," the woman asked, clearly not sure of what the protocol should be. "Do you want to leave?"

And stupid me, I was like, "No, I'll just switch rooms. It's no big deal." So Foxy and I ended up staying there. By then the guy was gone, taken to jail, and I was half-drunk anyhow.

Another time, a guy kept sending stuff backstage. Apparently, he'd taken a big liking to me. Almost as soon as I got up onto the main roster, he sent a big wooden chest backstage to me, like a massive treasure chest. It was insane.

Inside the chest were a bunch of clothes for me and a notebook. My name—my real name—was everywhere in the book, and he'd written in a red ink that looked like blood. It actually *could* have been blood; I'm not sure anyone tested it. His writing was a series of storylines for me and him, things he'd like to see happen, all very sexy and relationship-based. And fucking disturbing.

The security guard we nicknamed "Sassy," because she'd fucking seen it all, told me she'd read through it and that I shouldn't bother. "It gets really crazy. You don't need those thoughts in your head." On the back of the notebook, the fan had taped six thousand euro. Was it supposed to be a bribe? It kind of freaked me out.

The fact I didn't respond to him didn't stop him. He continued to send me stuff all the time and travel hours and hours to see me wrestle. I just wanted him to go away, but he didn't.

Another time, we were in Vegas, I believe at the MGM Grand. Outside our locker room, there's always a guard the arena hires to make sure no one goes in or out. I went about my day, and I kept noticing this totally normal-looking guy sitting just outside the door. I was doing my thing, and he was always there. Back inside the locker room, I happened to look at Twitter. And I saw this string of tweets from some guy, tagging me and basically live-tweeting my every move along with his commentary. *I like the way you smell.* And *You look really good today.* The tweets got creepier and creepier.

What the fuck was going on? My heart sped up, and my hands started to sweat. I looked at his profile picture. It was the fucking guy sitting outside the locker room door.

Oh my God! I was totally flipped out. This guy could kidnap me or whatever. Fuck.

I texted our producer at the time, Dean Malenko.

> This fucking guy is right outside my locker room. He's tweeting me all these creepy things, like really creepy things.

The police came and took him away. And I had to be escorted to my car after the match. These were issues I never dreamed about when I was dying to make it to the main roster. Back then, I had no way to know that, when you make it big in the wrestling world, you'll have a bunch of incredible fans, but you'll also be dealing with an influx of fucking crazies.

A little before my twenty-second birthday, August 2014, I was told I'd be wrestling AJ at SummerSlam, a pay-per-view and livestreaming event, dubbed *The Biggest Party of the Summer.* It's WWE's second-biggest event of the year behind WrestleMania. This would be a match to see if I could win the Divas Championship back from AJ, who currently held the title.

But in the days leading up to SummerSlam, AJ was thinking about pulling out of the event altogether. "It's my neck, it's bothering me," she told me. "I don't know if I can do it."

"If you don't want to do it, it's fine," I said. "If you do, I'll protect you. You don't have to take a single bump, we can make a match where you never hit the mat or mess with your neck at all. It's your call."

She decided to do go ahead with the match. We worked out our moves to ensure she'd be able to wrestle without ever bumping her head, hitting the mat, or tweaking her neck in any way. For me, it was a total win, both emotionally and literally. In that match, which happened on my twenty-second birthday, I was named the Divas Champ for the second time, yelling at her the line she'd gifted me: "This is *my* house."

Shortly after that, AJ took time off to heal her neck injury, but the writing was already on the wall. Neck injuries are pretty common in wrestling and can be career busters, as I'd later come to fully appreciate.

AJ came back for a few more matches, and by the following spring, a year after I'd beaten her to be bumped to the main roster, we allied again together to triumph over my girls, the Bella Twins, at WrestleMania 31. The next night, at *RAW*, AJ wrestled in a six-woman tag team in what would be her final match.

Before she retired, though, she ruffled some feathers and taught me a bit about what it looks like when women stand up for themselves and their sisters. She vocally criticized WWE's treatment of female wrestlers, pointing out the discrepancy of wages and screen time compared to male wrestlers, even when the women generated record-breaking merchandise sales and their broadcast segments were top rated. I was just starting to see these facts in my own life and cheered for her.

Still, life wasn't the same after that. She'd been my mentor, my best wrestling friend, my co-conspirator, my sister in crime. Without her, I was utterly lost. I still flew across the country on a regular basis, still drove with another wrestler or by myself to venues in every possible city and town. The pace of the life was wearing me down. We got little rest and were always on the go. Sometimes it was a struggle to stay awake on long drives, and I scared myself a few times starting to nod off behind the wheel. I was exhausted, sleep-deprived, and lonely. I should have known it was bad when, just before a major match, I fell completely asleep in the makeup chair. The makeup artist had a hard time rousing me. I was spiraling down, completely overworked, and I didn't have a fucking clue. Everything moved so fast, I never had the time or energy to really think about it.

Baby Raya.

My godfather, Mickey, and his wife, Sylvie.

My parents' wedding, surrounded by all their troublemaking friends.

I was always obsessed with any animal I could get my hands on.

Daddy's girl.

From left to right: My uncle Jimmy, my mum, and my Daddio in their wrestling gear.

Zak and I were a year apart, but practically twins and inseparable.

◁◁◁◁◁◁◁◁◁◁◁◁◁◁◁◁◁◁◁

Clockwise from top left: Me, Zak, Asa, and my dad and mum in front of my parents' old pub, the Wrestler's Arms.

Me as a bridesmaid (right) with my niece Terri (left) at my sister Nikki's wedding.

My brother Isak.

Me and my older brother
Roy and his infamous mullet.

Another training day at my
parents' wrestling school.

Our family friend Klondyke Kate.

My mum, my sister Nikki, and me in our wrestling gear.

I was a menace with a hair straightener as a teen.

My first-ever wrestling promo picture.

Me and Zak
dressed up for
our WWE tryouts.

My mum and me as a tag
team for Shimmer.

One page of the mood boards
I made, dreaming of the future.

Myself (far left) and the girls at FCW (left to right): Christina Crawford, Summer Rae, Audrey Marie, and Ivelisse, with a member of the WWE production team.

My first dog I had as an adult, Sooki, keeping me company after moving to the U.S.

Me (bottom right) with the girls from my parents' wrestling company. Fun fact: I had my WWE tryout with the girl in the bright teal sweater.

Me and my favorite FCW coach, Norman Smiley.

AJ and me showing off our belts before I moved up to the main roster.

←

At twenty-one, I became the only woman to hold the Divas and NXT Women's Championships simultaneously.

Me and Mum after I won my match at WrestleMania.

Me and AJ before my first WrestleMania.

Filming in Lake Tahoe with the *Total Divas* crew.

Myself, Bayley, and Becky
backstage at WWE.

Myself and
Goldust, one
of my biggest
supporters
since day one.

Messing around
with Big Show
backstage at WWE.

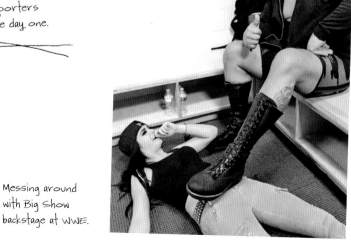

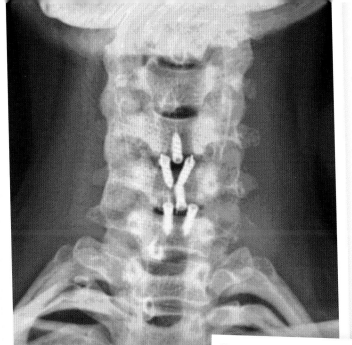

The screws that were surgically placed in my neck after my injury.

Me, stick-thin during the worst stage of my drug and alcohol addiction.

Myself and Stephen Merchant at Sundance for the *Fighting with My Family* premiere.

Myself, Joey, and Raquel during the early years of our friendship in Orlando.

Myself and Florence Pugh meeting for the first time to film promotional material for *Fighting with My Family*.

The day I adopted Lobster.

Accidentally got
shit on my hands.

With Ronnie at the county
fair for my birthday.

Me and the
surprise birthday
confetti from
Ronnie before we
were dating.

In disguise before my first
appearance at AEW in 2022.

Me and Renee on the day
of my debut at AEW.

Out for lunch with one
of my dogs, Ozzy.

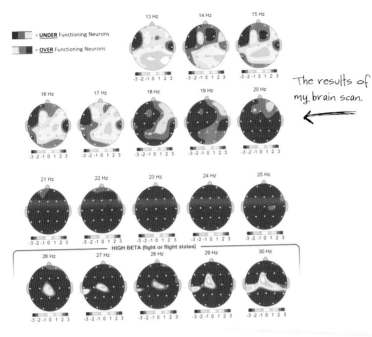

The results of my brain scan.

My sweet boy Sunny.

My older brother Asa and me.

Me with the whole family during a recent visit to Norwich.

Raquel, Roy, myself, Taylor, Lizzy, Zac, and Camilo visiting the Norwich Cathedral in 2023.

On the steps of Wembley Stadium the day before winning the AEW Women's Championship there.

YOUTH GONE WILD

I was summoned by Kevin Dunn, Vince McMahon's right-hand man. I had no idea what he might want from me, but I hoped it was something good. I knocked on his door backstage at *RAW* and when I entered, Mark Carrano, the head of talent relations, was also there.

"Paige, it's so good to see you." They both welcomed me and asked me to take a seat, offering me a drink, making small talk. Soon, though, they got down to business.

"You're familiar with *Total Divas*?"

Of course I knew about the reality TV show. *Total Divas* had been airing on E! for about a year at that time. It was designed to give viewers an inside look into the lives of WWE female wrestlers, covering not only their work with WWE but very intimate details of their personal lives. The cameras followed the girls everywhere. When I was getting ready to win against AJ Lee at *Raw* the night of my debut, the cameras had followed the girls into Mark's office as they complained about me and tried to get the producers to reconsider allowing me to win. Inside the ring and outside the venue, no part of a girl's life was off-limits for the videographers.

"We were wondering if you wanted to be part of the cast?"

Maybe given all the attention I was getting, I should have expected this to come along, but really, it hadn't crossed my mind, and now that they were raising the possibility, I wasn't sure it was a great idea. I was exhausted all the time just with wrestling and trekking about the country. My typical week included five days of traveling. I'd often have to take a flight or two to get to a town where a show was scheduled, then have to drive three or four hours to the next town, where another one was on the docket, my workdays extending until at least ten each night. I repeated this pattern for five days until I took a flight or two home. I was tired all the time.

How would I fit filming *Total Divas* into this life? From day one, my first priority was and always had been my wrestling career; that's what really mattered to me.

"Would it affect any of my storylines?" I asked. At that time, before AJ Lee retired, I had a fabulous storyline going with her, but she wasn't part of *Total Divas*. I was hesitant to do anything that might endanger my real focus.

They assured me it wouldn't. I thought of AJ, who never participated in *Total Divas*, and kept herself apart from all the drama. Famously, a year prior, in 2013, she'd slammed those who participated as "a bunch of cheap, interchangeable, expendable, useless women who have turned to reality television because they just weren't gifted enough to be actresses, and they weren't talented enough to be champions."

Damn!

Had that rant been scripted for her? Probably, as a way to elevate the drama and hype the show. But maybe some of her distance from that turmoil was due to her own wisdom guiding her. Looking back, I wished I'd had some of her smarts because the allure of more fame, more money, and more exposure was a siren song calling to me.

Plus, it was a good look in front my bosses. So I did what they asked and joined the cast. At age twenty-two, from the get-go, I was a bit of a prankster, which was obvious in the recap of my first episode:

[T]he midseason premiere . . . introduces one half of the cast's new dynamic duo, the troublemaking British Diva Paige. Already a divisive presence in the Divas locker room thanks to her hyper-speed rise to the Divas Championship, Paige goes about causing a ruckus almost instantly by playing a prank on Natalya. It goes so fantastically awry that it leads Natalya to fake a car accident to avoid its repercussions. The fallout is so instantaneous and absolute that even the ultimate peace offering—a gift for Natalya's cats—can't smooth things over, and by the end of the episode, Natalya has found herself a brand-new enemy to carry her through the remainder of the season.

I was that enemy and now had a camera crew following me around. When I went to the gym to work out, when I got ready for matches, when I was back in my apartment, as well as tons of filming when I was with the other girls.

For better or for worse, I soon became very good at creating full-blooded, real-life spectacles.

Part of the problem was that the producers supplied us with massive amounts of alcohol. Before this time, I'd mostly been traveling with AJ, and since she didn't drink or do drugs, I was insulated a little from the partying side of wrestling, which was always a big part of the lifestyle. Once I signed on with *Total Divas*, though, the floodgates opened. I was traveling and working with Foxy, and she and I drank and partied similarly: a lot. And all the time.

Given my family history with alcoholism and drug addiction, should I have been a little hesitant to jump with both feet into this lifestyle? Absolutely. But when you're young and on top of the world, you feel invincible. Nothing could fucking touch me.

The producers kept alcohol around all the time while filming, a way to loosen us up. I was a Jack-and-Coke girl, but soon the crew started to refer to my cocktail of choice by what it really was . . . a "Jack and Jack."

I was half-drunk most days, and particularly whenever we filmed. Which, to be honest, I think the producers loved. The more I drank, the more outrageous my behavior became and the more the fans ate it up. Isn't that the whole reason people love messy reality TV? And I was a sucker for giving fans what they wanted.

If you watch a reality TV show like, say, *The Real Housewives of Orange County*, you'll see a lot of the cast are all together in one place where there's a lot of alcohol flowing. It's a winning combination because the alcohol gets you comfortable. I am not afraid of confrontation, which worked really well because I'm the kind of person who will never talk shit behind a person's back. I will say it to your face, especially if I've been drinking. I'll approach whoever and say "Fuck you!" before I've had a chance to think about my actions. And the producers knew that. They were constantly egging me on. It was their job; I get it. I just wish I'd been more mature at the time.

Meanwhile, with AJ Lee retired, Foxy and I were traveling together a lot, and our partying was getting in the way. One time, we were in Louisiana and had to be in the Florida Keys the next day to shoot *Total Divas*. We had been out the entire night in New Orleans, drinking our heads off. Is it any surprise we didn't get to the airport in time for our flight?

"Fuck. Now what do we do?" We looked at each other, dumbfounded.

We called in to the show to tell them what happened and that we'd be late, as we tried to get a flight that would take us at least part of the way there; there were no other flights to the Keys that day. We'd have to drive the final stretch. It was a wrestling version of *Planes, Trains and Automobiles*, only with us completely hungover and feeling like shit.

Did the producers at *Total Divas* yell at us? Did they punish us or in some way try to impress upon us that this behavior was unacceptable? No. They sent a camera crew to be with us in our rental car as we made the final leg of the journey, loving that we'd added this new twist to the plot.

That wasn't the only flight Foxy and I missed. We weren't the best influences on each other. We did it again and again because, on some level, it seemed like the producers loved our fuckups. And I was only too happy to oblige, making a fool of myself on camera.

I can't blame Foxy, though. In any heated moment, I follow my old family motto of "Don't start it, but if it gets started, be sure to finish it."

One time, Joey, my friend from Orlando, and I were sitting in a bar, having a good time, when this girl next to me flipped her hair right in my face.

"What the fuck?" I said.

"I'm so sorry," her boyfriend immediately apologized. "She didn't mean to do that."

But the girlfriend was not having it. "Don't fucking apologize for me!" she slurred, clearly about as wasted as I was. "I did nothing wrong."

"Oh really," I said, reaching for my beer and taking a big drink from it, my face as calm and relaxed as if nothing was going on. The minute the girl seemed to think our little interaction was over, I spat out all the beer in her face.

She completely freaked out, and her boyfriend grabbed her and pulled her away. Joey picked me up and spun me around, sending me out of the bar. It was a mess, and I was a total menace. I'm fortunate I didn't go to jail back then or that a lot of my misbehavior didn't end up on TMZ because, at heart, I was a fucking troublemaker. To be fair, I wasn't looking for the trouble. At least not in the beginning. Still, if trouble found me, I was all ready to jump into the ring and wrestle with it.

And sometimes, TMZ *did* cover my shenanigans. One time, Foxy and I were at a bar (notice a theme here?), singing karaoke, which I enjoy doing especially when I'm fucking drunk. I love nothing more than to sing my brains out for a bunch of wasted people, all harmonizing off-key. But then a girl nearby, who'd been loud all evening and super fucking annoying, spilled an entire drink on Foxy's head.

"Oh my God!" Foxy said. "What the fuck?!"

The girl took offense at Foxy's accusation and, within seconds, started a fight—which was a total mistake on her part. Sure, Foxy's not a big, imposing woman, but she's the strongest person I know. She may not look intimidating, but you better watch the fuck out if you annoy her. In no time, the entire bar joined the fight, everyone raging. And while the spilled drink had nothing to do with me, I'm loyal to a fault and had to support my Foxy. So I was in there, swinging punches with the best of them. Soon, the cops were called.

Before they arrived, Foxy and I smartened up enough to run out the back door and just keep running. We laughed our heads off, thinking we'd gotten away with it. But in all the chaos, we forgot that earlier that evening we'd taken a picture with one of the waiters who was a big fan of *Total Divas*. He quickly sold that photo and his story of the bar fight to TMZ.

We, of course, had no idea. Until we showed up at work the next day and the office wanted to see us.

"What the fuck?!" They showed us the TMZ story.

"You can't do these things!" Mark Carrano gave us a mild talking-to. "You're in a different caliber in life right now. When it comes to your job, everything you do is under a microscope. You're going to end up ruining your career if you keep this up."

We nodded and tried to look apologetic.

"I'm not saying you can't drink," he continued. "You just have to not get involved in this kind of stuff. You have to learn how to walk away."

We left that meeting, and I didn't know how to process the information he'd given us. Growing up, I'd learned to never walk away. That wasn't how I was raised.

I tried to take Mark's words to heart, but I was getting mixed messages. The producers for *Total Divas*, on the other hand, loved the fact we'd been in the bar fight and had been featured on TMZ. They decided to capitalize on it and include the fight in the next episode.

On one side, I knew I should learn to keep my cool. But on the other, I was rewarded for being obnoxious, for getting mixed up in shit.

Foxy and I were out at a bar one night when a pervy guy approached, wanting to chat with me. Foxy knew how much I hated when this happened. He was super persistent and wouldn't leave me alone while I just wanted to chat and laugh with my girlfriend and have a good time. So when this guy kept at it, she grabbed him by the collar, yanking him back like a scene out of a superhero movie. He just went flying past me.

"Oh my God, Foxy!" I shrieked.

She just shrugged.

Luckily for us, the guy didn't get too crazy mad, because he definitely could have.

It's so fucking crazy to watch reruns of *Total Divas* now. Half of me is embarrassed; the other half feels weirdly sympathetic and sad to see myself that way. I'm just not that person at all anymore.

During this time, the movie of my life being made by the Rock was moving forward. At SummerSlam, I'd gotten to meet Stephen Merchant, the film's writer and director. He'd interviewed me a bunch, asking for all kinds of details from my life and questions about how I felt or what did I smell, think, or see during certain moments. I thought the movie should have been done by then, but I had no idea how long these things take. Apparently, it was all moving ahead on schedule and he was doing his work. He'd even flown to England to have a look around my hometown, and gone to NXT to watch the training there. He was immersing himself in my world so that he could portray it accurately on the big screen.

While all that time I was busy on the small screen making an arse of myself.

Just as I was losing control of my drinking and drug use, my career was fucking taking off. Before, I might occasionally be recognized on the street for my wrestling. But now, thanks to *Total Divas*, I was noticed regularly, everywhere I went. Even people who didn't care much for wrestling had become hooked on the reality TV show and knew me from it. Apparently, *Total Divas* had incredible ratings—sometimes even better than *Monday Night RAW*, which meant that millions of people, mostly women, were watching it.

If I went out for drinks or dinner with friends, inevitably, I'd be asked for my autograph. Earlier, I'd made a vow to myself. As a youngster, I'd once asked Baby Spice, Emma Bunton, for an autograph and she'd turned me away, breaking my fucking heart. I promised I'd never do that to a fan, even if I had to sign shit all night long. (Later, Emma Bunton apologized to me for that incident, and I accepted her apology.)

Total Divas was influencing every aspect of my life—even my romantic relationships. Kevin was from a band I had grown up listening to, a Day to Remember. We met through social media and then dated for a little while. He was a total sweetheart. Too much of a sweetheart, actually.

Soon, the producers for *Total Divas* wrote him into the current episodes, and though it was fun at first, at a certain point, it morphed into becoming fun at his expense. The producers wanted him to propose to me, which was really kind of cruel. Kevin was older than me and ready to settle down, but the producers knew I wasn't interested in that kind of commitment. Still, they went ahead with the storyline. He proposed on camera, and I accepted, knowing that by the end of the episode, I'd have to tell him I'd changed my mind. It was not cool to do that to him. Years later, I apologized to him, and he accepted my apology; we're good now. But I never should have put someone in that position on a TV show with millions of people watching. I should have protected him better.

And though Kevin and I didn't stay together, he introduced me to a bunch of people from outside of my wrestling circle. Given the trouble I was getting into in the wrestling world, I thought it would be good to have some non-wrestling friends.

I had found a group of girls who were young and just wanted to have some fun, and drugs and alcohol were the thing in downtown Orlando. Going to bars was the only social life I knew. I ended up paying for our nights out, picking up the bar tab, doing whatever was needed to keep my new friends. I was never popular in school, fell out of touch with the early friends I'd made at FCW when we relocated to Orlando, and was separated from my NXT friends when I was bumped up to the main roster. I didn't see AJ as much after she retired. I was not going to go back to being so fucking lonely all the time. For the first time in my life, it felt good to have friends outside of wrestling. After years of being an outcast, tomboy, weirdo, it felt good to have some girlfriends, and I would have done almost anything to keep it that way.

These girls liked to go out and drink, and let me tell you, if someone wanted to go out for a night of fun at that time, they didn't have to ask me twice. By this point, I had been doing *Total Divas* and drinking a lot. Too much. I needed alcohol all the time. I couldn't sleep without it, couldn't be filmed without it, couldn't operate at all without it.

Something had to change. And it did, when these new friends of mine eventually introduced me to cocaine.

We'd go regularly to this bar, Sly Fox, and we'd drink there. Cocaine was always around.

"Let's take a bump so then we can continue drinking," they would say.

That was the idea: Take a bump and sober up a bit, and that shift would allow us to keep on drinking, often staying up all night. Which sounded fucking great to me. But the repercussions quickly became problematic. Doing coke whenever I wasn't away wrestling, I chewed my lips raw; it looked like I had lip liner on at all times. Whenever I looked in the mirror, I was super wide-eyed. Plus, I became paranoid, thinking everyone in the bar knew who I was and was watching me, secretly taking pictures of me. Whenever a fight broke out or a confrontation occurred, I now had even less patience for people. For the first time in my life, I wasn't just finishing shit. Occasionally, I was starting it.

I'd gone from a Jack-and-Coke girl, to a Jack-and-Jack girl, to now a Jack-and-Cocaine girl.

My career was skyrocketing in ways I could never have imagined. But not all of it was good. And now many, many people were watching.

At the time, I told myself I was just being young and a little wild. . . . I'd never really gotten to have a traditional childhood, and now I was living it up like a spoiled kid, trying to make up for that lost time by allowing myself to pursue whatever looked like happiness, like a kid in a candy store.

But life had other ideas in mind.

By this time, I was starting to notice pains in my neck. I stretched it out and tried to shut up the voice in my head that said I was in trouble. Sometimes, it would wake me in the night, like a knife rammed into my cervical spine. Other times, the pain would travel down my left arm, making my fingers tingle. I'd watched AJ go through all kinds of problems with her neck. I'd watched when my friend Nikki Bella went in to have neck surgery. Was I next?

My wrestling career, the one thing I had sacrificed everything for over and again, was now on the ropes in just about every way, but I was too wasted most of the time to notice.

Though *Total Divas* is called a "reality" show, it wasn't depicting fully the reality that was unfolding all around me. Things had started to get all fucked-up. My image, my career, my very life was a mess. My drinking and drug use were out of control. I was losing my voice constantly, losing weight quickly. The tabloids of wrestling news, otherwise known as the "dirt sheets," published my every embarrassing moment like it was breaking news. I was quickly on my way to becoming the Amy Winehouse of the wrestling world.

POPULAR MONSTER

Chapter Thirteen

Besides, I had other things to worry about.

"Something's wrong with my neck," I finally told the trainer at WWE. The pain had been getting worse over the past few months.

He looked me over, felt the bones, measured my range of motion, and ordered an X-ray.

"Everything's looking okay," he told me after he'd reviewed the film.

I wanted to believe that, but it didn't feel okay. I couldn't sleep at night. I had to hold my arm a certain way, propped on a pillow to even drift off for a little bit. I was in pain all the fucking time.

"Can we do an MRI, just to be sure?"

"I'll order one. We can try some physical therapy in the meantime."

I did their PT but wasn't improving, and I was frustrated. Maybe the doctors don't believe me? I'd had a similar experience with ovarian cysts and the agony they eventually caused—not being believed, doctors thinking I was making shit up or overexaggerating. If anything, my way of dealing with pain went in the opposite direction. I might deny the shit out of feeling pain, but I'd never, ever overhype it.

Part of the problem had been my dad's method for dealing with injuries. "Can you wiggle your toes?" he'd asked after I'd been hit by a car as a kid. "You're fine."

I sucked the pain up and wrestled that night because that's what you do. Part of being a wrestler is steeling yourself to put up with pain, to learn to drown it out, to toughen and numb yourself to your body's cues. And I had been sucking it up ever since I was a kid.

But there's only so much gritting one's teeth a person can do when they're in fucking agony all the time. Later, I'd read how several studies say there's a gender bias in medicine. This often leads to doctors and health professionals denying women pain relief for a range of health conditions.

To be fair, though, I also think the doctors worried I might be seeking drugs for non-health-related reasons. My crazy lifestyle had raised a lot of eyebrows, and now, maybe they thought I was making up an injury to get opioids to get high.

I was at an IHOP the next week when I lifted a plastic tumbler of Coke to my lips. "Shit!" It slipped from my grasp, slamming the tabletop and spilling all over the table full of pancakes. The waitress rushed over to help contain the mess.

What the fuck was that about?

My arm was too weak. I couldn't hold the glass. I knew immediately it was my neck.

I took it as a sign. If one of my arms had gotten that feeble, it was only a matter of time before I would be seriously hurt in the ring or do real damage to another wrestler because I couldn't count on my own body. Part of my job was to make sure my opponent didn't get hurt. Now I couldn't be sure an injury wasn't just around the corner.

I went back to the trainers. "Really, something is wrong. I want to see a doctor and have them review my MRI."

The WWE gave me a choice between two doctors: Dr. Maroon or Dr. Uribe, who'd done the necks of wrestlers I admired: John Cena, Nikki

Bella, and TJ Wilson. I asked for Dr. Uribe. I wanted the real story and someone who would take my pain seriously. At that time, his office was in Tampa, so I made the hour-and-a-half drive to see him.

"Oh no, baby." He shook his head looking at my MRI on the screen before us, almost chuckling at the ridiculousness of my situation, his Cuban accent inflecting his words. "No, baby, no, no."

"What?"

"You can't wrestle like this. You need surgery, and you need it now. If not, you're going to have long-term damage. If you don't take care of it now, you'll probably never wrestle again."

Dr. Uribe was a total sweetheart, and since he'd done such a great job with the other wrestlers I knew, I believed him. Immediately, I was scheduled for surgery and removed from the WWE rotation, since it was no longer safe for me to be in the ring. I didn't know how long I'd be gone, or even if I'd ever wrestle again, but I took a break from my active wrestling career with the full support of the WWE. They had my back.

While Dr. Uribe was hopeful I'd make a full recovery, he couldn't promise anything. Recuperation, I was told, could take a while—up to a year and a half. I was super bummed to be away from wrestling, but if that was what was needed to ensure I'd have a long and solid career, it was a price I was willing to pay. By this point, I hadn't been wrestling much anyhow. The pain had been too intrusive.

They went into my neck through the front and used three screws to fuse my vertebrae on the left side. The weird thing was that it didn't freak me out or worry me at all. I knew I was in good hands with Dr. Uribe.

As I recovered, I pulled away from all my friends, from all my loved ones. I became a hermit in the house. Zak and Nikki came to visit, but part of me just wanted to be left alone. Taking away wrestling meant also taking away the one thing that always kept me going. I abused prescription painkillers; I stopped going to physical therapy. My life got smaller and harder and more awful each day. At first, I fought back against the darkness that was closing in on me. After all, I'm a fighter. But eventually, it felt as if all my efforts were for nothing. I couldn't keep the depression from swallowing me whole. The only solace was drugs and alcohol.

By this point, I had become totally numb to my life and that was the way I preferred it.

Before I moved to Texas, back when I'd still lived in Florida, I'd had a regular routine, with workouts and some glancing care of my well-being. Sure, I'd been abusing alcohol and drugs then, but I was still wrestling and needed to keep it together, keep myself relatively healthy. Now I was home all the time, no daily regimen to follow, and everything fell fucking apart. I was losing weight like crazy, unaware I looked like a scarecrow, feeling utterly alone and trapped. I got more and more scared, and more and more unable to care for myself.

Meanwhile, my parents and brothers in the UK were going crazy, trying to help me. I ignored their calls. I found out later they reached out to wrestlers they knew across the US. They asked them to go to where I lived to try to catch a glimpse of me or get some information, to see if I was okay. They were that worried.

A year and a half after surgery, the WWE asked me to fly to their offices in Connecticut, where they'd since moved, to talk about my recovery and career. This was my first visit to the company's new offices, and I was on edge about being there, sure people were talking about me behind my back. I met with Mark Carrano, who got to the point after first setting a digital recorder on the table and switching it on.

"I'm hearing from other wrestlers, Paige. They're worried about you. You've gotten so thin and you look unwell. . . . I'm sorry to be that blunt." I hadn't been responding to anyone's texts, but pictures were circulating online of me looking like a wreck. I wasn't surprised people were talking about me, but I didn't want to hear it.

"I'm fine. Really."

"Please, Paige. I want to help." He waved away my excuses. "We want to help."

"I'm totally fine. I just need a little more time to recover."

"We can intervene," Mark pleaded. "We can help you. But you have to tell me the truth."

What Mark didn't know was that I couldn't speak the truth. I couldn't admit to myself what was really going on. It was just too fucking painful.

"I'm gonna be in town for a show. I'd love to see you!" Renee texted. She'd been one of my best friends, a ring announcer and backstage interviewer. We'd started at WWE at about the same time and had been on *Total Divas* together. I reluctantly agreed to let her come over.

By this time, most of my friends had stopped calling and texting. I didn't return their calls and, in some cases, even blocked them, so it wasn't their fault. But a few were stubbornly persistent, including Renee.

She rang the doorbell.

I opened the door, and when she saw me, Renee's face lost all its color. She's a beautiful perky blond woman with a thousand-watt smile and sweet eyes, but now she looked like she'd had the worst scare of her life. She folded me in a hug, and I could feel her hands assessing me, how skinny and bony I'd become, how unwell.

We sat on the couch with drinks, trying to make small talk, but I couldn't even do that. I was too disconnected from who I used to be.

Renee had kept texting me through it all, sometimes two, three, four times in a row, even when I didn't reply. She made sure I knew I was loved and that she had my back. But now I could see how uncomfortable she was, how pained she was at seeing what was really going on with me. I wanted to be present with her, wanted to remember the me I had been before all this got started. I knew she could help me resurrect the person I used to be.

Recently, Renee told me about how worried she'd been to come visit me, unsure of what she'd find . . . and that day went beyond her most overblown fears. She was utterly horrified, and I could see it on her face.

She left soon after, and I was relieved. No one wants to be seen when they're in the space I was in.

"Hi, Ms. Bevis, this is Danny from Aegis."

It was my twenty-fifth birthday. The minute I saw the number on my phone, I knew it was bad. Aegis never called unless you failed a test. I'd been randomly tested for drugs since I'd joined FCW, and I'd never before been called. Cocaine doesn't stay in your system long, so I'd always managed to pass, but now I was getting sloppy and doing it the day before a show.

"So we got the results back of your drug test and found benzoylecgonine in your system; it's the main metabolite of cocaine." He was clearly loving this gotcha moment, and his smugness made me so mad.

"No, that's wrong," I said. "I was at the dentist last week. It must be from the Novocain or something."

"I don't think so," he said. "Either way, you'll have to take it up with WWE."

I talked with Mark, and there was no getting around this. "It's your first pop, so it's going to be a month's suspension, no pay. We might send drug testers to your house at any time, just letting you know." He warned me that I'd be suspended for two months if I popped a second time. And if I popped a third time, there'd be no out. I'd be fired. "I'm just giving you the rundown," he said.

Then they announced my shame to the world in a press release.

> WWE has suspended Saraya-Jade Bevis (Paige) for 30 days effective tomorrow for her first violation of the company's talent wellness policy.

A reasonable person would decide that doing coke was not a good trade-off for the career I'd built. A reasonable person would simply stop doing coke and get her life back on track, but I worried I was a washout and that my career was over. I had left the realm of being a reasonable person a long time ago.

So, what the fuck! Why work hard to rehabilitate my image? I was done anyway.

Two months later, I popped drug test number two. The dirt sheets went wild. My parents were not pleased. Not after all the work they'd put into my career, all the ways they'd supported me. I felt like shit, and more than covering my own arse, I wanted to protect them from what I'd done.

"WWE has suspended Saraya-Jade Bevis (Paige) for 60 days effective immediately, for her second violation of the company's talent wellness policy," the WWE said in a statement.

I took out my anger and frustration via Twitter.

> Same shit different day. Kids . . . Please don't get prescriptions or doctors notes. Not acceptable.

Then I added, Rules apply depending on your status.

My dad immediately came to my defense, writing on Facebook that painkillers I had been prescribed for my long-term neck injury were responsible for the violation. He said that because that's what I'd convinced him was true. But it wasn't.

It took no time for WWE to slap back at my tweet.

> Saraya-Jade Bevis tested positive for an illegal substance, not a prescription drug. In addition, WWE is providing world-class medical care for her in-ring injury.

They basically told the world I'd done coke. And they were right.

WHERE IS MY MIND?

Chapter Fourteen

I went to visit my parents, making amends to them after distancing myself for a year and a half while my life was going to hell, and they were concerned with what they saw. I was clearly very sick. They convinced me to be checked out at the hospital. But the medical professionals there thought I was fucking loony tunes. I tried to tell them I was Paige from the WWE, but they didn't believe me. Why should they? I looked a sight. My hair had a massive knot in the back from where my hair extensions hadn't been tended. I was supposed to go back every three months or so to have them redone, but I had neglected them. Now I had to wear baseball caps all the time to try to keep the awful state of my hair hidden. I was skin and bones with dark circles under my eyes. I looked homeless. The doctors and nurses all thought I had some kind of delusion that made me think I was a famous wrestler.

They decided they needed to section me for three days because I was genuinely unwell. Apparently, there was some serious shit wrong with me, including stress-induced anorexia. My hair had been falling out by fistfuls for some time, big patches of my scalp almost bald where the hair extensions didn't cover, and my body was in a bad way. I hadn't been able to eat in forever and had lost way too much weight.

Eventually, the doctor googled me and saw it was really me. The next time I tried to tell him I was Paige from the WWE, he softened his tone. "So you are."

I stayed there a few days before they released me.

For months, I had been in almost daily contact with Stephen Merchant, who was writing the film about my life. He'd ask all kinds of questions, and I enjoyed speaking with him. But around this time, he simply stopped calling, as if the connection went dead. . . . I was too busy self-imploding to really notice until Mark Carrano left a message.

"Production on the movie has been halted," he said. "Everyone is worried about you. They don't want to finish the movie if the real-life person it's based on is not gonna survive to see it through."

I was crushed, but what the fuck could I do about it? Pass me another drink. Line up another line. Reader, I know it sounds pathetic. It was.

One morning, back in the States, I was doomscrolling on social media as everyone does. Things had started to calm down a little. Twitter was a cesspool of hatred as usual, but unbeknownst to me, things were about to get devastating for me on there.

I saw one tweet, a picture of me naked—*What the fuck . . . ?*

Nah, that can't be real. Someone made a fake picture of me. But the more I scrolled, the more my heart sank, the more a cold sweat took over my body. There were so many pictures.

So. Many. Pictures.

Ones I hadn't seen in many years. Pictures that I never thought would see the light of day. I had actually forgot about them at this point. *Why are they popping up now? Who could've even got ahold of these?* I didn't even have them saved to my personal iCloud, so I couldn't have been hacked. So many questions were running through my head.

Then it got worse.

Videos started appearing.

Extremely personal videos. Seeing parts of myself I never wanted the world to be able to see.

I was completely humiliated. Mortified. Heartbroken.

It went viral very fast. People were tearing me to shreds, calling me a porn star (which is the nicest thing they threw at me), sending it all to my family instantly. My phone was blowing up. People calling, texting, trying to get ahold of me.

I was in a full spiral panic. Sobbing, sweating, pacing.

Everything that had happened in the past year and a half already had me at my worst. Or so I thought. . . . But I had barely scraped the surface of the rock bottom I was about to hit in my mind.

Am I gonna get fired for this? Is my family gonna hate me for this? Is the world gonna turn on me for this?

My mind wouldn't stop racing, and I felt nausea take over my body.

I ran to the bathroom and threw up, still sobbing. I was a broken woman.

I ran out of the house and just kept running. I didn't know where I was gonna go, but I felt so trapped in that house. Felt like I was being swallowed up into a dark hole.

That's when I found myself outside a grocery store, an H-E-B. Standing at the edge of the parking lot, I looked around and felt like everyone was staring at me. So I ran and hid in the hedges and just sat there, trying to get my breath. But I couldn't. It felt like my lungs had caved in. Sitting on the ground, hiding from the world, I wanted to bury myself right there under the dirt and never think about any of it again.

Just repeating to myself . . .

I don't want to be alive anymore.

It felt like it took forever for my family to answer the phone. My heart was racing. I felt like I could hear it beating through my chest. My whole body was shaking. *If my dad is ashamed of me, this might just very well tip me over the edge. This will be the end of me.*

My dad answers.

"Hello, princess."

I start instantly sobbing uncontrollably.

"I'm so sorry, Dad. I'm so sorry."

And what he said next saved my life.

"Sweetheart, it's very normal to have sex. Unfortunately, you're just in the public eye, so people are making a bigger deal about it."

He continued with a joke in my perfect dad fashion. "Might even make you more famous! Look at Kim Kardashian."

Even through my uncontrollable sobbing, he still managed to make me laugh (and question how the bloody hell he knew who Kim was).

"I love you so much, and don't ever be ashamed of something that's normal. I'll forever be proud of you, and I wish I was there to give you a hug. Keep your chin up, princess. Don't let this break you."

My family all appeared on the screen telling me how much they loved me and how much they wanted to squeeze me.

I'm the luckiest girl in the world.

I put down the phone and start walking back to my house. Still ignoring everyone who was blowing up my phone. Until Mark Carrano called.

Oh no. Here come the cold sweats again. My heart that had just slowed down was now beating rapidly.

Am I about to get fired???

I answered. "I'm so sorry, Mark! I don't know how this happened."

He instantly said, "Don't worry, Saraya. This stuff happens. I just wanted to check on you and see if you were okay, and give you an idea of what we are gonna do next."

Wow. What I thought was gonna be the end of me was just showing me who the fuck was in my corner. Finally.

I told him I was having a hard time but ready to try to fix this, and he explained that social would write a tweet for me to put out regarding this humiliating leak and they'd try their best to get it taken down.

The sense of relief I felt was unmatched. My family loved me, and I still had my job, albeit not in the ring.

But I knew that it was gonna be a long road. This kind of stuff never goes away. It dies down, but it never goes away. So I started to train myself to not care in public.

But even to this day, I'll get a pit in my stomach anytime I think about it, but at least I can joke about it now, right?

This isn't the end of you yet, Raya.

I tried to believe that. To tell myself over and over. To hear my dad saying, *You think you're the only person who ever had sex?*, reassuring me that the way he saw me had not changed.

But I had changed. My neck was fucked, and so was my wrestling career, the only thing I had ever known. The big, exciting Hollywood movie about my life had already come to a screeching halt because I was too much of a mess. Instead, the "movie" that had just been released was sex tapes that had been taken when I was still a teenager, only nineteen, and now they were all over the internet for everyone to see. For *my family* to see. I couldn't function without alcohol. Fuck, I could barely function without cocaine. I couldn't stand being in my own skin for a moment longer. I didn't even look like myself anymore. . . . I didn't want to be myself anymore.

A while later, I was talking with my mum on FaceTime, and I just kept crying into the camera, telling her how hard my life had become, how I simply didn't want to keep going. To make my point, I pulled out a bottle of Percocet I'd been given for the neck pain and started to eat them, just chewing them up as she watched, one after another, handfuls at a time. She was crying, begging me to stop and get help. God, what torture I put her through. No mother should have to see her daughter try to overdose in front of her eyes while she's five thousand miles away. That's downright cruel, but I was hurting and didn't know how to deal with it. Just like when she had disappeared when I was a kid, now I was putting her through the same kind of hell, just trying to escape my own demons. I was desperate to disappear, too, right in front of her. I am my mother's daughter. And like her, somehow, I came back to myself. I spat out the drugs and we both bawled. How much lower was I going to have to go before I got help? Let's suffice it to say that attempting suicide over FaceTime with my mother was enough to wake me the fuck up.

PART *Three*

IF YOU COULD READ MY MIND, LOVE

For over a year, Mark Carrano had been sending emails, calling, checking in. "When you're ready to come back to work, we'll be here for you." WWE was still paying me, since I was technically employed by them, but I pretty well ignored his every attempt to reach me. Though I appreciated the sentiment more than he'd ever know, I hadn't been in a position to reach out to him. Yet. But now, for reasons I didn't fully understand, I was.

I pressed the speed dial on my phone and rallied my courage.

"Oh my God, Paige! I'm so happy to hear from you!" He sounded so fucking pleased to be in contact with me, I couldn't help but smile.

"I'm ready to come back," I said. "If you'll have me."

"This is so great!" Immediately, he made plans for me to be checked out by a doctor to be sure it was safe for me to start training, and to begin regaining my fitness at the Performance Center in Orlando, where NXT had moved a few years earlier and where I'd trained as an up-and-comer. Only now, I would be going back as a disgraced two-time Diva Champ.

Looking back at this time, I sometimes wonder what the moment was that broke the spell, that propelled me to pull myself together. Certainly that attempted suicide via FaceTime with my mum had been rock bottom. But there'd been a day shortly before then that stuck with me and may have been the turning point, though I didn't realize it at the time.

I had gone to the grocery store looking like absolute shit. During that time, I woke up every day fucking hating myself, hating my life. My hair extensions by then, months and months after they'd last been sorted out, were a fucking mess. I literally couldn't get the back of my hair, beneath the top layer, untangled. As a result, I had this hideous bulge at the back of my head where it was all irredeemably matted. I tried to keep the snarled ball hidden by wearing baseball caps. I'd looked in the mirror before leaving the house for the grocery store, and my eyes were all droopy and dark. I was extremely skinny and looked like a fucking cokehead alcoholic. But in the moment, I needed more to drink. It was a Sunday, and all the liquor stores are closed on Sundays in Texas. Beer or wine from the grocery store were my only options. The plan was to jet in and out, fly under the radar, and get the fuck out of there.

With dark glasses and my baseball cap, I headed to the beer and wine aisle. I turned one of the corners and almost ran into a little girl and her mum picking out cereal.

"You're Paige!" the girl squealed; she was about nine or ten. "From the WWE! Oh my goodness! I love you!"

Her mum pulled her back a little, taking note of how messed up I appeared. But the little girl's admiration was pure and joyous. She looked at me as I'd once been able to look at myself, as someone who was inspiring and doing kick-ass shit.

Unlike the rest of the world, who all seemed to know about the sex tapes that had dropped and that I'd already popped two drug tests, this little girl knew me only as a female wrestler she looked up to. It had been way too long since anyone had gazed at me with that kind of unsullied admiration.

"I want to be a wrestler, too, someday," she said, flexing her tiny bicep. "Like you."

Her mum put an arm around the girl's shoulder, as if to protect her from me. The mother could tell I wasn't in the best place, and she seemed to want to get her little girl outta there, fast.

"Are you in training?" I asked, remembering how to interact with fans, getting outside myself and my miserable condition for half a second, thinking about someone else besides me.

"I've been doing push-ups and running in our backyard, but none of the girls I know want to wrestle with me."

"I hope you find someone to train with soon," I said. "You'll make a great wrestler, so don't give up, okay?"

"I won't. I promise! When I grow up, I want to be just like you!"

Her mum steered her away from me before we could prolong the conversation, making sure the girl didn't see what a total fuckup I was.

I got my beer and headed back home, thinking, *Fuck. I'm this girl's role model.* At first, that thought made my heart feel good, and I smiled to myself. And then I realized the truth. If I was that girl's role model, then I fucking needed to start acting like one. . . . This was not role model behavior by a long fucking shot. *I* didn't even respect me.

As soon as I got home, I pounded a few beers and did a few lines to numb away all those feelings. What else could I do? I was stuck and didn't know how to extricate myself. I couldn't see a path forward . . . but somewhere inside me, meeting that little girl planted a tiny seed of hope. She saw someone different in me. Maybe I could be that person again one day?

The shame I felt at all I'd done threatened to swamp me. I almost hung up the call. I kept picturing myself back in the Performance Center, imagining all the trainers and trainees talking behind my back, saying the shit everyone was saying online . . . calling me a porn star, telling me I was totally washed-up and a druggie. That my best days were far behind me and I should just go home to the UK with my tail between my legs. I did what I could to put those thoughts out of my mind. I just needed to take the next step.

Mark promised to have a plane ticket booked ASAP from Texas back to Orlando. I was gathering all my resources to do what I'd wanted to do since day one but had lacked the resolve. I was finally ready to make my getaway. Before we ended the call, I kept waiting for Mark to ask for details, to pry into what had happened with me, to ask questions that would make me feel like shit. But God bless him, he didn't. He knew I needed to be handled with kid gloves and I appreciated that.

Next I called my friends Joey and Raquel. Like Renee, they had never stopped calling and messaging me:

> We're thinking of you! Hope you're doing okay. We're here whenever you need us!

So many of my friends had stopped checking in altogether—and to be fair, when my life was a wreck, I was the one who fucking ghosted them, so I don't blame them. They had no way to know I needed them, nor how to support me. No one had known how to help me, myself included. But through it all, Joey and Raquel kept up a string of texts, saying hi, checking in, letting me know I wasn't alone, even though I almost never replied. I knew they were people I could count on.

"I'm coming back to Orlando," I told them. "I'm ready to start training again."

"Yay!" Their genuine joy screamed at me down the phone.

"I could get a place of my own. That would be super easy and not a problem. But . . ." I hesitated. How much should I reveal? Fuck it! I was tired of hiding, of pretending I was okay when I wasn't. If I couldn't tell the truth to Joey and Raquel, my closest friends, I couldn't be honest with anyone. And now, after all this time of lying and hiding, speaking the truth seemed important in a way that was new.

"Actually, I'm a bit worried about living on my own," I confessed. "I don't know if I can make good choices for myself after all the fuckups. I was wondering—"

Raquel is an angel. She cut me off before I could even ask. "Raya, you come here. We would love to have you, and we'll be by your side. We're gonna have so much fun. I'll get the guest room ready for you."

"Really?" My heart felt as if it had just filled with helium. I was going to be okay!

I was learning a lot about who was a trusted friend and who was just along for the ride. During the time I'd been in Texas, my former room-mates had all but disappeared from my life. Joey and Raquel, however, had stuck by me. They really didn't give a fuck about my wrestling career. Sure, they'd watch a match if I sent it to them or asked them to, just to cheer me on, but they didn't give a shit if I was famous, or consider how my fame might benefit them. They just loved me for me. And that's what I needed in my life going forward: more friends like that.

Joey picked me up at Orlando International Airport, and I pretty well collapsed into his arms. When we got back to Joey and Raquel's place, I found a beautiful bedroom all set up for me. I told them I had quit the drugs cold turkey and was trying to stay clean. They agreed to help me and to stay clean themselves to make it easier. I felt so loved and accepted. And I kept thinking of that little girl in the store. What I came to realize is that everyone thinks a role model should be perfect, but maybe the opposite was true. Maybe it was just as important to let people see where I'd fucked up. To show them it was okay to be imperfect, and to make a comeback from that position.

"I have some really great news," Mark said when I met with him a few days later at his office. We were there to chart the path of getting me back to work. "If you stay clean for a year—don't pop any more tests and keep out of trouble—we'll take off one of the strikes against you. What do you say?"

"I would love that, Mark! Yes." I wanted to rebuild my career and prove everyone wrong. I had come to see that, though I had many fans who wanted the best for me, there was also a huge contingent just aching for me to fuck up again in a big way. For whatever reason, a ton of people wanted to see what happened with me. Some to celebrate my comeback, and others to gloat if I were to fall on my face. I wanted to be able to tell them all, *I'm not who you think I am. I am better than that.* Plus, I wanted to be off the drugs for me. I wanted to be healthier and happier.

Since touching down in Orlando, I'd been clean and doing okay without the drugs, but I was still drinking. The idea of going to sleep without a drink was completely unthinkable. How was I supposed to do public appearances, interact with people, celebrate the victories in life, and console myself when things didn't go my way? How did people do these kinds of things without drugs or alcohol?

I think Mark could pretty well hear the conversation going on in my head, because he pushed a business card across the table to me. "This is Bob Killer," he said, pronouncing Bob's last name like "Keeler." "He's a sober coach who we employ. Give him a call. He'll help you figure out how to do it."

I had been living at Joey and Raquel's for about a week, but I thought about going back to the drugs. This business of changing everything about my life, of letting go of the drugs and the numbness they created, was fucking hard and uncomfortable. And even though I had Joey, Raquel, and Renee all in my corner, I still felt way too alone a lot of the time.

But that's when the switch flipped. I finally had some good influences around me. I knew if I continued doing the same things, my life would stay the same or only get smaller and more miserable. I didn't want that.

Walking up to the Performance Center for my first day back at training, I was terrified. And excited. First thing, I texted the trainer called Mooney. He'd been there on my very first day with NXT.

"Hey, can you let me in the side door?"

He was so sweet and welcoming. I was to meet with Tara Halaby, the doctor who was going to do my PT and set up our schedule. I said hi to her and to Norman Smiley and walked past Dusty's old office—they'd kept it exactly as it had been after his death in 2015. My heart swelled with gratitude for all he'd given me. To be honest, though, I was so glad he hadn't been around to see me go through the past year and a half. But I also knew how fucking proud he'd be of me for coming back and working to get myself together.

Walking through there, I felt every emotion you can think of all wrapped up in a little bubble. I was terrified because I didn't know what people were gonna think of me. Were they gonna think I was the worst human being in the world?

I was also really excited to get my life back and get back in the wrestling ring. I've always been happy when I'm wrestling.

Plus, it felt so damn good to walk into the Performance Center. It was a whirlwind of emotions.

As I walked through the facility, all the newer trainees seemed to shyly eye me, following my every move. So many new faces! They had all watched my career previously and had also witnessed my public breakdowns. What did they think of me? I squirmed, knowing they knew I'd been a fucking mess.

That first day was just to get the lay of the land, but the next day we started with PT, doing tons of exercises with bands to get the small muscles in my neck and all the muscles supporting my neck in good condition for the serious training. Then we added in cardio and weight training, all of which would continue for a month before I'd be allowed to step foot back into the ring.

One night, Joey and Raquel were out. I was on edge and knew that even a beer or a glass of wine would calm my nerves, but we didn't keep any in the house. I opened my phone to order some. But in that moment, I thought about Bob Killer. I'd called Bob, and he'd been talking to me since I got back to Orlando, helping me as I got clean from the prescription painkillers and the coke, but I told him I was still drinking. He didn't give me shit for it but pointed out all the ways it wasn't helping me. I listened, and I believed him, but I still needed a drink now and then to get through.

Another night when Raquel was working, Joey and I decided to go out and party. He and I hit up bar after bar, and we had a fucking blast. *This* was why I liked to drink. *This* was fun! But it was only fun until it wasn't.

The next day, I woke up with my mouth as dry as the Sahara and tasting like absolute shit. What had I done last night?

"Good morning, sunshine." Raquel came into the living room, but her sweet voice was like an ice pick in my head.

I peeled my eyelids half-open. Apparently, I had made it only to the couch the night before. The sun coming through the blinds felt like it was going to gouge out my eyes. I tried to sit up, and she just started laughing, though not in a mean way.

"What?"

"Joey, come here," she called. He, too, wasn't feeling so great after our evening and stumbled in looking pretty much how I felt. When he saw me, he started laughing as well.

"What?" I demanded.

"You have McDonald's stickers in your hair," Raquel said.

I reached up and, sure enough, my fingers found the stickers from the pile of Big Macs I had devoured the night before. Fuck. I laughed, too.

Maybe Bob was right and the alcohol wasn't helping me.

I texted Bob straightaway, and when he called me back, I told him about my little excursion the previous night. When we'd started working together, he'd told me, "You have to be a hundred percent truthful with me, or this won't work." I must have wanted to be clean and sober enough to have believed him. He listened kindly, but again pointed out how I wasn't doing myself any favors.

"I'm not angry with you," he said, "but I am disappointed." He never yelled at me or tried to strong-arm me, which wouldn't have worked, but reasoned with me. "It's a slippery slope. You drink like that, and then you might find yourself wanting the drugs again. And if you really want this life you say you're trying to build, you won't do this stuff."

I felt even more guilty after our conversation, but I heard what he was saying. And I'd like to say I didn't drink again after that, but I'd be lying. Still, whenever I had slipups like that night, though I wished I could hide that stuff from Bob, I couldn't. Because really, I wanted to be better for myself, for my own reasons, and I knew I needed his help to get there.

I didn't want him to be mad at me, only for him to be proud. Whenever I was struggling, I'd send him a text and he'd hop on the phone with me. If I was really in a bad place, he'd have me breathe with him, and that helped. I was determined to show him I could do it, but I mostly wanted to do it for myself. I had too much going for me to throw it all away again.

My palms were sweaty as I pulled on my kneepads. This was the day they were finally gonna let me back into the ring, and I was really dreading it. I hadn't wrestled for a year and a half and knew from previous experience that if I was away for even a little bit, the exact timing of my moves would be off. How bad would I be after such a long absence?

At first, they'd just had me running the ropes; the kind of cardio needed in the ring is different from what you get on a treadmill, and it took some time to regain that fitness. But after the doctor's okay, it was time for me to take my first bump. That's when you're thrown to the ground, landing on your back, often having the wind knocked out of you. When I was wrestling regularly, I took bumps all day long and didn't really feel them. And since I started at such a young age, when my teen body simply bounced rather than slammed the mat, I'd never had the experience of taking a bump that completely knocked the stuffing out of me. But that first bump after my hiatus? Holy shit. Adrenaline pumped through me like I'd jumped out of an airplane, and I lay there gasping, thinking, *How have I done this for so long? This is really fucking awful.*

I worked with a bunch of the trainees at that time, and these girls were so sweet and wanted to help, but they could see I was suffering.

The coaches had me throwing those girls around. I wanted to apologize to them for all the bumps they were having to take for me because I was out of practice, now that I could feel how awful the bumps were. But I needed to be ready for the main roster soon, and the only way to do that was to get good again at throwing women about.

Two months after I'd moved back to Florida, I was invited to a taping of *RAW* in Atlanta, which I'd do with all my colleagues from the main roster. The plan was that, this first day, I'd come and make an appearance on TV, saying, "I'm back . . . !" but I wouldn't actually wrestle until the following week. I got ready to go and at first was super excited. But when I tried to walk into the arena before showtime, my heart felt like it was going to blow up in my fucking chest. The anxiety gave me full-body shakes, which took years to completely go away. I was about to see all my favorite wrestlers, many of whom I'd ignored in the past year and a half, all of whom had seen the sex tapes and knew of my popped drug tests and heard all the rumors, seen the YouTube videos of me behaving badly. I was so sure they'd hate me, think I had no business returning after not respecting our sport and myself enough to have acted better.

I stood outside the arena, utterly unable to move. I wanted to run away, but my legs refused to cooperate. My breath caught in my throat, and my hands shook; I was certain I was going to have a major breakdown right there and then.

I pulled my phone out of my bag to text Mark Carrano.

I can't go in there. You have to help me.

I was absolutely fucking terrified, and my body convinced me that to take a step either toward the arena or away from it was to ensure my sudden and very painful death. I lowered myself so that I was sitting on the step outside the arena and tried to take the deep breaths Bob had shown me, afraid I might pass out at any minute.

A few minutes later, Mark was by my side. "Everything's going to be okay," he said, helping me stand.

I was shaking so badly; he could feel it.

He looked me in the eye. "You're okay."

I raised my eyebrows, not sure I could trust him, but his face was calm and welcoming. He meant it. He held my arm, and together, we entered the arena.

The first person I ran into was Triple H, and he immediately wrapped me in a massive bear hug.

"I'm so glad you're here!" he said as he squeezed me. He whispered the next part of his greeting: "We were all so afraid you were going to die."

Hearing that, it felt like I was loved there more than I realized at the time. And also stung a bit, reminding me just how bad I had let things get.

The other wrestlers, one by one, came up to me and welcomed me back, and you know what? They weren't fucking faking it because someone had told them to. They really meant it. At times, I thought that they all hated me and would be happy to see me crash and burn, that they'd cheered my every fuckup. But that had never been true. They cared about me! They were glad to see me.

The best moment of the night came when I saw Stephanie McMahon. She also wrapped me in a huge hug and then pulled back to look me in the eye.

"Welcome back, Paige," she said. "This is still *your* house."

And this time, I allowed myself to feel the love and acceptance. She was right. I belonged.

UNDER PRESSURE

It started with an Instagram post. I don't even remember what the photo was that I'd put up, but Ronnie, a friend from a while back, a musician I'd always admired, added a comment: *I hope you're well.* My heart sped up the minute I saw it.

Ronnie had been a good friend for years by then, but now I can say how it really went down. Reader—I don't think you truly understand how long I have been head over heels in love with this man. The first time I saw him was at a music festival his band was playing, and I swear, he was walking in slow motion toward me, wind in his hair, smoke billowing, doves flying, somewhere "(I Just) Died in Your Arms Tonight" playing in the background. . . . He was the most handsome man I had ever seen, the only person to ever take my breath away.

But the timing wasn't right for us both. We met right as things in my life were headed into a downward spiral. We became best friends instantly, but nothing romantic would happen for five more years. In the meantime, I had lost his contact info.

In the time since I'd moved back to Orlando, I was overjoyed to have friendships again. People I'd cut out of my life came flooding back in. My phone blew up all the time with texts from people I adored checking on me, seeing how I was doing, sharing their love. For that year and a half when I'd been isolated, I thought everyone I knew hated me, but now I saw that that wasn't true. Not at all. I was loved and admired and missed and cherished.

So when I saw Ronnie's Instagram comment, I instantly wanted to be back in touch with him. At the time, I was visiting our mutual friend Bobby, and I begged him, "Please, reconnect us."

Bobby saw the glint in my eye and knew that my interest in Ronnie wasn't totally platonic.

"I'm not sure that's such a great idea," he said. "You're one of my best friends. And he's one of my favorite people. If you two got together and then broke up, I wouldn't be able to choose sides. Plus, you both have such similar personalities, you might clash."

"I just miss talking to him."

Despite his reservations, Bobby reconnected us and immediately, Ronnie and I started talking. All the time. I wasn't looking for a hookup but friends to surround myself with, safe people. He lived in LA, and I was in Orlando, but we found time regularly to chat and reestablished our friendship. Ronnie had been one of the people who I knew I wanted to be in touch with again. There was something about his gentle spirit, his wisdom at managing life, that I admired. I realized how very much I'd missed him.

We talked all the time and supported each other long-distance. I told him how much I loved singing but that I couldn't do it publicly (sober, at least) because I'd likely hyperventilate and pass out, it terrified me so fucking much.

So, when it came time for me to make my first *RAW* appearance after I'd been gone a year and a half, the night Triple H told me he was glad I hadn't died and Stephanie said, "This is *your* house," I wanted to tip my hat to Ronnie. I dressed in a black leather jacket, open down the front and studded with silver spikes, the hood pulled over my head. And when I walked out onto the ramp to greet the thousands of fans pleased to see me again in person, plus all the others watching on TV, I asked, "Did you miss me?"

They roared their joy at seeing me again, and I felt their admiration ripple through every cell in my body. The moment was utterly electric. Then I held the microphone to my face, offering my greeting with a line from one of Ronnie's songs, doing it in the same singsong rhythm he'd do. "I'm baaaack!" I crooned. The crowd went wild. And I hoped that somewhere, Ronnie was watching and knew I was sending him a message.

That night, I also sent a message to all the fans. I had paired up with two wrestlers who were just now being bumped up to the main roster from NXT, Mandy Rose and Sonya Deville. Together, we formed a team that Vince named "Absolution." I think the name was meant to play up all I'd been through. Now I was back, playing a heel and guiding these younger wrestlers forward, while looking for some kind of pardon or absolution of my own. I was on the road to something better.

After that reintroduction to the wrestling fans, I had one week to cram any final preparation for my first real match. And in some ways, it was like riding a bike; it all started to come back to me, the moves, the timing, the cadence. But as we worked through our spots, I still didn't have my cardio all the way back. It didn't take long for me to feel blown-up, gasping for air, trying to regain my strength and focus. For as hard as I was training, I still got tired very quickly.

I'd been working out like crazy, but the kind of endurance needed in a ring is very different. I could do all kinds of running on treadmills, but when I got into the ring under the lights, there was so much more I needed to be able to do: lift people and put them back down. Run. Hit the ropes, roll across the canvas, so many different maneuvers within a wrestling match. I had to relearn how to get up quickly. I couldn't be slow, but needed to make everything very snappy. If I fell to the ground, there was a way to spin and then roll to my knee and my elbow, as well as moves to help me get up. So I would do drills like that, where I'd be on my back, and the coach would yell go, and I'd have to stand up quick, and do that over and over again from a full-out lying-down position. I would also need to be able to lift someone safely, even if I was tired. For what seemed like hours at a time, I did drills, picking up a wrestler in a body-slam position and then putting them down again. Pick them up and put them down, over and over again.

And then there was the Brookside Shuffle, where I had to hold my hands above my head and shuffle to the side, but all the way around the ring. And then switch from clockwise to counterclockwise, before switching back in the other direction. That was to help me regain spatial ring awareness. And if someone was going to be flying, I had to learn how to stop on the spot or move somewhere else, developing an almost psychic awareness of where my fellow wrestlers were at all times, as if I had eyes in the back of my head. There were so many different things to relearn.

Plus, as wrestlers we have to be able to talk to each other while in the ring, so one of the things they had me do was to run the ropes, counting aloud with each hit. It was a way to get me reacquainted with talking even when winded. Because if I were to do almost any kind of cardio training like running or hiking and really push it physically, I'd get to this place where I couldn't talk anymore. I'd need to give 100 percent of my concentration to what I was asking my body to do. In wrestling, though, I would have to be able to talk the whole time so that I could work out moves with my opponent. Or, if I'm playing a heel, as I was at that time, I needed to be yelling and screaming at the other person as part of my character. I also needed to be able to talk to the ref, to ask how much time was left, or, as in the case of my first big match upon returning, to let the ref know I heard him when he said they were adding six additional minutes to the match right in the middle of things.

Fuck! Six extra minutes. I was already so fucking tired in this first singles match back, this time against Sasha Banks. How could I go six more minutes? Even with all the training, I was fucking dying, but I gave it my all.

To complicate matters, I was wearing a pair of shorts that, in the midst of this now-longer-than-expected wrestling match, felt like they had split apart at the crotch.

My Absolution team—made up of girls who were new to televised matches, having debuted just one week earlier—was gathered and cheering for me from one side of the ring. I rolled to be next to them.

"Hey, are my shorts split?" I asked without letting the audience know I was talking to them. As professional wrestlers, we get really good at communicating with one another without letting on that's what we are doing. But since these girls were super new to televised matches, they didn't want to chance talking to me and being caught on camera doing so. They just smiled at me blankly. That was of no fucking help.

I rolled to the other side of the ring where, among the female wrestlers we were up against, were Bayley and Mickie James, both of them old-school pros.

I called out to them. "Hey, can you see my gimmick?" I asked, trying to be subtle. I was afraid that if I wrestled with my usual vigor, I'd be giving the TV cameras a full shot. And remember, this was being filmed for a family-friendly audience.

"You're wearing a red thong," Mickey said in reply.

"Damn it!"

I spent the rest of the match trying to keep my lungs from exploding while working to hide the fact my shorts were split. At one point, I was on the top rope and had to sit down instead of standing because if I'd stood right then, the cameras would've gotten a decisively non-PG-13 view. The whole match was crazy. We ended up going for something like seventeen minutes, and when it was over, I had triumphed. But at what cost? I was completely toast.

The minute I got backstage, I ran into Vince McMahon.

"Were you blown-up out there?" he asked, referring to whether I had run out of energy in the middle of the match.

"Six extra minutes when I'm just coming back was fucking hard," I admitted. "But the real issue was my shorts. They split in the crotch. I just wanted this to be the one time I'm on the internet without showing everyone my vagina."

He laughed, and so did I. As much as the leak of those sex tapes had destroyed me, and I was afraid I'd never get out from under the shame of it all, I was able to joke around with him about it. Maybe I was making progress.

By this time, the Women's Revolution at WWE was building up steam. Back in 2015, before my neck injury, we'd gained attention for the plight of female wrestlers in a male-dominated sport when I was put in a match, paired with Emma, and set against Brie and Nikki Bella. At the last second before we took the ring, we were told our match had been cut down significantly in time. Instead of wrestling for the reduced time frame they'd allotted us, we decided to make our anger known by doing a very abbreviated match, no more than about thirty seconds long. It was our way of protesting how little time women were given. We were the only women featured on *RAW* that night, and though our merch sales and the fan attention we garnered were incredibly high, WWE kept cutting into our time, not giving us the respect we deserved.

When we got backstage after our truncated match, the producers had been pissed. "What the hell was that?"

We were mad and didn't care that they knew it. If, as punishment, they decided not to use us in future matches, well then, fuck it.

But in no time, the fans picked up on our anger and added a megaphone with the Twitter hashtag, #GiveDivasAChance. All over social media for three days, that hashtag reigned, and the fans let the WWE know they valued and wanted to see more women wrestling. At last, we were no longer just a sideshow for sex appeal, a chance to feature a bikini contest, but real athletes and entertainers who could pack in the fans just as much as the men did.

In recognition of this fact, by the time I returned to the ring, Stephanie McMahon announced that on January 28, 2018, *RAW* would host the first-ever all-women battle royale, giving fans what they'd been asking for. By this time, the Diva Championship title had been retired, replaced with the RAW Women's Championship, putting us on par with the men. Every female wrestler on the roster was excited about the all-women event. I trained harder than ever to get ready, excited to work with my Absolution partners.

WATCH THE WORLD BURN

L ife as a working pro wrestler resumed, and I felt great. I was getting stronger every day, enjoying being back at work with my friends, relishing the love from the fans. I didn't even realize how much I had truly missed it all until I was back, but now everything felt right again. I'd first reentered the arena on November 20, and by December 27, I was doing an untelevised live event: Absolution (me, Mandy Rose, and Sonya Deville) in a match against Sasha Banks, Bayley, and Mickie James at the Nassau Coliseum in Uniondale, New York, just a couple of days after Christmas.

It was a planned kick from behind.

We'd done this move and ones like it thousands of times, and many much more dangerous ones. Sasha Banks was in the corner. I was walking away from her, toward the center of the ring, yelling to the crowd. Using the ropes on either side, she lifted herself up and connected with both feet right between my shoulder blades, sending me flying face-first into the mat. My head snapped back violently, as if I'd been in a car accident and been given whiplash. Immediately, an electric shock ran through my neck and into my head, then ricocheted throughout my entire body.

Fuck.

Suddenly everything was in slow motion.

I was face down, gasping for breath. At first, I thought maybe I'd just had the wind knocked out of me and I would be okay in a minute.

I tried to crawl, to stand up, but I couldn't control my limbs. Still on my hands and knees, I stumbled forward, trying to shake the pins-and-needles feeling out of my arm. My hands felt numb, like they weren't mine. I couldn't control them. I paused for just a second, but it seemed like minutes.

What the fuck was happening to me?

I tried to move again, this time toward Sasha, trying to grab her leg. I wanted to reach out, to grasp on to her boot stretched out in front of me, but I couldn't. I tried to tell my arms to move, but they didn't listen. I just fell forward onto my elbows. The ref knelt down to check on me, but I wasn't registering what he was saying. My mind was going a million miles an hour. I'd been hit much harder countless times in my life but had never felt out of control like that before. Everything felt wrong.

I tried again, and for just a second I managed to somehow get to my feet. But I couldn't stand up straight. I was bent over at the waist, unsteady on my feet, reeling sideways into the ref. Immediately, I collapsed under my own weight back down to the mat.

The ref put up his arms in a crossed position to signal a serious injury in the ring, and suddenly I was lying face up, curling up like a match on fire, with medical hovering over me. For a moment that stretched out into what seemed like forever, all I could think was: *Am I paralyzed?*

And then the truth tore through me. It was *really* over this time. My career. All these years of wrestling, all this training, all the hell I had been through, all the hard work to make my comeback. Everything was just starting to get better. Wrestling was all I had ever wanted, and I was finally in a good place. Healthy. Sober. Back in the ring, where I belonged.

Now, in one split second, my neck was messed up and I'd never fucking wrestle again.

The entire stadium held its breath. The ref called for a stretcher, but there was no fucking way I wanted to leave the ring like that. I was going to walk out if it took the last scrap of life in me to do so. After a few minutes, the feeling began to return to my limbs and I was able to push myself up to a seated position. With help, slowly, I fucking walked away from the ring.

It felt like I was walking away from wrestling forever.

Just like my first day at FCW, Bray Wyatt was the first person to come up to me, checking to see if I was all right. I hobbled to the trainer's room backstage to be checked out. Plans were put into place immediately for me to get to a doctor in Pittsburgh for an evaluation, and even as all the trainers tried to tell me it would be okay, I already knew what the neck specialist would say.

It was over. I had spent a year and a half trying to return, and my comeback had lasted all of two and a half weeks. And now, it was over.

Sure enough, the next day the doctor in Pittsburgh confirmed that I would never wrestle again. The scans showed that I had absolutely no spinal fluid protecting one side of my neck. I was lucky I hadn't been paralyzed, he said. I could have another surgery to improve things, but I could never safely go back into the ring again without that fluid. I called my parents, and we bawled together.

It felt like it would be so easy to just let it all crash and burn. To take whatever painkillers this new injury would require, swallow them down with some alcohol, and just let my whole life go to shit again. Why not? Every good thing in my life came from wrestling—my family, my friends, my success . . . my whole identity. I know injuries are a part of wrestling, reader, I do. It's just the risk you take. But this was more than that to me. I didn't even know who I was without wrestling. What if I couldn't do anything else? Female wrestlers were just starting to be properly respected. Hell, I was just starting to have some respect for myself again.

And now what the fuck was the point? I had done everything I could to turn my life around, and it was all for nothing. I could feel the weight of everything bearing down on me again, threatening to crumble my spine into dust, to crush me for good.

Somewhere, on the other side of the familiar, never-ending pit of despair I was quickly falling into, my phone rang.

It was the WWE. "Okay, we want you here for *SmackDown* tomorrow night."

It should have felt like a ladder being thrown down to pull myself back up on. But honestly, in that moment, it didn't. *Fuck, I don't want to go to* SmackDown. *I've just gotten this news, and I'm fucking devastated.*

"Why?" I asked. "What do you need me for?"

"We can't tell you."

When I walked backstage at the arena, I was swarmed straightaway by writers and producers.

"We're gonna make you a general manager!" They were so excited.

I couldn't believe it. . . . They still wanted me even though I couldn't wrestle. The timing, as it turned out, was perfect. Be a boss, make matches and fire people in character, stay out of the ring . . . I could do that. The current general manager at the time, Daniel Bryan, had taken that role due to what had seemed to be a career-ending neck injury of his own. But somehow, he had worked hard to heal and had returned to the ring at WrestleMania a few nights earlier. I was inspired by that. They asked me if I would take his place. *Don't be a dumbass, Raya,* I thought, *they are throwing you a lifeline, take it.*

I accepted, and I was honored to do so.

In the weeks that followed, I was able to participate in the all-women battle royale I had wanted to be in, though not as a wrestler. I was super bummed, but I'd take it. As a general manager, I was able to help the younger, less-experienced women wrestlers make their marks, and I was so very proud of that fact. I was still in the game, though not doing what I would have preferred to do.

At the time, Vince didn't want me telling people publicly that I was retiring yet. He had decided to bestow on me a huge honor. Four months after my injury, he allowed me to do what had almost never been done before. Usually, when a female wrestler retired, WWE would just post it on social media. Until then, only the men got a stage to say goodbye to a live crowd and on television. But Vince gave me the *Monday Night RAW* following WrestleMania in New Orleans to make my retirement speech.

"It was really hard for me to stay at the sidelines yesterday at Wrestle-Mania," I said to the crowd. My tears started almost as soon as I began to speak. My voice was raspy. I felt such gratitude for all I'd been given: my career, these wonderful fans, my spectacular brother and sister wrestlers. I would miss it so much; it hurt physically in my body to think of a life without wrestling. But I had been invited to the biggest stage of them all as a wrestler and had been embraced. I had triumphed many times and given my all to the sport. I was so thankful, even as I was crushed.

"I love this ring," I cried out with every ounce of my being. "I was born to be in this ring. This is my heart. This is my soul! And this is my blood!"

The crowd cheered, and I tried to keep it together.

Then came the words I'd practiced and still could hardly spit out, choking on every syllable: "But unfortunately, due to neck injuries, I can no longer perform as an in-ring competitor."

The entire arena, tens of thousands of fans, started chanting, "Thank you, Paige! Thank you, Paige!" Tears streamed down my face. I thanked every single female superstar I'd worked with. "I am proud to be part of this division." I thanked my family and Daniel Bryan, who'd had his comeback after a career-ending injury, for giving me hope. I thanked WWE for letting me entertain fans for the past four years.

"New Orleans four years ago is where I debuted and won the Divas Championship. And four years later, New Orleans is where I want to retire."

The crowd started chanting again, and I was too overcome to even speak. As I tried to regain myself, they changed the chant. "This is *your* house," they called out to me. "This is *your* house."

The tears really gushed then. "Thank you," I said. "And yes, this will always be *my* house!"

I put down the mic and my comeback T-shirt on the mat, and just like that, I exited the ring for the last time as a WWE wrestler.

STAYIN' ALIVE

After the year and a half of pure nightmare for me, coming back to Orlando and to Joey and Raquel felt like pure bliss. Something was missing, though. Reader, you might remember that I'm a *huge* animal lover. I just wanted a furry best friend back in my life. I know, shocking!

So I had a bright idea. I asked Joey if he wanted to go to the Humane Society with me. I did this a lot. Usually, I just would go up there and give the animals some snuggles. It gets rough for those babies in there, and without constant love and attention, they become less adoptable. So I would take some time to go there just to love on them.

We got there, and I made my rounds like usual, but this time was different.

I walked past the most beautiful blue pit bull. He had a gray coat with a white streak that started right between two big, expressive puppy dog eyes and ran down the middle of his head, nose, and chest. I don't know if you have ever had your soul dog before? The kind of dog that comes around once in a lifetime and you know was meant to be yours. I knew that minute I saw him, he was meant to be *my* dog. He was meant to come home with me.

I went inside his enclosure, and he instantly jumped up on me and gave me kisses. I could see his previously cropped ears were freshly cleaned and had a gooey substance on them. The lady working there told me he was in a dogfighting ring, used as a bait dog, and his ears had been hanging off, so they had needed to fix them.

My heart broke. Who could ever do this to this sweetheart of a baby? Even with all the hardship he'd ever known, he still was such an angel and so pure of heart.

What an inspiring, strong boy. He had to come home with me.

I instantly went to the office and signed his documents. Joey, supportive as always, loaded him into the car, and with his head hanging out the window, we drove off. Joey asked what I was going to name him. The Humane Society had given him the name Tonka. But he didn't feel like a Tonka to me. Then I had it. I am obsessed with the TV show *Friends*; I've watched it over and over. There's a scene where Phoebe is talking about Ross and Rachel. She said, "He's her lobster!" because lobsters are one of the animals that choose to stick with each other forever. I gave Joey my answer to his question.

He's my Lobster.

That was honestly one of my best decisions. But not all of my adventures with Joey worked out as well as that one did.

"You know what would be a great idea?" Joey had said to me, some months earlier. He and I had been drinking and celebrating the online clothing and accessory company I'd been working on. "We should totally get tattoos!"

My company, the Saraya Store, had just launched, and I was so excited. Friends had all come to the launch party, and I'd felt so loved. One of the items we sold was patches—the kind you'd put on your jacket or backpack with sayings on them, funny quotes and shit. Joey and I were playing around with them when he had this brilliant revelation.

"We should go to Earl. Right now!"

Earl was the artist who'd done the tattoo I'd gotten as tribute to my adopted brother Isak, inking in words to remind me of him: *If you could read my mind, love.* I trusted Earl, and he did good work. But another tattoo? Did I need one? Did I even want one? I was pretty drunk at the time and didn't really take the minute or two needed to think it over. Next thing I knew, we were at Earl's shop.

"What are you going to get?" I asked Joey. He pointed to one of the patches from my new brand. The patch featured vampire fangs with the words "Talk Shit. Get Bit."

"I'm gonna do these fangs," he said, determined.

"Where?" I asked.

"The inside of my arm. How 'bout you?"

I really hadn't thought this outing through, but I pointed to the same patch. "Talk Shit. Get Bit," I said. "But I don't know where."

"On your hands!" Joey suggested.

Did I mention we were drunk? Sure, I was still talking with Bob Killer regularly and working on getting sober, but this wasn't one of my better days on that path.

Hands are pretty noticeable places on a person's body. Maybe that wasn't such a great idea. But I was having too much fun with Joey, too excited about my new company, to really think it through properly.

"Fuck it," he said. "Go for it!"

So I did.

Before long, "Talk Shit" was spelled out on the outside edge of my right palm, and "Get Bit" on the same spot on the left. Earl posted a photo of me and my hands to promote his business. And there, in this jagged-looking script on my fucking hands, was a permanent message to the world that a few hours ago I had no intention of getting.

Shit. What had I done? I thought it was hilarious at the time, but now not so much. Immediately, the photo went fucking viral and I couldn't figure out how to untag myself from it.

Remember, when I signed with WWE, they basically owned everything about me. My wrestling name, Paige, belonged to them. I also had to agree not to change anything about my looks without getting their prior approval. So, of course, as the stupid photo was shared all over the place, I soon got a text from Mark Carrano:

What did you do?

I lied.

What are you talking about? It's not real! Are you kidding me?

Thankfully, I'd gotten good with makeup, and I was able to hide the hand tattoos the next time I had to work. I used red makeup to help cover up the black ink and then put foundation in my skin tone on top of that. Then dusted it in powder to finish it off. My skin still looked a little crispy under the makeup because, obviously, it was a fresh tattoo, but I mostly was able to hide it. Only someone who looked closely would see it.

The minute I walked into work the next week, Mark approached me. "Let me see your hands."

I giggled and pretended it was just a silly little game we were playing, showing him my hands. Thankfully, he didn't look too closely.

"Oh good!" he said. "I was worried. You have a promo today. If you hold the mic with tattoos there, they'd be so noticeable."

"Ha ha! Yeah!" I laughed off his concerns. What an idiot I was. Every time I held a mic from here on out, I'd have to be careful. And since the tattoo included a swear word, it was definitely not okay for family-friendly entertainment.

A few weeks later, though, I totally forgot to cover it up, and I was busted.

"Saraya!" Mark almost passed out when he saw it.

"I'm so sorry!"

"You're going to be an older lady with this shit tattooed on your hands one day. You ever think about that?"

"I'll get them removed, I swear. But for now, I'll use makeup."

"Okay. Just make sure they're always covered."

Even though I was moving toward living my best, fullest life, I still fucked up from time to time. Again, Bob Killer was right. When I was drinking, the choices I mad didn't always serve me well.

It's funny because now people absolutely love my tattooed hands, but the truth is, I've always hated them. I still plan to get them removed, but for now, they're a great reminder to take my time in making decisions. To be a little more sober in my life choices.

While I was busy hiding my hands, I also needed to take care of my matted fucking hair-extension problem. When I returned to the WWE, I did my own hair because I was too embarrassed to have any of the hair and makeup people see how fucked-up the back of my head was. Having been neglected for so long, those extensions needed serious fucking help. I found a hairdresser who said he could fix me, and I believed him. But in order to deal with the mess that had been created, he said he'd need to give me a pretty radical haircut. The only real solution was to chop off that massive mat. We decided on a longish bob that he could construct with the help from some new extensions, a cut falling below my chin but much shorter than anything I'd had since I was a little kid and got that haircut I'd hated. I winced as foot-long locks fell to the floor.

But when I looked at myself in the mirror after he'd finished, I totally loved it. It was like being a new person. The scared girl I'd been didn't look back in the mirror at me now; instead there was a pulled-together young woman who looked like she could kick ass and cause some good trouble. For me, the cut represented my transition to general manager rather than wrestler. And the fans loved it, too. One post of the haircut received 400,000 likes, and the hairdresser, Wayne Tuggle, named the cut "the Paige."

Getting rid of that knot at the back of my head and the hair that had grown during that year and a half from hell was a turning point for me. I was a general manager now, someone the younger girls looked up to. Maybe I was becoming a role model again.

That is, if I didn't get any more fucking hand tattoos.

*

My judgment in other areas was suspect too. Having made my triumphant return to the WWE, I didn't want to lose my sense of humor. When I first came back after my year and a half of hell, I was traveling with Nia Jax.

"Should we just prank the entire backstage and tell them I popped another drug test?" I asked Nia. Everyone knew that I'd already popped the two drug tests and if I did it another time, I'd be fired. She thought it was a great idea and WWE social wanted to film it.

I had two partners at the time, Mandy and Sonya, and they were the perfect targets. They were told I had been fired, but meanwhile, I was hiding out in this tiny room right next to the girls' locker room. I sat in there for hours, Nia bringing me nuts every so often so I wouldn't die of starvation, just to be sure we could pull it off.

I could hear them. "Are you serious!? Oh my God!" They were heartbroken.

Meanwhile, I was cracking up.

When it was time for them to make their entrance, the music came up, and they walked down the ramp, and I came running up behind them with a camera. They were doing their wrestling poses, and you can see on the video (it's online) when they realize they've been pranked. Their faces said it all: *You fucking bitch!*

I guess I still had a sense of humor and didn't need any help being a menace.

One time, Mandy and Sonya were on their way to the venue. I called them and tried to convince them that they were late, we had to go on first. The schedule had been shifted, and they needed to change into their wrestling gear in the car.

"Now! You need to change now!"

It's an old-school wrestling prank I'd learned back in the UK. By that point, though, I'd pranked them so much, they were over my bullshit.

"We don't believe you."

I even texted the producers. "Please tell them they're up first." The producers did, but Mandy and Sonya didn't buy it. So I had to be constantly on the lookout for the next victim.

One time, I convinced Natalie the brownie she'd just eaten actually was a pot brownie. It wasn't, but it freaked her out, especially when she heard that WWE was conducting its random drug tests. In her panic, she ended up crashing a rental car into a huge trash can. Though she only dinged it a bit, she called WWE and told them she couldn't come in because she'd been in a car accident as her way of dodging the test. I think she eventually forgave me for that one.

One of my colleagues, the Irish wrestler Becky Lynch, always carried this insanely huge roller bag with her everywhere, bigger than any bag I'd ever seen.

I talked with Renee. "What do you think she has in that bag? She could have a body in there." And that's when the idea struck.

When Becky was out of the locker room, Renee and I removed all her stuff from the bag and I crawled inside. Because of my neck injury, though, I couldn't curl myself into a small enough ball to really fit. So Renee tried, and she fit! We zipped up the bag as far as we could and waited for Becky to return. The minute she walked into the locker room, Becky could sense something was up. She approached her bag warily and didn't even really laugh when Renee popped out. She was more pissed off that we'd touched her stuff and moved her things. We'd tried to be careful with it, but I get it now. I might not like someone messing with my things.

The pranking got so common that the writer and director from *Jackass*, Jeff Tremaine, at one point wanted to do a prank show backstage at the WWE. They gave me a cattle prod. Now really, you should never give *me* a cattle prod. I was just running around backstage, electrocuting everyone. To allow those wrestlers who didn't want to participate in this madness an out, the WWE had issued a "no prank" list and we were supposed to abide by that. And that's how Titus O'Neil got really pissed at me.

He's an angel of a man and this big, huge wrestler. I ran up to him and electrocuted him, not knowing he was on that list. I'd never seen him mad before but now he was fucking furious.

"What the fuck?" he screamed, absolutely losing his shit. "I said I didn't want to be a part of this!"

"Dude. Calm down. I didn't know."

He told on me to Vince McMahon, who called me into his office and handled it all in a jokey way. "Saraya, will you please stop picking on Titus?" he said, which was so ridiculous, since he's six foot four and 270 pounds. But to be fair, I did fucking electrocute the guy.

He had every right to be mad at me. I had no idea how much it hurts to be zapped by a cattle prod, and I would never do that again. I have always been a shit disturber. I came out of my mother's womb that way; my entire family will vouch for that.

And let it be known, sweetheart that he is, it didn't take Titus long to forgive me.

"We want to do something special," Ronnie and Bobby said that summer as my twenty-sixth birthday approached. They were so sweet, these friends of mine! I'd really never done anything for my birthday before. I had come so far and definitely wanted to celebrate. I loved the idea of a little party. So they planned one in LA, going out to a restaurant and some bars and then back to Ronnie's house after with just a few other friends.

I almost never splurge on myself and decided this was the moment to do so. For once, I was going to make my birthday a big deal. As a kid, I never had a party, and for most of my life, I'd been so busy working that I never got to celebrate. But this time was going to be different. I took myself out and handed over my credit card for a pair of Christian Louboutin heels with the famous red sole. I blew nearly $800 to make those shoes mine. It felt really good! Until I wore them and found out they are incredibly uncomfortable. . . . They looked good, though.

I got ready at Bobby's, put on my new shoes (*ouch*), and a group of us went over to Ronnie's house. When we got there, he had left the front door open.

I walked in to find the entire place was filled with black and purple balloons, the colors of my wrestling gear. As soon as he saw me, Ronnie yelled, "Happy birthday!" and sent confetti flying everywhere. Here he was, a guy who wasn't even my boyfriend but a person willing to go to so much trouble just to make my birthday special. No guy I'd dated had ever done something that sweet for me, much less a friend. I was completely fucking shocked.

When I hugged Ronnie, he ended up standing on my shoes. My feet were already so numb, I honestly didn't even notice.

"Sorry!" he kept saying. He felt really badly about having stepped on them. "Sorry!"

"It's no big deal." *Who gives a fuck about these shoes?* I thought. You should have seen the *house*!

Once we all settled in, Ronnie whispered to me, "Hey, I left something in the downstairs bathroom for you."

He had already done so much! I couldn't imagine what else he could have possibly planned, I was already so happy. But, like always, he was extra as fuck. I saw what he'd left for me. . . . He'd written me a fucking poem! He is a songwriter and has a way with words, and this was just so beautiful, hilarious, and touching. It was perfect for me.

A poem. A party. Balloons. *Fuck, I love this man!* And clearly, the feeling was mutual.

Of course, he didn't stop there, either. The next day he went out and bought me a replacement pair of red-bottomed shoes to make up for having stepped on my feet.

No one had ever bought me a nice gift like that. I was floored. And for weeks, I refused to tell him that the new shoes were actually a size too small. I didn't care. I shoved my feet into them, wore them to bars and restaurants despite blisters to show him how much I appreciated the gesture, even though they hurt like hell.

By that point, we had been seeing each other, but not officially, for a while. After spending a day hanging out together, Ronnie had asked me to be his girlfriend, officially. At a certain age, do guys even really do that anymore? I said yes, obviously, and we went to sleep for the night.

"Are you my girlfriend?" he said excitedly, first thing in the morning with a big, cheeky grin on his face.

I was so happy.

Later, when I finally told him the shoes didn't actually fit, he was mortified. I stopped wearing them because they fucking destroyed my feet, but I've hung on to them ever since. They mean the world to me. As does he.

"I hear you're back in Orlando. I'm going to be shooting some B-roll of the city, if you want to pop along," said Stephen Merchant, the writer/director of the film about my life. Production of the movie had resumed once I had cleaned up and started training to wrestle again. He said they needed to film a scene in which Florence Pugh, the actor who played me, was in the back seat of a car looking out at Orlando. As they didn't have Florence with them at the time to film the shot, maybe I'd like to help out.

"Do you want to sit in for her?" he asked.

I did! (So technically, I'm in the movie, but it's just the back of my head. I'm wearing a snapback cap, in case you're looking.)

Soon after that, the production was over, and they were finishing up the final edits.

"I'd like to know what you think of it," Stephen said.

He arranged to meet me at the Performance Center for the viewing. Thank goodness he'd decided to finish the film. After the production had stopped when I'd been a fucking mess, he'd been able to resume and now wanted me to see what he'd done. Stephen Merchant was a fucking angel.

When he turned up, he gave me the biggest hug. And he's giant, like a very tall man. I was to watch the film in a conference room that was surrounded by glass walls. The walls are all frosted for privacy, up to a height where, with a normal-size human, you couldn't see them standing on the other side. But Stephen was so tall, his head was well above it.

The screen lowered, and he cued up the film. Just as it was about to start, he excused himself.

"You're not going to watch it with me?"

"I can't. I can't watch you watch it. It makes me too nervous." He left. The room got dark, and the film began.

Within the very first scene, my breath completely left my fucking body. Oh my God, he got my childhood home in the UK absolutely perfectly! How did he do that? It was crazy! And then the characters playing me and Zak were wrestling with each other in the house, and it was all so real, I burst into fucking tears. I sobbed through the entire movie. I couldn't remember half of what I'd seen because I was just sobbing. Every so often, I'd see Stephen poking his head over the frosted glass, his big eyes and glasses watching for my reactions.

When the movie finished, he was right there. "What did you think?"

"I'm so sorry, Stephen, I cried the whole time. I need to rewatch it. It's just very surreal. I never thought my life was worth making a movie about, especially at my age, but you made it all make sense. And it's inspiring."

His body almost collapsed with relief that I liked it.

I not only liked it, I adored it. "You have no idea what this just did for me," I said. And it was true. The movie ignited a fire in me. Maybe I could live up to the expectations I had for myself after all, even if I couldn't wrestle anymore. He'd helped me see my life as a story of a girl trying to find her way, and damn it, that was still me and I was still finding my way. But having seen his interpretation of it on a screen, I suddenly felt that I was on the right path.

I also knew my family was going to be over the moon. "You did such a great job! Can I call my family? Now?"

I got them on WhatsApp immediately.

"I just watched the movie, and it's so beautiful and good. I can't wait for you to see it. Stephen will be flying to the UK soon, and he'll set up a screening."

He did, and when they saw it, they loved it, too.

When I left the Performance Center that day, I was flooded with gratitude. I was so lucky to be where I was in that moment in time. I couldn't fucking believe it. . . . I got out of the shit I'd been in quickly enough that the movie hadn't been canceled. It got fucking made! And it was going to come out soon and might actually spark something in someone. I thought of that little girl in the grocery store who hoped to be like me when she grew up. At the time, I wanted anything else for her. She should find another role model because I was fucking bad news. But now, having seen my life through Stephen's eyes, I felt like that was an okay thing for her to want.

I had come so very close to destroying my life. And I would have missed all this!

Within a few months, I'd moved in with Ronnie in LA and convinced Joey and Raquel to follow me to the West Coast. I helped them find jobs and get settled and was so thrilled to have these good people surrounding me. I'd let go of all the friendships I'd had earlier, those that hadn't been good for me. What I needed from here on out were people who would be in my corner, people who believed in me and wanted the best for me. I flew back to Orlando and all around the country for WWE, working as the general manager, and my life was about as good as I could imagine. Better than I could have dreamed.

I was sitting next to the actress Florence Pugh at the Sundance premiere of the movie, and she started sinking deeper and deeper into her seat.

"You okay?" I asked. We'd only just met each other, and I hardly knew her.

"It's just really weird," she said. "Sitting here, watching the movie with you. And you're not dead or anything, which is usually the case when someone has a movie made about them. I don't know how to act right now."

"Oh my God! You did such a great job. You made me look so much better as a person than I am. You do a better me than me!"

I loved her immediately.

I had come to Sundance with my crew—Ronnie, Joey, and Raquel, as well as Zac. For the premiere, Ronnie and I had picked out matching outfits, me in all black with a brown long coat on top, him in a brown suit that matched my coat with a black shirt.

On the flight to Utah, I'd seen Lena Headey, who played my mum in the film. I jumped out of my seat immediately when I recognized her.

"Hi!" I had to tell her that my friend Raquel was utterly obsessed with her and her work on *Game of Thrones*. And she was just like my mum in real life, such similar personalities, so positive and loving. "Raquel will be there, at Sundance. I can't wait to introduce you!"

She was so sweet, and all I could think was, *How cool is this? The plane hasn't even taken off yet and Lena Headey is right here!*

We were picked up and taken to Park City, where it's absolutely gorgeous, mountains and snow everywhere. The hotel was this amazing log cabin with ski runs out the back. I could watch people on the lift heading off for their day on the slopes.

Before the actual showing, we went to an amazing pre-premiere party. While there, the PR assistant who'd been assigned to me by WWE warned me to stay away from Vince Vaughn, who played the fictional trainer Hutch Morgan in the film. "He's not very nice," she whispered in my ear.

So when he passed by us, I kept quiet and kind of ducked my head. But he saw me and immediately called out, "Saraya!" He was so happy to meet me and so fucking nice. "I loved being a part of your story," he said. "I'm a big fan of yours now." And I just glared at the handler lady: *See. This is how people get bad names. People like you spread misinformation. Maybe you met him when he was having a bad day or a bad moment. But you just saw that. He was lovely!*

I got to meet Nick Frost, who played my dad, and Jack Lowden, who played Zak. I met the head of MGM and other corporate bigwigs. It was amazing. Sure, I was used to WWE events where there's red carpets, and they send you to the Oscars and that kind of stuff. But this just felt different. This was mine.

The handler woman still kept getting in the way. She wouldn't let my makeup artist into the theater. She was downright rude. "And you're not supposed to drink!" she hissed at me.

"You need to stop being a bitch." Ronnie got annoyed at her. "You're putting out too much negative energy and making everyone uncomfortable." She quieted down after that.

Earlier, I'd googled Sundance and had a blast figuring out outfits to wear, lots of black turtlenecks and big coats. But then I ran into Dwayne Johnson at the screening, and I almost died. We were both in black jeans, black turtleneck, black boots, the exact same outfit. Only my brown coat made it clear we weren't trying to be twins. We both laughed. And I thanked him again for making a movie about my life. I was so grateful he'd seen a story there and had championed this effort to bring it to the big screen. How could I ever let him know how much that meant to me?

And then it was time for the screening, where I sat next to Florence and told her how much I adored her work playing me. The lights got low, and I could hear the audience taking in the story—*my story*—and feel the compassion they felt for the character, this young girl, and all the ways they were rooting for her. My heart felt tender and raw.

Watching others experience my life was so cool that some of the cast members and I went around to the various screenings that took place in town after the premiere in order to surprise the audience at the end. It was the same every time. People laughed and cried. The story moved them. My life moved them. I couldn't get over it. We popped out at the end of the screening, when the whole auditorium was clapping, and everyone was so glad to see us.

I'd never thought people would be interested in a movie about someone like me. I mean, who'd want to watch that? For years, I saw myself as such a fuckup and a cautionary tale. But these actors, writers, and director, they fucking sold that shit and made it a movie. Number one in the UK even! I couldn't believe it.

And the whole time, I kept thinking that if I had continued on the path I was on, they either would never have finished this film—or it would have had a very different, tragic ending.

I was just so fucking grateful for my life.

MY WAY

Something's wrong!" I called Ronnie. "Something's really wrong. I'm bleeding all over the place. I keep throwing up. I can't even stand. And I'm in such pain."

Ronnie was on the final day of a tour with his band, and thankfully only an hour away by plane. "I'll cancel the last show and hop on the next flight," he said. "But first, I'm calling an ambulance."

I didn't know what the fuck was going on. I had started what seemed to be a normal period earlier but then all hell broke loose. I was getting lightheaded and losing a lot of blood.

In our relationship, I was usually never the one who had a health concern. Ronnie is super health conscious and almost a hypochondriac, while I paid absolutely no attention to my health whatsoever. But now I was in deep trouble. I'd never felt such pain. I was all alone in our LA house, just me and Lobster, and I didn't know what to do. I was glad Ronnie would be coming back soon, but I was still terrified.

I could hear my phone ringing. Ronnie was trying over and over to call me again, but I was on the master bathroom floor, curled up into a ball, throwing up. When I heard the ambulance, though, I desperately started to crawl toward the door to meet them.

The EMT people hadn't taken long to arrive, thank God. They examined me and said they needed to take me to the hospital, stat. I couldn't walk but I didn't want to get on the gurney they'd brought. Mostly, I didn't want anyone to see me like that, so I kept crawling out the front door. In doing so, and in trying to keep Lobster from getting in the way, I mistakenly elbowed the door shut behind me.

"Uh, can you open the door again?" one of the EMTs asked in a steady, kind voice. "All our equipment is inside."

"Shit! I didn't grab my keys. I'm locked out."

They were too scared of Lobster to do it themselves, so I had to squeeze myself back through the doggie door, my abdomen clenched in cramps, blood soaking my sweatpants, to unlock the door and give them access. After that, I couldn't make it any further. I pretty well collapsed on the gurney and allowed them to wheel me inside the ambulance.

As the sirens wailed through our LA neighborhood, I tried to talk myself down from the pain. One of the EMTs recognized me. "I can't believe it's you," he said. "I'm a huge fan."

"Please. Don't tell anyone about this." I was really embarrassed. I didn't know what the fuck was going on—there was blood everywhere, and I don't know a whole lot about medical shit, but I know for sure a person isn't supposed to lose blood like that. The last thing I wanted to worry about was seeing it all over social media later.

"Please," I begged. "Keep this quiet."

"Don't worry," he reassured me. "I couldn't say anything even if I wanted to. It's part of the job."

When I got to the hospital, a nurse set me up with an IV right away.

"What's that?" I asked.

"Morphine," he said. "For the pain."

It scared me because the doctors had to keep topping up the morphine bag, and topping it up again. Maybe it was because I'd developed a higher tolerance from all the drugs I'd done? Shit.

All the while, the nurses were cleaning me up, doing swabs. I still didn't know what the problem was. A nurse came in and did an ultrasound. I tried to read her face, but still had no answers.

About thirty minutes later, a doctor came in.

"I'm sorry to tell you this, but you're having an ectopic pregnancy," she said. I didn't know exactly what that was, but from the way she looked at me, I knew it was serious. Ronnie and I weren't trying to get pregnant, and I had always been told that I'd have a hard time conceiving.

"Should I be worried?" I asked.

When she didn't reply, I pressed her.

"Could I die?"

"Yeah. Yes, you could."

Oh fuck. I started to freak out. Where was Ronnie? When would he arrive? I texted him in a panic.

I'm gonna die. I'm fucking gonna die.

I was *beyond* terrified.

Eventually, Ronnie walked in, and I could see the terror I was feeling all over his face. He started sobbing. We were convinced it was the end of everything.

Soon after he arrived, another doctor came in, calm and relaxed, and introduced herself as the main doctor on my case.

"How are we doing?"

"They said I'm gonna die!" I was hysterical by this point.

"No, you're not, you're in safe hands. Who told you that?" she asked, confused.

"The doctor who came in earlier did."

She was not impressed. "She's an intern. She shouldn't have been telling you anything."

She put me at ease immediately, explaining the actual situation—I was having a miscarriage of an ectopic pregnancy, which can in some cases be fatal, but I also still had cysts everywhere, and one of them had ruptured. It was serious, but not life-threatening. I had gotten there in time. She explained that I would need surgery right away, but I would be fine. Her whole vibe was nurturing and peaceful. I was exhausted and wanted to fall asleep to the calming sound of her voice. Just her presence made me feel so much better.

She was such an angel. She knew how to speak to people, how to ease my fears. And she even stayed in touch with me afterward, texting a few times to see how I was. I loved that woman. She saved my life.

She was also the first person to explain to me that I had endometriosis and that that was the cause of a lot of pain and suffering I'd been through for years. Endometriosis, she said, is a disease in which tissue similar to the lining of the uterus grows outside the uterus. It can cause severe pain in the pelvis and make it harder to get pregnant. I'd had years of pain, and none of my doctors had believed me. I mean, come on, I'm a fucking wrestler for fuck's sake. I know how to put up with pain. But they always dismissed me and said it was normal to have discomfort with a period.

I had the surgery to remove the cyst and clean out what was remaining of the ectopic pregnancy, and stayed in the hospital overnight. It was a horrible experience, but understanding I had endometriosis was a big deal for me, a turning point. I wasn't fucking crazy when I complained about the pain I was in. I'm now working to help raise awareness about this condition and trying to make sure women like me don't suffer unnecessarily. Plus, I'm getting active in the whole abortion rights movement. Because I needed health care in that moment and if this were to happen to me again, in a state where abortion is illegal and I was not able to terminate the ectopic pregnancy threatening my life, then I really *could* die. It's a human rights thing.

Still, that event was pretty scarring. . . . For hours, I felt like I was on a fucking roller coaster, positive I was going to die, bawling my eyes out. Even Ronnie, who never cries, had been a wreck from the moment he saw me. We were a fucking mess. And then I was fine again. Go figure.

The next morning, Ronnie put me in a wheelchair and got me the fuck out of there. I hate hospitals.

Ronnie did a lot to protect my health. After all, he was the one who had decided earlier on that we should both be sober—as in really, completely, totally sober. When we first started dating, we'd both been drinking here and there and vaping regularly, staying away from the hard stuff but not as sober as I should've been. He didn't drink as much as I did. I was still drinking a lot of beer because it was less likely to fuck me up than hard liquor, but still. I'd gained a lot of weight from that beer. I was up from 130 pounds to nearly 155, though Ronnie never noticed. For him, cleaning up our acts wasn't about how we looked or anything external; it was all about our well-being.

"We need to stop drinking and cut out the vaping. And start a vegan diet. I'm serious. It's time to be healthy. I feel ridiculous with these giant vapes and big clouds of smoke wherever we go. We look stupid. They're like fucking pacifiers."

He wasn't wrong. We kept our vapes on our pillows or on our chests when we were falling asleep; they were always within reach. But that day, he decided he'd had enough. And when Ronnie makes up his mind about something, that's all it takes. He gathered up all our vapes and threw them into the bin.

"And no more drinking!"

And that's exactly what we did. We just stopped. I have to give him credit. He has much more willpower than me, and he led the charge. Plus, I knew he would hold me accountable. He's brutally honest. If I fucked up, he'd tell me. I needed that.

So he was the one who kept us both honest. And even a few years later, in 2020, when his friend passed away from complications due to alcoholism, Ronnie didn't waver in his commitment. Some people, in a hard moment like that, will take it as an excuse to get loaded for a bit and let the feelings just dissipate. I know I did. But no, he hated alcohol even more after that tragedy.

"It ruins lives," he said.

He didn't want drinking on his tour bus. And while he didn't mind if his bandmates went out for drinks on their own, he didn't want it around him or me. At first, it was hard. I never would have made it through those early days without him. I had gotten clean from drugs, which was hard enough, but drinking is so much more socially acceptable. I don't know if I would have had the willpower to stop completely on my own.

"Let's avoid these situations," he'd suggest. "Let's not put ourselves in that position."

He kept us away from places and people that might have tempted me to give in. And in the meantime, he encouraged me to see therapists about the things that were bothering me, to explore the scary shit from my past, to make peace with the elements of my life I'd been trying to run from. I was still working with the sober coach Bob Killer, who was thrilled with this new decision. Seriously, I don't know if I would have gotten this far if it hadn't been for Ronnie and Bob. They have always been super encouraging and only want me to be my best.

Things were good in our life, and after doing it for a few months, sobriety became a lot easier. I don't feel the alcohol calling to us anymore, and because everyone around us knows we're sober, they don't offer us alcohol and drugs. Getting sober with someone else was easier than doing it alone, or even with a coach like Bob. We hold each other accountable.

Being sober, being healthy, I really started to feel like myself again. I was worried that being sober might turn me into someone righteous, with a stick up her ass, but that hasn't been the case at all. I was worried I wouldn't be as fun to be around when I wasn't drinking, but it turns out that wasn't true. I've always loved a good prank.

GIVE 'EM HELL, KID

Why don't you try making all your favorite British dishes but vegan?" Ronnie asked. He was back at it with the healthy shit again, but I appreciated his good influence on me.

My mum was a fantastic chef, so of course I had eventually picked up some cooking skills, but lately I had gotten lazy and become much more skilled at ordering on DoorDash. But it was the beginning of the pandemic, and I was going out of my fucking mind trying to keep myself occupied. So why not try cooking? Sure, I could try eating healthier.

When I'd retired, though I could no longer wrestle I'd felt alive with purpose working as the manager with Absolution and later with the Kabuki Warriors. But then WWE got rid of the manager role after a few months and I was left with nothing to do, no tangible way to participate in the wrestling scene. I'm happiest when I'm being helpful, being productive, earning my keep. The fact that WWE didn't really need me, but also had me signed to them and yet weren't using me, was hard. I felt like a bum. Sure, I was still getting a paycheck, but I wasn't being helpful. I'd float ideas and storylines past them and come up with ways for them to put me to work, and inevitably they'd say no. They basically owned me. I couldn't do anything else, like write this book, without their permission. I felt absolutely stuck. I had been working since I was thirteen. Being a hard worker was how I proved my worth to the world. And how I proved it to myself. Without that role, I was fucking lost with no place to put my skills and talents, and no ability to go elsewhere as long as WWE still had me under contract.

And then the shutdown happened. Fuck. Being stuck in a house 24/7, not being able to travel, not being part of a larger something, was a huge test, even after all the work I'd done on myself. How was I going to keep myself occupied? How was I going to be okay with myself through all this?

At first, I got really good at video games. And then, every time I turned on social media, people were making banana bread or sourdough bread. That looked really good. Ronnie and I loved this vegan restaurant, Crossroads Kitchen, and I got their cookbook and started learning vegan recipes. I watched YouTube videos perfecting how to dice and cube, to sauté and broil, how to parboil and to roast. I wore this fabulous apron and moved around the kitchen like I owned the joint, which I fucking did! It was great and kept me focused.

And then Ronnie came up with the idea that I could adapt all kinds of traditional British meals like shepherd's pie and find a way to make them vegan. Challenge fucking accepted!

At the time, Ronnie had been doing a lot of music-related stuff on Twitch. Twitch is a streaming platform that allows creators to broadcast live video content—gaming, entertainment, music, sports, whatever. Viewers can chat in real time, pay for a subscription, buy your merchandise, or donate as a way to interact with creators during livestreams. When Ronnie does something, he never does it at less than 1,000 percent. Soon we had a room filled with top-of-the-line video equipment.

Ronnie's fans could win one-of-a-kind memorabilia from music videos, band merch, and even some of his personal belongings. He has an awesome online community, so he was an instant hit. He would even raise money for smaller bands and people struggling with money during the pandemic. Plus, he was having a blast in the room he'd set up to stream content.

Should I do something like that, too? I needed something that felt like it was mine.

Ronnie was encouraging with the first steps I took into the gaming world. *Fortnite* and *World of Warcraft* were my favorites. And crazy as it sounds, it turned out people wanted to watch me play video games. Okay. That was cool with me.

I decided a little "Cooking with Saraya" segment would be fun pandemic content. I could have had my own daytime TV show; I was killing it. Ronnie and I had been dating since 2018, and we became vegan not much longer after that. People watched as I developed a great new vegan take on an old British classic. I made an amazing vegan Bolognese (not very British, but I adore pasta) and a god-awful pad thai (okay, so I maybe didn't kill it every time . . .) that Ronnie still ate, which was sweet. Either way, people loved it.

In some ways, Twitch was like the attention I usually got in a wrestling ring. Some people loved me, some people hated me, but very few were indifferent. Our friend Omar is a computer genius, and he got us all set up; he even made green screen backgrounds and stuff, and people fucking loved it. As long as I kept producing new content and didn't mind looking like an idiot for the sake of entertainment from time to time, we were good.

The cooking was so popular, we started to do other real-life segments, streaming as we went to the park to fly a drone, or drove in our cars, grocery shopped, toured our house, played with the dogs. Our fans got to come right along with us, making inside jokes and being a part of our lives.

At the time, we were living on a cliff overlooking the ocean, and we posted a picture of the view. Big mistake.

The doorbell rang, and I ran to answer it. I was expecting Postmates, or I never would have opened the door so casually. It definitely wasn't Postmates. Some random guy was just standing there.

He looked really weird. He wore a shirt that was completely unbuttoned except for one button that had been shoved into the wrong hole, making the shirt lopsided. I looked down and he had no shoes on his feet.

"The symbols led me to you," he said, a creepy-arse look in his eyes.

The symbols? What?! Well, tell the symbols to get the fuck off my property.
This guy looked fucking crazy.

"Can I help you?" I edged away from the door and partially shut it, trying to keep him away from me.

"I don't mean you any harm." He tried to reassure me, but that only freaked me out more. "I know I'm supposed to be here at this time because the symbols told me so." Immediately the little hairs on the back of my necks stood at attention.

"Just a moment," I said, and held the door mostly closed with my foot.

I texted Ronnie.

> There's a weird guy at the door. Come upstairs!

Ronnie came bolting up the steps. He ran after the guy, who immediately took off. In a split second, Ronnie caught him in a headlock and shoved him into his car. "I'm gonna fucking kill you!" Ronnie screamed in his face, holding him there. Immediately, I called the cops. The guy was arrested, but that didn't make me feel all that much safer,

Ronnie was utterly freaked out. We both were. We didn't know who the guy was but whatever he wanted from us wasn't good. It wouldn't be until later that we figured out that someone had used that photo of our cliffside view from our house at the time and, from that tiny clue, determined exactly which house out of the many that lined the cliff was ours. It was really freaky, and I was totally on edge.

Thankfully, by then, the cops in the neighborhood knew us because of fans. They'd had to come to our address a few times before. The first time had been when we'd just moved in and Ronnie had been messing with the fire alarm when it went off. We didn't have the code to interrupt it, so we contacted the Realtor, but it took her hours to get back to us. Eventually, she did, and we put in the code and that was that. We got in our car to go to the grocery store and were halfway down the block when the neighbor across the street texted. "There's a bunch of cops swarming your house right now."

Fuck! We turned around and went back. I was freaking out, worried they'd harm Lobster. I remembered the cops Tasering my dogs back in the UK. Lobster's a big, beefy pit bull, and a lot of people have issues with those kinds of dogs just because of how they look. They don't know what a sweetheart he is. I was so worried they'd fucking shoot him.

When we pulled up to the house, all the cops were inside. "I'm going to go in first," I told Ronnie.

"Fuck no," he said, but I was already running toward the door—not because Ronnie couldn't handle the situation, but he is covered in neck and face tattoos. Like Lobster, the look of him can put some people, cops especially, on edge. The last thing we needed was for them to think we were fucking breaking into our own home.

I pushed open the door, my heart jackhammering in my chest.

"Hell-oooooo?" I called before carefully stepping inside. When I rounded a corner, two cops were facing me with grim expressions and their fucking guns drawn in my face. My heart completely stopped beating.

I pointed to the living room wall where a big painting of us hung over the fireplace: me; Ronnie; his daughter, Willow; and Lobster. "This is my house," I choked the words out. "We live here."

After what seemed an eternity but was likely no more than five seconds or so, they seemed to believe me and holstered their guns. "Your fire alarm went off, and we had to check on it. Then we thought someone was breaking in."

"I'm so sorry. My boyfriend was fucking with the freaking alarm. I thought I should come in first because I worried you'd think he was a burglar."

Ronnie was right behind me.

"That was a good idea," one of them admitted. "We definitely would have thought that."

"See," I said to Ronnie. He was a bit frustrated that I had thrown myself in there ahead of him.

As my breathing returned to normal, I noticed Lobster. There he was pretty much between their legs, looking happy as shit. *Look! I've got someone to play with me!* So much for the idea he'd be a good guard dog.

That day we got to know the officers, and our familiarity with them grew a few months later when we had to call them back because a guy kept sending me disturbing stuff in the mail, iPhones, letters, weird shit. By then, the cops knew what we did for a living and recognized we'd become a kind of magnet for overzealous fans. There'd also been fangirls who kept tabs on Ronnie. One night, they hid in our bushes and our assistant, Lizzie, caught them and had to tell them to get out. So the cops knew us well by the time Mr. The Symbols Led Me to You arrived.

I told the police what had happened, wanting to be clear that Ronnie had chased the man as a form of self-defense. I worried for Ronnie. In 2008, before I knew him, he was the lead singer in the post-hardcore band Escape the Fate and got involved in a violent situation. He'd gone with a group of friends who were about to fight an adversary in Las Vegas, thinking it was just gonna be a fistfight. He was fucking wrong. Things escalated out of control, and an eighteen-year-old man was shot and killed. He had shot first, but one of Ronnie's friends ran to the car to get his firearm and shot back.

Later, during the investigation that followed, both sides described the situation happening the same way. It was determined to be self-defense.

Ronnie hadn't even known there would be guns there. *Nobody* had expected it to end the way that it did. But because police found brass knuckles (which are illegal in Vegas) on him, he was sentenced to prison, where he served two and a half years. Locked up, he struggled with isolation and the difficult conditions, feeling depressed, anxious, and overwhelmed. The last thing we fucking needed was for him to be in trouble again. He'd worked so hard both in his personal life and with his music to spread a message of redemption, of personal growth and overcoming adversity. It was something we had in common.

When I finished telling the officer about the psychopath at our door, it was clear they understood the situation and they gave us their direct numbers. "If you have any more trouble with the symbol guy or anyone else, call us."

From that point on, we were super careful never to show shots of the house or the neighborhood, not to give rabid fans a way to track us down. Just because we're in the public eye doesn't mean we don't have a right to live a life free from crazy fucking people showing up on our front doorstep.

Still, we kept up the Twitch livestreams and I was grateful for the outlet. Besides a handful of crazy people here and there, I enjoyed the chance to spend time really getting to know my fans, and most of them were respectful and supportive. Sometimes, we would stream for twelve hours or more at a time. I still have an online server where we talk often, and I give them sneak peaks of whatever I'm up to. I adore them.

But I guess WWE saw things differently. Or, at least they did after a data breach occurred, allowing them and others to see exactly how much money streamers were making on Twitch—not just wrestlers, but everyone. Turned out that I was the number one wrestler on the site, income-wise. But I was still an employee of WWE, which meant they had a say in anything I did, including my online presence.

A representative called me. "We know about your stream, and we're not asking anything of you right now, but we're going to make you a deal about your stream."

"Well, it better be a good deal," I said. I was pissed. They weren't using me on TV; they weren't using me to do media. I wanted to be useful, and this was the only thing I had. No way I was going to let them take it from me.

After that, though, things changed. A bunch of wrestlers had their streams shut down, and my friend Thea, Zelina Vega from the WWE, refused to shut her stream down and was fired. (She was later rehired.)

The same guy called me back. "We need to have a part of this money."

"No." I was stubborn as anything about this. "You can't have my stream, and I am not shutting it down. I'm not wrestling, I'm not on TV anymore. It's the one thing I have that's keeping me going."

After that conversation, I did a livestream where I fucking completely broke down because I was so mad. I was just like, "*I gave my neck to you guys TWICE!* And the fact that you're trying to take this away from me when I have nothing else is infuriating. In life, sometimes you have to pick your battles. And this one is fucking mine. I'm going to fight to hold on to my stream because it's literally all I fucking have!"

The livestream went viral, and after that, WWE never said another word about my Twitch.

"We're not going to renew your contract." I got the call from Johnny Laurinaitis, one I'd been expecting for months. I'd contacted the company over and over as my contract was coming to its end in July 2022, and no one was getting back to me.

"Don't worry. It'll be fine," they'd all said, but now, it was clear, it wasn't fine. They were fucking letting me go.

I went into full panic mode, but I kept my manners. "Thank you," I said. "WWE has been amazing. You helped me with a lot of shit behind the scenes, you helped save my life when it came to drugs and alcohol, and gave me chances and chances, especially after my public meltdowns. You really took care of me since I was nineteen, and I'm grateful."

The minute I hung up the phone, though, anxiety grabbed at my windpipe, threatening to never let me breathe again. What was I going to do now? Wrestling was all I'd ever known. I had money in savings, and Ronnie was really sweet, taking over paying for the house and big shit like that, but this was about more than a paycheck. This was who I saw myself as.

A month and a half later, Triple H called. "Hey, Saraya. Why aren't you with us anymore? Don't you want to be here?"

"What do you mean, Hunter? You didn't renew my contract."

Apparently, Triple H had been all caught up in other things. Vince, by the time Triple H called, had stepped down. Plus, Triple H had had health issues of his own that had taken his attention.

"What?! That's so bizarre," he said. "Listen, I want to bring you back. And we can put you in a general manager role on TV."

I had enjoyed being the general manager before and would have loved to return.

"We won't bring you out every week, so you won't have to be flying all the time. I just want you to come back. And if you ever feel like getting into the ring again, I mean, if a doctor gives the okay, we'd be down for that, too. Just think about it, okay? And I'll come up with a number for you."

The way things had been left when I retired nearly five years earlier, the doctors had said that there was no way I'd be able to wrestle again in the near future . . . but long term, there might be a chance. Still, every time I'd asked WWE if they'd cover the cost for me to have another MRI and see a specialist, they'd said no. Maybe they were finally changing their tune.

I was thrilled. They wanted me back!

But for the first time, I could feel the hesitation in my body. If I went back, I wouldn't have the freedom I wanted. I would be restricted again and, who knows, might find myself sitting on the couch wondering when and if they'd ever use me again. I hated that feeling. Also, I didn't want to have to ask for permission for whatever the fuck I wanted to do. I was tired of being owned. And then it hit me.

I also wanted to be Saraya now. I didn't want to be Paige anymore. After more than a decade of being someone I wasn't, I was ready to just be me.

I went to sleep that night making a list of pros and cons. Sure, WWE could offer me a huge platform. But was re-signing with them taking a step backward? Besides, there might be another offer on the table.

ONE WAY OR ANOTHER

A few days before Triple H's call, another wrestler, Chris Jericho, had called. He'd left WWE for All Elite Wrestling (AEW), a new company created in 2019 as a competitor to WWE.

"Hey, would you ever come to AEW?" he'd asked. He knew my contract with WWE hadn't been renewed.

"I don't know. The whole wrestling thing for me is kind of tainted at the moment," I said, and I meant it. I had been looking at alternate career options—maybe acting?—and thinking my days in wrestling arenas were in my rearview mirror.

But Chris kept calling every day and giving me reasons to join AEW. By that time, the husband of my dear friend Renee Paquette, Jon Moxley, had also landed AEW, and those two started calling me every day as well. Renee hadn't yet decided for herself, but said, "If you go there, I'll go there." Even Britt Baker called, trying to get me to lean toward AEW. I didn't know if I could wrestle yet, and I wasn't sure what they wanted me for anyway.

I told them all I was thrilled they wanted me to join them, but the head of AEW, Tony Khan, hadn't contacted me. Until he did, this was just fantasy shit we were throwing around. They all told me how busy Tony was—he's the owner of AEW, an NFL team in the US, and a Premier League football club in the UK. He's a busy, busy man.

And yet the very next day, guess who called?

"I think you'd be really great for our women's division," Tony said.

He made a strong offer and promised not to restrict whatever I wanted to do outside wrestling and AEW. And get this: I would appear as *Saraya*. I could finally be myself. Not half-bad for a girl from Norwich.

No more taking backward steps for me. Let's fucking go!

In discussions with both companies, each had said that I'd be welcome to return to the ring as a wrestler if the doctor gave me the okay. One of the first things Tony Khan had said was they'd like for me to get my neck checked out either way. It would be good to know exactly what my limitations were. At AEW's invitation, I saw a doctor who did an X-ray straightaway.

"Your neck looks really great. The fusions look perfect. But to make sure, we're going to have to do a CT scan and an MRI."

The doctors sent me downstairs that very moment, and I had them done.

Back in his office to review the results, he marveled at all the fluid surrounding my cervical spine. "It looks perfect!" he said.

I was blown away, not sure I could believe what I was hearing. "Will I be paralyzed if I wrestle?" I was still terrified I wasn't okay. I had gotten so used to believing that if I hurt my neck in anyway, it might be a life-destroying injury.

"No, look. See all this fluid around your spine? That's a cushion. To save you. To protect you. Your neck looks absolutely perfect. You can wrestle."

"Really?" I wasn't sure I could trust this.

"Move forward at your own pace. Do as much or as little as you want. If you feel anything at all, call me. But you're good to go." He wrote out a note to that effect.

I had not woken up that morning expecting to hear this news and was in total fucking shock. I had long ago learned to live with the fact that I likely wouldn't ever wrestle again. It had been five years since I'd retired. . . . And now I could return to the ring?

I got my parents on FaceTime immediately. I took a picture of us because I was fucking bawling and they were fucking bawling and we were all absolute messes. Then I texted Sasha Banks, the wrestler whose kick had retired me.

> I wanted you to hear the good news as soon as possible! You don't have to stress. I can wrestle again!

I wanted to absolve her of any guilt she still felt, to know I was good.

I couldn't fucking believe it. I was texting Tony, my coworkers, my friends—everybody all at once. They all wrote back excited, saying how amazing it was.

I posted the doctor's note online, and immediately, people started to shit on me, saying it was a fake note because of a minor typo.

Oh my God, can't you just be fucking happy for me?

The work started immediately—and, reader, if taking a bump had hurt after a year and a bit off when I was younger, it was *much* harder now. I hadn't wrestled at all for five years. Plus, I was older, and my body was slower to bounce back. The last time I had returned from an injury, I pushed myself too hard, too fast and ended up temporarily paralyzed in the middle of the ring. I found out I was cleared at the end of October and was booked to wrestle three weeks later. Things were moving quickly, but this time, I had done all the tests, all the physicals, done more training. I was being cautious, but still, no one could deny it was taking a risk.

Zak had flown in, there to make sure I was ready and to be by my side. Just like my first match when I was barely a teenager and he was a Pink Power Ranger, he was the only person who could truly put me at ease about being back in the ring. Honestly, even with him there to help, it sucked training again. But I knew it would be worth it.

As my match got closer, though, my body didn't want to cooperate. I was so stressed out, and it was showing up in all kinds of fun ways. Just a few days before my debut match at AEW, my wisdom teeth suddenly decided to start cutting their way through my gums, making their own surprise entrance. My face was insanely swollen. I looked *nuts*.

Great. Love that for me.

But the show must go on, so a couple of days later I got on the plane to New York, still feeling awful—anxious, sore, and still swollen. As the flight across the country dragged on, I felt more and more nauseous. I didn't make it to the terminal. Just as we landed, I was throwing up in the tiny airplane washroom.

I was a nervous wreck. My anxiety was out of control.

The next morning, on the day before the pay-per-view, I went to the arena with Zak to prepare for the match. I planned to do moves that specifically targeted my neck. Stupid? Maybe. But I wanted to prove a point—I was *back*, 110 percent.

But was I? About two months earlier, AEW security had snuck me into an arena in Queens wearing a hoodie and sunglasses, tucked away in a tiny room so no one, not even the other wrestlers, would see me. Midway through a heated women's match, I took my place backstage, just steps from the entrance ramp. On my side of the curtain, I was completely in the dark. On the other side, ten thousand fans. I didn't know if they would even still recognize me.

Here goes nothing.

The first few notes of my new entrance music, Ronnie's song "Zombified," filled the arena. The song made me come alive, and it made perfect sense. *Here I am, back from the dead.*

My name—my *real* name—appeared in huge, bold letters across the massive LED screen. As I walked out below it, the crowd exploded to their feet. The noise was deafening, and it went on and on. Standing alone in the middle of the ring, I felt that sound reverberate in every atom of my body.

Now, back in New York for my first actual match, the same sound felt like it was crushing me under its weight. I'd never been this nervous before. What if I couldn't live up to their expectations? What if I didn't live up to mine?

Center ring in my signature Doc Marten boots and studded leather gear, I stood face-to-face with Britt Baker. As soon as the match started, a "Welcome back!" chant broke out. Wrestling fans are very fickle, but they can be kind, too.

Most of the match, I took a beating: twisted neckbreaker onto the floor. Stomp to the back of the neck. The Lock Jaw. Bump after bump. But near the end, just like in any good story, when all hope seemed lost, the momentum changed.

I won the match. I was exhausted, and a little rusty, but it all went pretty much as planned. I celebrated with my brother and my friends, who had been watching from their ringside seats, just as nervous as I was. Backstage, the adrenaline and anxiety finally subsided. I could breathe again. I was happy, but more just overwhelmed with relief.

Not for long though. Online, almost immediately, people were tearing me apart. *Too slow, too fragile, too overrated.* The criticism cut through my relief like a razor blade.

Did I make a mistake coming back?

Fine. You want to hate me? No problem. I love playing a heel.

That same year, Ronnie and I did two things together that changed me. The first was that I got up the courage to sing for him. I'd conquered the fear of getting back in the ring, so what was one more? Here he is, a musician with an amazing fucking voice, and I adore music, but I have a very real phobia of singing in public. Back when I was drinking, if I was fucking wasted, I loved to sing my head off at a karaoke bar. But to sing sober with anyone else within earshot? Absolutely not.

He wanted to hear my voice, but that would require I sing in front of him, and I just couldn't do it. End of conversation.

He was away on tour and down in the dumps a bit about something, and for the first time I thought: *Maybe I could cheer him up by sending him a little video of me singing.* I wanted to show him I was willing to try, and to give him something that might make him smile.

I had to point the camera away from me—I could not possibly have my face filmed at the same time, too—and I sang an a capella version of "Running Up That Hill," made famous in the eighties by Kate Bush. I was terrified, my hands shaking, but I did it anyway. Then I hit send.

I kept looking at my phone. It showed the little checkmark that meant he'd seen the message. But he wasn't writing back.

What if he thinks I am awful? Oh fuck. What have I done?

Minutes passed. Still no reply. I was sweating and pacing, walking around the living room. I couldn't sit down, and I was freaking out, totally in fight-or-flight mode. My hands shaking, my jaw clenching.

When I finally heard from him, he said he hadn't listened to it yet. "Sorry, I had a meet and greet. I'll listen now."

My stomach clenched as I waited. A minute or two later he texted back.

Oh my God! That totally made me tear up. That was really good.

He's always brutally honest, so I knew he wasn't messing with me.

I can tell you haven't had vocal training, but what you're doing is really, really good.

You're lying!

It was so fucking hard for me to take the compliment. I don't know why.

240

No, I'm not.

After that, Ronnie arranged for me to record myself in his studio with just him and his producer there.

"That means I have to sing in front of you two?"

"You can do it."

I got into the booth, but I was sweating and panicking. Ronnie kept rubbing my back, helping me relax. He gave me random words to say at first and then to sing, just one at a time to get me comfortable making sounds, but I couldn't get anything out of my mouth. My hands started to shake, and I covered my face. I was hyperventilating.

I do love to sing. I had put that picture of a CD on my vision board back when I was younger, but even then I always had incredible stage fright. I can walk out to the ring in front of thousands of people and wrestle every week, but the only times I have ever actually sung in front of people were when I was absolutely wasted doing karaoke at some bar.

Ronnie made up a little song on the spot and asked me to sing just the first line of it. I did it, and somehow I didn't pass out from the pure anxiety. Then he sang the next line, and I followed him. We were just messing around, but I was getting comfortable and having fun.

Before we finished, I asked if I could record myself doing the Kate Bush song I'd sent him. I really liked that song, and they let me.

A few days later, I overheard Ronnie playing the clip for his music video director, Jensen. "Do you know who this is?" Ronnie asked.

Jensen shook his head.

"That's Saraya!"

He was pleasantly surprised. My accent doesn't come across much when I sing, so when Ronnie was showing the clip off again later to his band, they had no idea it was me, either. It's sweet that he's so proud of it, but a bit embarrassing, too. Still, though, I felt like I had conquered another fear.

Reader, if you think he was just blowing smoke up my ass because I am so gorgeous (*duh*) and he loves me (*obviously*), you're wrong. He is just not the type. It wasn't all talk, and he proved that in a crazy way. In the summer of 2024, Ronnie's next album, *Popular Monster*, came out. I genuinely love his music, and I never get sick of listening to it over and over, blasting from speakers into every corner of the house, while he dissects every note before the songs are released. He is a perfectionist. This time, though, I had to get used to hearing myself as well. Ronnie actually put my vocals on a song called "Bad Guy," with a feature credit on the album and everything. It wasn't the earlier sample he had been showing off to everyone, but a part he had written specifically for me. (I did a bunch of takes trying to get it right, but his main note was just to sound more and more British each time.) Lots of my friends and family and our fans were so excited for me, understanding that it was an honor to be included in his art like that—but only a handful of people know what a huge fear that was for me to overcome. Singing publicly like that was one thing on my bucket list I honestly never thought I would be brave enough to do, even if I had the chance to. I honestly still can't believe I did it.

Before the singing, though, there'd been another vulnerable moment that put things into perspective for me. Ronnie had suggested we have our brains mapped at a brain performance center nearby. "They've done work with UFC fighter Chuck Liddell, and their neurofeedback exercises can retrain a brain and help us be healthier," he explained.

He was always looking for ways to optimize our health. "Both physical and emotional trauma can alter the brain," he told me. "After all the hits you've taken, and all the traumas we both dealt with, it might be good to know."

We went into the center and were hooked up to machines with electrodes all over our skulls. The results would be available in a few days.

We settled down for the Zoom session to review the results. Ronnie went first. They'd found a very specific spot on his brain that was bright red. This was where his anxiety was located, the doctor explained, and talked him through the kinds of biofeedback he could do to lessen that anxiety. When it was time to review my results, the doorbell rang—Ronnie had ordered food—and he left to get it.

"And Saraya, this is what we saw with your brain." The image that popped onto the screen was nothing like what we'd seen with Ronnie. His had been mostly cool-toned colors, blues and greens with just this one spot of red. But not mine. The image on the screen took my breath away. The entire fucking thing was red.

I was expecting our brains would look much alike, but from what I was seeing, I was so much worse than Ronnie.

"Look!" I almost screamed when Ronnie came back into the room. "I'm more fucking damaged than you!"

The doctor explained it wasn't so much about being "damaged" but that Ronnie's scan explained why he was more fidgety and prone to anxiety: because that one part of his brain was affected. And the reason I always *appeared* like I was able to handle shit was because my trauma was spread out and well dispersed. Lucky me!

I had stopped the drugs, tobacco, and alcohol. I was living a really clean life, and this was still my fucking brain?! But the doctor talked me down. It was a good thing I had stopped all those damaging habits, and here was proof that I should never ever return to them. So many things had shaped what I was seeing on the screen—physical trauma, emotional trauma, the drugs and alcohol. I was shocked to see all of that red, but at the same time it felt like validation. It felt like the pain I had gone through wasn't all just imagined in my head . . . it was *literally* part of my brain. Weirdly, that was kind of reassuring.

Because, the doctor said, there was an upside called neuroplasticity—the ability of the brain to form and reorganize its connections following injury. If my brain could be hurt by all the things I'd done to it and had done to me, it could heal.

WE ARE THE CHAMPIONS

The plane took off from LA to London. It had been eleven and a half years since I'd boarded that flight from the UK to Florida to start my new life in the States. At that time, I'd been just a kid, nineteen and afraid, leaving everything and everyone I knew behind me. I was trying to map out a new life for myself, but I couldn't yet see what it looked like. Over the years I'd been back to the UK to visit and occasionally to wrestle, but now I was making the reverse trip under fucking weird and wonderfully different circumstances.

I had just turned thirty-one, and for that birthday Ronnie had gifted me a pair of ducklings, Jammy and Dodger. (His habit of going overboard on my birthday hasn't died down even years later.) Animals have always been my love language, and I could picture no better way to say "I love you." I had made a comeback as a wrestler after the supposed career-ending injury and a five-year hiatus. Now I played a heel in the ring, yelling at the crowd, being the bad guy, loving the character I'd created. I was having fun again and living up to the name William Regal had hit me with back when I'd first trained at FCW, "Hell in Boots."

Today, Hell in Boots was flying back home for her biggest match yet: Wembley fucking Stadium.

I hadn't wrestled in the UK in eight years, and I would never have imagined as a kid that one day I would be wrestling on the iconic stage of Wembley. Yet now it was happening. I would wrestle as part of AEW's pay-per-view event *All In*, in front of a crowd of more than eighty thousand fans, said to be the largest ever gathered for a wrestling show—and in my fucking home country!

I was bummed Ronnie wasn't sitting in the seat next to me; because of the felony on his record he couldn't easily get a tourist visa outside of the US. He'd been told that if he accompanied me and they turned him back, he'd never be allowed in the country again, not even on a work visa to perform—a risk we both agreed wasn't worth it. But I would have my group of true and loyal friends with me: Raquel of course came, while Joey had to stay home to look after their two dogs (one of which was a new dachshund puppy that Joey and I had just recently surprised her with as a birthday gift). Taylor, who had shown up randomly on Twitch one day during the pandemic but quickly became a real-life friend. Lizzy, a long-time friend I met through Ronnie. And last but not least, my incredibly talented makeup artist and dear friend Zac, and his boyfriend, Camilo. Plus, Renee and all the wonderful AEW family I'd acquired since joining them.

When we first arrived in London, the hotel was quiet, but I couldn't sleep. I was jet-lagged, tossing and turning all night.

The next morning, starting at four thirty, I did media all over the city. Talking to radio hosts, reporters and podcasters, traditional media and social media. Interviews by folks in my home country, glad to see me again and wishing me luck in my match. Almost twelve hours later, we finally headed back to the hotel. I fell asleep in the car on the way.

I woke up to the car pulling into a swarm of fans already filling the valet area outside the hotel. They started calling my name as soon as I stepped out of the car. "Saraya! Saraya!" It was wild. I stayed and took selfies and chatted until all were satisfied, reminding myself again of my favorite Maya Angelou quote: "People will forget what you said, people will forget what you did, but people will never forget how you made them feel."

The next day, my friends and I snuck away from the media circus and headed to Norwich. We hopped on a train, and poor Raquel, who had arrived a day later, had literally just jumped off the plane and came straight to the hotel when I dragged her right back out to the train station. Just as we got to Norwich, my brother Roy was there waiting for us.

With Roy leading the way, I took my friends around to show them my stomping grounds. The sun was shining, and it was a gorgeous day. If you've spent much time in the UK, you know the weather can be dodgy, but that day it was perfect.

I showed my friends the pub I went to at fourteen, where I had a dance-off with a drag queen and then was learning to pole dance before Roy dragged me out by my ear. He'd taken me to that gay pub, telling me this was the safest place for me because no guy would hit on me there, but then he was dragging me out, telling me, "Don't you fucking dare!"

I pointed out the Prince of Wales Road, where all the pubs were located, the shopping area, and the big open-air Norwich Market, with all its colorful tents. Then I took them to the cathedral that dates back to 1096, where we stared in awe at the crazy amazing architecture, the stained glass, the sense of beauty. The cathedral had its own cat, Budge, who first wandered in back in 2018 during Good Friday service and had made the place home ever since.

I took them to the Forum, which has a huge library, coffee shop, and pizza place. Raquel ordered iced tea and the server just looked at her like she was mad. I had to explain to Raquel that the idea of iced tea is blasphemy in the UK. We went to a rooftop bar for a bite to eat. Roy was newly sober, and my friends asked if we would be comfortable around them having a drink. I was proud that we could both say yes, and we meant it.

And yet, in that moment, it was really difficult to not have one. Drinking is a cultural thing in England; it's everywhere. It's the "normal" thing do to. It was harder to say no there. But I did.

The night before, we had been at a restaurant and I had confessed how much more difficult it was for me to not drink, being in England.

Taylor pointed to the nonalcoholic beer on the menu and told me to get one of those, if I thought it would help, and she promised she wouldn't let me have a real one even if I was tempted to. So I ordered one. It's good to have friends who are supportive like that.

"If this were years ago," I told my friends, "I'd be taking you on a pub crawl." I laughed, but inside I was missing it for the first time in a long time. But I wouldn't be here, having this incredible moment if I had kept on drinking. I knew it wasn't worth it.

I had hoped to surprise my dad and just show up unannounced, but I'm an idiot and posted a picture of all our train tickets on social media. Dad's friends were all texting him, asking him when I'd arrive. I asked Mum to tell him that I'd had to stay behind in London because of the media requests, but I don't think it worked.

We all landed then in my parents' gym, where my nieces and nephews had gathered. Raquel was super sweet and had thought ahead, getting gifts for all my extended family and made the visit extra special.

We saw a local footie match where Roy and my nephew Ricky played and Dad coached. Meanwhile, Mum ran out to get enough authentic British fish and chips to feed us all for a week. We chowed down on chips, mushy peas, curry sauce, all the good stuff. And it was delicious! To share my old life with the friends who had come to mean so much to me, who had seen me through such dark times, was fucking amazing. And they were soaking it all in, genuinely happy to see me at ease, in my hometown, happy and healthy and surrounded by the people who love me.

At one point, my mum pulled me aside. She gave me a crystal necklace and told me to put it under my pillow at night so I'd sleep well. I hadn't told her about the sleeping issues, and here, she knew I'd needed her help. She also gave me a bracelet that had some special metal in it that would trigger a reminder in me, always telling me how much my parents loved me.

We hopped onto the last train back to the city, and when I got back to the hotel I put that necklace under my pillow, and fell asleep instantly and completely, like a child.

The next day was the run-through at the stadium, and only official wrestlers and crew were allowed in. I stood on the ring they'd constructed in the midst of this fucking Grand Canyon of a stadium with my fellow wrestlers Toni Storm, Britt Baker, and Hikaru Shida. Jumbotrons towered next to us where our images would be projected to those in the farthest seats along terraced steps that seemed to reach to the sky. We gasped. How amazing it was that we were there.

We needed to work through our match, and though the other wrestlers, producers, and I knew some of what would happen and were set on our spots, we still didn't know how it would all pan out. I had come up with the idea that I'd like to use my mum in the match if possible, and so it was decided that my partner, Toni Storm, would take a swing at Britt Baker standing in front of my mum. When Britt ducked, Toni would end up clocking my mum, enraging me and putting our partnership to the test. Because to hurt someone I love, of course, was the worst offense a person could inflict. I would defend my parents and all my loved ones to the death.

But what would happen after that, we had no idea.

As all these details were being finalized, we were still waiting for Tony, our boss, to tell us who would win. He also owns the Fulham Football Club, which had a match that day, so it was after ten that night that he finally arrived.

"I have good news for you," he said.

For at least a month, I'd been asking if I could have "We Will Rock You" by Queen as my entrance music. I knew it would cost AEW a fortune, but it seemed so appropriate. I was planning to come into the ring wearing a jacket that read "Queen of England" on the back. It would be perfect. But weeks earlier, he'd told me he couldn't get the song. So when we'd rehearsed earlier that day, I'd come out to Ronnie's song, my usual entrance music, "Zombified."

But I guess the prank was on me this time because his face broke into a huge smile. "I got you the music," he said.

I was beyond excited. I didn't want to tell my family or friends because I wanted them to fully experience it in the moment. It was going to be absolutely fucking magical.

Then Tony moved on to other business.

"So, this is what I'm thinking for the finish. You'll do these spots we've agreed on." He turned to me. "Then you're going to grab the spray paint and spray Toni in the face, and then you'll hit your finisher."

Sara, our producer, turned to me smiling. I realized later that she'd known what he had in mind.

"Okay, and then what?" I asked, wondering what the fuck was happening because I was a bit shocked to find out that I was going to spray Toni. She's my partner, my friend, my teammate. (Toni and I had been incorporating spray paint into our matches recently because we were heels, and heels can do all kinds of shady shit.) But now I was going to turn on my teammate? Well, I guess that's what a heel does.

"But then what?" I asked again.

"You hit your finisher," Tony repeated.

Sara translated. "You win."

Of course, I had hoped they'd let me win since I would be on my home turf, but I hadn't expected it. Immediately I teared up. Toni and Ruby Soho wrapped me in a huge bear hug.

How was this happening? I was never supposed to wrestle again and yet here I was. I had just come back from being away from the ring for five years, and now I was in Wembley *fucking* Stadium. My family would all be there, and my friends, adding to the huge booming sound of the crowd. I had been with AEW for only like nine months and they believed in me enough to give me this honor. I was floored.

People always say that wrestling is fake. And yeah, the outcome might be predetermined, but what's at stake is very real for those of us who live it. That AEW trusted me to be the face of their company, to be their champion, was overwhelming. They were putting a lot of trust in me, and

I felt every ounce of it. But by this this point in my life, I absolutely knew I was trustworthy. I had learned to trust myself.

"You have no idea what this means to me," I said through tears to Tony. "Do you realize what you've done for me?"

He smiled. "Let's fucking go!"

The evening was like none I'd ever experienced. My family and friends all gathered in their special VIP box, overlooking the massive crowd. I snuck up for just a second to say hi to everyone.

When it was time for me to make my entrance, the crowed screamed out the lyrics of Queen's "We Will Rock You" while the foot stomping felt like a fucking earthquake. I was sure I'd died and gone to heaven. My parents, my brothers Zak and Roy, and two of my wrestling nephews, Ricky and Patrick, on either side of me as I made my way down the entrance ramp. It felt like an army behind me. They had been behind me every step, every fuckup, of the way here. They took their seats ringside as I pulled myself up into the ring.

The match started, and all the moves went off as planned. When my teammate Toni hit my mum, Mum played it like a champ, riling up the crowd. And that was the moment I turned on Toni. From that point forward, you could hear the entire stadium, all eighty thousand fans. When she hit me, they all responded with a "boo!" and when I hit her, a resounding, echoing, reverberating "yeah!" rang in my ears.

The hometown crowd was behind me, the heel, the one who'd brought on so much disgrace, the one who'd fucked up time and again. They were right there with me.

And then it happened. I won, and all pandemonium broke lose. There I was in the ring, holding the championship. The tears I cried were genuine. I was so grateful.

When I got backstage, Renee was waiting for me and almost knocked me off my feet with her hug; her eyes were full of happy tears. Years ago, she'd seen me at my absolute worst, had insisted on visiting me when I wasn't letting anyone catch a glimpse of me, and she'd loved me every step of the way. To share this triumph with her was everything.

Backstage, my parents and the rest of my wrestler friends were everywhere, congratulating me. My dad especially was blown away by the kindness and excitement he saw showering down all around me, surrounding me.

"You really are loved, aren't you, Saraya?"

He was right. I had such good people. Ronnie FaceTimed me immediately, and we celebrated the win long-distance.

When the initial chaos died down, I went up to the box where the rest of my family and my friends were waiting. I wanted to thank them for coming and loving and supporting me. They all but swarmed me when I arrived, and I ate up their joy. I have been fortunate enough to have some pretty incredible moments in my wrestling career, but never with all of my family there to celebrate with me. I can't even begin to describe the feeling.

I was the champion again, and I knew that in the near future, the championship would move on to someone else, as it has to. But for the moment, the immortal words of Freddie Mercury keep ringing in my head, about so much more than a wrestling match.

I came through so much to get to this place. So many times when I was headed in a wrong direction, so many chances I had to permanently fuck up my life . . . and somehow I got through to the other side. Wrestling may have a predetermined outcome, but it's really just like life. It's about the story of how we get there. Knowing who is in your corner and really cheering for you. How you come back after life knocks you down. How you recover, lace up your boots, and get back in the fucking ring, no matter what.

If you can do that, then you have won.

"We are the champions, my friends."

EPILOGUE

Almost exactly a year later, I was back at Wembley Stadium for another show. More specifically, I was at Wembley station, waiting for a train to take myself and my friends Zac and Taylor to Norwich. As usual, my first priority when I landed in England was to go visit with all my family, and my friends were more than happy to join me on the trip back to beautiful old Norwich. I never really thought much of it when I was growing up, but now I can appreciate how charming of a place it really is, with its winding cobblestone roads and picturesque old buildings. Despite the chaotic excitement that always came with visiting my ever-growing family, I couldn't wait to go home and see everyone over a heaping plate of Mum's roast dinner.

While we stood on the platform, I noticed a girl out of the corner of my eye. She was maybe just a few years younger than us, pretty, and nicely dressed with pearls scattered across her sweater and her dark hair half-pinned back.

She was staring at me.

"Do you see that girl? She keeps looking at me," I whispered to Taylor. It wasn't making me uncomfortable, but I had a strange feeling about it.

She stated the obvious. We had been being stopped, politely, by fans all over Wembley for the past few days leading up to the pay-per-view show. "She probably just knows who you are."

I sort of shrugged, thinking she didn't give me much of a classic wrestling fan vibe. Besides, I don't like to assume everyone knows who I am, even as surrounded by wrestling fans as we were.

At the same time, Zac noticed her and gave her an encouraging smile. She peeked her head around him.

"Are you Saraya?" she breathed. "Oh my God." And then she immediately burst into tears.

Reader, the weirdest thing happened just then. It turned out that this was not the first time I had met Carmen. We had met ten years before in Malaysia, when I was there with WWE. The very same year I became the NXT Women's Champion and the Divas Champion. And now we were crossing paths again, a decade later and halfway across the world. We couldn't believe the crazy coincidence.

"Mind the gap." The quintessential British announcement rang out to signal the train's arrival as we hugged.

No shit. How many crazy things had happened in my life in the gap of those ten years? We all got on the train car together, headed for a moment in the same direction. We reminisced, and I asked her all about herself. It was like running into an old friend, from another lifetime ago. The kind you lose touch with but are always happy to run into. She was on the way to write her bar exam to become a lawyer. I was on my way to see my family just before another show at one of the biggest stadiums in the world. Before she got off at her station, I had already started arranging tickets for her to come to the show. I had to share this full-circle moment with her.

As the train carried us forward, I couldn't help but think about all the twists and turns that had led me to *that* train platform on *that* day at *that* time. The little girl who looked up to me in the grocery store, the little girl petrified in my bed back in Norwich. How small I felt when my body and addictions were on display for the world to see, and how much larger-than-life I felt when I was back in the ring again surrounded by my family and the roar of Wembley Stadium just the year before. All those moments that felt like I was heading in the right or wrong direction, in between now and then.

Mind the fucking gap.

Even just in the time since I was in England the summer before, things had come a long way. I had flown home to California to our crazy menagerie of animals. I was wrestling again, and even singing—somehow still checking things off my bucket list.

Crazy things have continued to hurl themselves at me—a cancer scare with my mum (she's okay), a stolen car (they found it!), even more pets (hell yeah)—but overall, life has been good. I am still sober, and so are my brothers. My parents are together and as infatuated with each other as ever. I have the support of good friends around me, encouraging me and loving me for all the right reasons. Things are better than I ever thought they would be.

There was another huge moment after I got home, too. As you know, reader, my brother Zak has been fighting the good fight to get into WWE for many years. As much as I love WWE and adored my time there, I wish they would've given my brother the chance to showcase what he can do. Bias aside, he's one of the best wrestlers in the world. When I asked Tony Khan if he could give my brother a chance, he agreed without hesitation. I couldn't believe it! After twelve years, we were finally doing this together like we'd always dreamed of.

I got to work on Zak's visa, and about four months after Wembley, he was in America with me, waiting for his first match.

Let me tell you, it's very hard to get a crowd to react the way Zak made them react. When he walked out, the crowd wasn't overly familiar with him just yet. But he charged down the ramp with so much energy and determination, you would have thought it was a world title match. As soon as the bell rang, he hit the other wrestler with a Spear—flinging his whole body forward at full speed, parallel to the mat, straight into his opponent's midsection within in the first ten seconds. The crowd *erupted*! I erupted! This time I was cheering him from the sidelines, as thousands of people cheered his name. I sobbed watching it finally happen for him. The crowd was on fire. People online were actually bloody nice! This was his moment.

After he won, I ran to join everyone backstage, who were already cheering for Zak. I came around the corner to catch him, but before I got there, Dean Malenko (one of my favorite people and wrestlers on the planet, may I add) was already congratulating him. He'd instantly fallen in love with Zak. I snuck through the crowd of people around Zak and gave him a huge hug.

I'M SO PROUD OF YOU! Both of us were in tears. No one else could have known at the time everything we had fought through to have that moment together.

This year, back in Wembley, another crazy thing happened. My friends and family were all piling into a restaurant the night before the big show, and fans were stopping my brother and me to say hi. (How cool is it that people recognize my brother now?! I was living for that!) One couple spotted me in the doorway, and I recognized them, too. They said they had met me at that exact same spot, on that exact same date and almost even the exact same time, the year before. *Weird*, right?

You can spend so much of your life feeling like you are going in the wrong direction, just to end up in the right place at the right time.

Sometimes I still beat myself up, to be honest, wishing I could have chosen an easier path. I don't know, maybe it's all fate. That everything I went through, and everything I did—right or wrong—was exactly what got me where I needed to be.

I'm not sure what comes next, reader. But isn't that the point? Thirty years ago, even if that crazy old fortune teller told me, I never could have guessed how my life would turn out today. Ten years from now, I can't even imagine. Hell, I don't even know what next week might look like. How am I only thirty-two? I feel like I have lived nine lives already, but you really do get only one, so might as well make the most of it.

Just like when you're in the ring, you already know the ending. But I promise you, I am going to put on a hell of show until I get there, wherever that is.

ACKNOWLEDGMENTS

First, I want thank my family. My dad, my mum, Zak, Roy, Nikki, Terri, Ricky, Patrick, and all the babies. Without every one of you, for different reasons and the same, I would not have made it through my life. My hardest times and my highest times, you were there clapping me along from the sidelines. Lifting me up when I needed it and always making sure I'm being the very best I can be . . . and when I wasn't, still loving me. I love you all so much.

To my friends who have been there since day one of my move to America. Raquel, Joey, and Renee. Thank you for being my place to stay, my shoulder to cry on, and my place to vent. You guys have not judged me once and support me in everything I do. When I think about it, we've never bloody argued once? Ha ha. Even when I was in my highest fight-or-flight mode. As a famous wise man once said, "Who'd of thought? Not me!" Love you guys.

I cannot continue with the book until I thank my newer friend of the past four years, which is Taylor. Someone who knew nothing about wrestling. Knew nothing about me. And when she found out about my life and controversies, she still did not give a flying fuck. Dear reader, she did not watch my movie until I put it on at my house because, in her words, "I already know your life story." (Which she does.) She edited this book with me for days and hours to get it perfect after getting the original draft. I'm a perfectionist, and luckily so is she, so we both tackled this head-on and got it bloody done. So thankful for you, sister. Forever friend.

To the WWE, especially Stephanie and Hunter, thank you for giving me a chance. Even looking like a scruffy emo teenager, you saw something special in me. You created and gave me the pedestal I needed to really flourish as a performer and person (sometimes, ha ha, sorry about the times I was a royal pain in the arse). I was pretty much raised in the spotlight with you guys, and you did everything you could to always make sure I was healthy and comfortable. You never gave up on me. For that I'm forever thankful to you.

To Tony Khan and everyone who made me coming to AEW happen, thank you so much for bringing me in and treating me so kindly. It's a huge family, and I can really feel it as I'm walking in every week. Thank you for giving me the freedom to do whatever I need to do workwise outside of this company, and thank you so much for giving my brother Zak a chance and letting my whole family be involved in Wembley fucking Stadium. Not only that, you went and bought the bloody rights to play "We Will Rock You" by Queen as my entrance music?! Absolutely bonkers. Thank you for all you do for me and my family.

And lastly, a huge thank-you to my team at Gallery Books, United Talent Agency, and my manager, Meech Golden.

ABOUT THE AUTHOR

Saraya-Jade Bevis is a British professional wrestler, known for her time in World Wrestling Entertainment (WWE) under the ring name Paige. Saraya was the youngest and two-time WWE Divas Champion and inaugural NXT Women's Champion. Her career was brought to the silver screen in 2019, when Dwayne "The Rock" Johnson produced *Fighting with My Family*. She made her wrestling debut in 2005 at the age of thirteen, announced her retirement in 2018 following a neck injury, and made an unlikely comeback in 2022. Follow her on Instagram @Saraya.